Syntax: A Linguistic Introduction to Sentence Structure

Second Edition

TITLES OF RELATED INTEREST

Essentials of English Grammar
Otto Jespersen

Towards a Contextual Grammar of English
Eugene Winter

Syntax: A Linguistic Introduction to Sentence Structure

Second Edition

Keith Brown and Jim Miller

HarperCollins *Academic*
An imprint of HarperCollins *Publishers*

Published by
HarperCollins_Academic_
77–85 Fulham Palace Road
Hammersmith
London W6 8JB
UK

First published in 1980
Second edition 1991

P 295
B 7
1991

British Library Cataloguing in Publication Data

Brown, E. K. (Edward Keith, _1935–_)
  Syntax: a linguistic introduction to sentence Structure.
  2nd ed.
  1. Syntax
  I. Title   II. Miller, J. E. (James Edward), _1942–_
  415

  ISBN 0-04-4455615

Typeset in 10 on 12 point Times by Fotographics (Bedford) Ltd
and printed in Great Britain by Billing and Sons, Worcester

Contents

Part three: Functional relations

Preface to the first edition

We would like to explain briefly why we have decided to write an introduction to syntax when there are many such books already on the market.

This volume arose from the teaching of syntax to first-year undergraduate students at the University of Edinburgh. Since the first-year course is designed to give students a general overview of linguistics, we thought that the syntax component should cover those basic concepts that have been and still are being used in the description of the syntactic structure of languages. This decision rules out those many textbooks that purport to be introductions to syntax or to grammar in general but are really introductions to transformational grammar. Of course, many basic concepts – constituent structure, embedding, recursion, inter-sentential relations, and so on – are integral parts of transformational grammar, but they are not exclusive to this particular approach to description. Other equally basic concepts – dependency (syntagmatic) relations, propositional processes and participants, the notions of theme and rheme, topic and comment, and so on – are not well handled in transformational models. Of the other textbooks available, none treats the range of concepts we want to consider in enough detail to form the single text round which a course could be built.

We recognize the commanding position that the transformational approach has assumed in the field of syntactic description over the past decade. It is still the dominant linguistic paradigm and has contributed more to our understanding of the nature of language than any other single model; indeed, the companion volume to this is a fully formalized transformational grammar. But the concepts we wish to discuss are independent of and prior to any single model of grammar; it is precisely notions such as constituent structure, embedding, recursion, dependency relations, and so on, that any model seeks to account for, and linguists criticize one or another model precisely because it deals with one or another of these concepts inadequately. Our approach does not rule out formal grammar. A formal approach to language description is one of the corner-stones of linguistics, and we hope to encourage students to look at the formal structure of language. It will be clear that much of the formalization we introduce in Parts One and Two derives from a transformational approach, and we introduce some trans- formational rules. This book is not intended, however, to be an introduction to a fully formalized transformational grammar, and a formal approach is not exclusive to transformational grammar. The companion volume, however (Brown and Miller, 1982), discusses the problem of constructing a fully formalized transformational description of constituent structure, compares two trans- formational models and explores ways of formalizing other aspects of syntax.

There is another reason, external to linguistics, why we take this approach. At least half of the students who take a first-year course do not proceed any further with linguistics, though many do continue language study and have occasion to use grammars. Most, if not all, detailed grammars of English or other languages are not set out as a formalized transformational grammar, but rather make informal use of such concepts as constituent structure, subject and object, complement and adjunct, agent and patient, government and concord, and so on. At least part of our purpose therefore is to train students to understand such concepts, so they can make the best use of the grammars they come across.

This book has been written with undergraduate students in mind, but it should be suitable for beginners at any level. We think it appropriate to have as few references as possible in the actual text, as our subject-matter is those basic concepts that have become the common property of linguistics. The references at the end of the book give some idea of the sources from which we have drawn inspiration; they are not an exhaustive list of the writings on each topic, but an indication of books the student should find accessible.

Preface to the second edition

It is now some fourteen years since the first edition of this book was drafted and ten years since its publication. On re-reading our preface to the first edition, we have found many comments that are just as valid in 1990 as in 1980 and there is little to be added. Indeed, developments in linguistics over the last ten years have, we feel, supported our general position on the purpose and content of a basic textbook on syntax. Formal models have multiplied, but they all try to handle the constructions and concepts described here. Functional models have been developed, based on grammatical functions, participant roles and thematic organization, and there is a large body of ongoing research on discourse which also draws on these concepts. That is, whereas in 1980 Part Three of our book could have been seen as peripheral, certainly with respect to formal models, it is now central.

A number of introductory textbooks reflect the view that, from the beginning, syntax must be taught within a particular formal model. We have consistently taken the view that, while beginning students (let us emphasize the word 'beginning') should be encouraged to be explicit and should make contact with basic rewrite rules, formal models are not relevant to them and indeed obscure what is relevant. In 1980 we talked of the concepts that would enable students to use and understand grammars of English and other languages: constituent structure, grammatical functions, dependency relations, word classes, grammatical categories. Given the new policy – at least in Britain – that schoolteachers should have an understanding of 'grammar' and that 'grammar' should have a place in the English class, these concepts are clearly regaining lost ground in the intellectual landscape. In 1980 we failed to mention speech therapists, sociologists, social anthropologists, interpreters and translators; they too need the basic concepts of syntax.

Although the first edition did not present a formal model, it was heavily influenced by classical transformational grammar. This edition is different. The detailed transformational rules have been excised and only the general notion of transformational relation is discussed, in the chapter on sentence relations. In contrast, this edition does make students aware of X-bar notation and analysis. The essential point is that the X-bar approach is independent of any formal model and is now so widespread that we would be failing in our duty if we excluded it. In the interest of balance, however, a number of comments in the chapter on syntagmatic and paradigmatic relations (Chapter 17) make it clear that the definitive treatment of constituent structure and dependency relations has yet to be found. If the book (and the authors!) survive to a third edition, it may turn out that dependency relations have to be given more detailed and prominent discussion than they receive now.

Finally, we have continued to exclude such matters as language acquisition and language competence. Although these issues are exceedingly important and fascinating, the contribution of linguistic analysis to them is controversial. We believe that most students who study linguistics are looking for analytical tools to apply in other enterprises, and that the concepts and the structures to which the tools relate are important and fascinating in their own right.

Introduction

It is indisputable that language is central to all communities of human beings. One of the first tasks of the young human being is to learn the language of the society into which he or she is born, and it takes many years to acquire the mastery of language expected of mature adults. Language is essential for the regulation of every community: the instruction of its young, the creation of laws, the development of its culture, the identification of its members. Consequently, language, as well as being a fascinating phenomenon in itself, is a necessary part of any investigation into human social organization and psychology.

This book is concerned with language for its own sake. To be more accurate, it is concerned with one part of language, namely, syntax. But before we embark on the study of syntax, we should consider some general questions about the nature of language study. Let us begin by examining an instance of one person talking to another. If both speaker and hearer are mature speakers of the same language and neither suffers from any defects – such as deafness or laryngitis – that impede the production and the hearing of speech, we can say that the speaker produces a sequence of sounds, and that the listener hears the sounds and understands the message. This rudimentary account ignores many factors necessary in a detailed description of communication by language, but it will suffice for present purposes.

If both participants were literate, and perhaps not in close proximity, the speaker could have decided to convey his or her message in writing. The person receiving the message would then have been required to read a series of marks on paper, the marks being organized in sequences of different lengths separated by spaces. If the message was a long one, there might be several series of marks, each series being separated from the other by a space on the paper. Of course, the sequences are ordinarily called words and the series are ordinarily called sentences.

If we compare a written message with a tape-recording of a

spoken message one obvious discrepancy is that nothing in the series of noises corresponds to the spaces between the words on paper, not even a pause or a slight cough. Furthermore, while there may be slight pauses corresponding to the gaps between the sentences, there need not be. The machine records a sequence of mere noises. If the language being spoken is one we know, we can interpret the noises, reconstructing the words, phrases and sentences encoded in them. But if we know nothing of the language being spoken, we will make nothing at all of the transmission.

It is obvious – once it has been pointed out – that the same message can be conveyed either in speech or writing. This suggests that the notion of 'language' is rather more abstract than one might suppose. Language, we might say, does not intrinsically depend on either speech or writing (or indeed on any specific means of expression, like the system of manual signs employed by the deaf), but is a more abstract notion. We might say that a language is the system of relationships that speakers have in their minds, and that the language can be expressed in speech or writing or by another medium. The linguist usually works with this more abstract notion of language. At the same time much can be said about written and spoken language in general or about a particular written and spoken language, witness the success with which linguists write descriptions of other languages from which assiduous students can acquire enough knowledge to communicate in them.

These remarks about a speaker and a listener have an important consequence for anyone who wishes to study language. To talk about language in any sensible fashion we have to draw a number of distinctions that are not normally drawn overtly in school grammars of languages.

In the first place, languages are organized on two levels: the *level of expression* – to put it crudely, the level of the noises in which the message is encoded – and the *level of content*. The word 'content' is unfortunate, since this level encompasses both the organization of words into sentences and the meanings that are associated with these words and sentences, but it is the standard term.

The linguist needs a sound knowledge of both levels of organization. Since language may be viewed as something abstract and messages can be encoded in sounds or writing, in principle the study of the level of expression will extend to both writing systems and sound systems. In practice, most attention has focused on the expression of language in sound, reflecting the general consensus among linguists that spoken language is more basic than written language. The study of the level of expression of sounds belongs to phonetics and phonology. Phonetics is concerned with the description of physical sounds, the functioning of the organs that are involved in their production and the range of sounds the speech organs can produce; phonology is concerned with how different languages systematically use sounds for the transmission of messages. We will not be directly concerned with either in this book.

We said in the previous paragraph that spoken language is more basic than written language, yet the written language enjoys greater prestige in all communities in possession of a writing system and a literature. Written language has a greater range of vocabulary, a more complex syntax and, except perhaps in hastily composed letters, none of the stops, starts and repetitions of spoken language. So great is the power of written language that in some formal situations, such as delivering judgments in court or preaching sermons, it is felt appropriate to use the syntax and vocabulary of written language for proceedings conducted in speech.

Nevertheless, it is the spoken language which is fundamental. Every normal human being learns to speak before he or she learns to read and write. Even where literacy is universal most people conduct most of their communication in speech (typically face to face, but also via radios, television sets and telephones), and many books and newspapers are written in a style that approaches the style of spoken language.

The history of languages contributes two facts that put the primacy of spoken language beyond doubt. First, no case is known of a community that had a written language before it had a spoken one. Speech always developed a long time before the emergence of a writing system. The second is that changes in language over time by and large originate in the spoken language and gradually find their way into the written language.

From the level of expression let us pass to the level of content, bearing in mind that the term 'content' is too narrow. Study of the content level has traditionally been split between syntax and semantics. Syntax is concerned with ways in which words combine to make sentences, and semantics deals with meaning. Traditionally a third component was also recognized – morphology, dealing with the structure of words. It is evident that if sentences can be split up to make words, words can be split up into smaller units. For example, *ineffectiveness* consists of four parts: *in, effect, ive* and *ness.* Morphology is the subject of Part Two of this book. It is in many ways a sort of 'bridge' between the content and the expression level. It is related to syntax in a natural manner since the parts of words can be considered as participating in the structure of sentences along with the words themselves. Morphology is also relevant to the study of the expression level, because the structure of words is relevant to the functioning of systems of sounds. However, that aspect of morphology is not of major concern in this book.

The relationship between syntax and semantics is difficult and controversial. It has always been recognized that there is some distinction to be drawn between the meaning and the structure of sentences, but it is far from clear just where this boundary should be drawn. Language is a means of conveying meanings of various kinds, and it would be surprising indeed if considerations of meaning and of structure were totally separate. This book takes the view, however, that syntactic and morphological structure should be studied in their own terms as far as possible, the results furnishing a basis for investigations into semantics. Syntax and morphology are gateways to meaning, and it is important to have secure syntactic and morphological criteria against which intuitions about meaning can be measured. But, as we shall see, discussions of syntax cannot, and should not, totally exclude considerations of meaning.

In the course of our discussion we will need to redefine and refine a number of concepts and terms commonly used in language description. One we can usefully tackle immediately is 'sentence'. In ordinary usage this term refers sometimes to the actual sequences of sounds produced by a speaker, sometimes to an orthographic unit and sometimes to something much more abstract. In this book we use the term 'utterance' to refer to actual sequences of sounds, and restrict the term 'sentence' to the more abstract use. We consider the sentence to be a unit described in the syntax at the abstract level of content.

In order to understand why we make this distinction, consider the relationship between a sentence and its corresponding utterances. More than one utterance corresponds to a given sentence, in fact, a multitude of utterances. Take the sentence which we may represent orthographically as *What did you think of the programme on China?.* Even in the speech of one and the same speaker this sentence may be expressed (or realized) by a large number of different utterances. In slow speech there may be a sound in the utterance corresponding to the last letter in *what* and a separate sound corresponding to each of the letters in *did*, to the first letter in *you* and to the last two letters in *you*. (To talk of 'separate sounds' in this way is to skate over some very formidable problems in the analysis of speech.) But if the speaker speaks at even ordinary conversational speed there may be only one separate sound corresponding to the last letter in *what* and the first letter in *you*. This part of the utterance might be represented as *whadja* with *dj* representing one sound.

The discrepancy between the number of 'letters' and the number of separate sounds in our sentence may be considerable. Moreover, other factors increase the number of possible utterances corresponding to our sentence – all within the speech of our one speaker. For example, the speaker's attention may be distracted, causing him or her to repeat a word, or perhaps to miss out a word entirely. The speaker may inhale a crumb of toast and finish the utterance in gasps and coughs. The speaker may suffer from laryngitis that has all but paralysed some of the organs of speech, so the utterance is deformed.

Furthermore, different speakers can produce a range of utterances that are interpreted as realizations of our original sentence. The quality of voice, for instance, is clearly different between men and women; and no two men or women have exactly the same quality of voice. Similarly, speakers of the different accents of English may not aim at the 'same' sounds. If all these factors are put together the utterances which can realize our sentence vary enormously.

Yet all of these different utterances are related by the hearer to the same, abstract sentence. Native speakers clearly practise such an abstraction in everyday conversation. Normally we simply do not notice if a word is repeated or a couple of sounds are slurred (unless the interference is so great that the intended sentence cannot be reconstructed). Indeed, we are often able to guess at the complete sentence after hearing only part of the utterance. It is this abstract notion of the sentence that the linguist usually works with.

Let us accept then that the sentence is an abstract unit. Linguists set up such a unit to explain how we relate a range of utterances to the same abstract sentence, and to explain patterns within the sentence. For the moment we can suppose that these patterns are built up of words; it turns out that the only satisfactory way to make sense of the arrangements of words is to consider the patterns they form within sentences.

Words are dependent on each other in many different ways. For example, they may have to occur in a certain order. In English, words like *the* and *a* precede the nouns they go with, but in some other languages what corresponds to *the* in English is placed after the noun. Again, one word may not be able to occur unless another word is present. In the sentence *Foreign books are expense, foreign* cannot occur unless there is a word like *books*. The forms of words may also differ according to what other words are present in the sentence. In Latin, for instance, the adjective corresponding to *good* is *bon-*, the hyphen indicating that various items can be added. If the adjective goes with a noun such as *puer* ('boy'), it has the form *bonus*, but if it goes with a noun such as *puella* ('girl'), it has the form *bona*. These relationships or dependencies between words can be sensibly described only if we establish the sentence as a unit in our description. We define the sentence then as an abstract unit postulated in order to account for the dependencies between units of syntactic structure.

When the abstractness of language was first mentioned, along with the distinction between the levels of content and expression, there was a short discussion of the relationship between written and spoken language. Linguists, it was argued, have good reason to assign priority to spoken language. Closely related to the linguists' attitude to spoken and written language is a very important point concerning the task of describing the syntax of a language.

To a great extent we treat the topics that used to be gathered together under the heading of 'grammar', a word that for many people has a strong association with the idea of 'good grammar'. The popular understanding seems to be that the grammar of a language, whether your native language or a foreign language, contains information that enables its user to write and speak the language correctly. This understanding has some foundation, but the notion of correctness is far from simple.

The complexities of the notion can be illustrated by the situation in Britain. Children learning English in Exeter, Manchester, or Edinburgh produce utterances that satisfy the expectations of the people they come in contact with: relatives, the children they play with, the local shopkeepers. (This is the simplest of cases. For many children the learning of the appropriate English is not so straight-forward, for instance, the child of Bengali-speaking parents in an area inhabited by English speakers.) Children cannot string any sort of noises together in any order. They must produce approximately the noises produced by the people around them, and the noises must be combined into sequences as they are by those other people.

Every community has rules of language that have to be observed by its members. The person who does not observe them is not understood and, more seriously, is open to ridicule. Conversely, the child who produces appropriate utterances speaks correctly from the point of view of the local community.

When children go to school, they may speak incorrectly from the point of view of this new community. At some stage in their education children are encouraged to adapt to a new standard of correctness, usually that of the literary language. Different children adapt to different degrees. The question whether adaptation is necessary or desirable is highly emotive and divisive, and one we do not tackle here. From a linguistic viewpoint, the literary language is only one dialect of English, even though many may consider it the 'correct' form. All dialects of English, literary and non-literary, have their own rules, and these rules are capable of description. The grammar itself makes no evaluative judgements – it is users of the language that make such judgements, for reasons (for instance, social prestige) external to grammatical considerations.

What is considered to be 'correct' usage can change over time. Let us illustrate this. Twenty years ago linguistic observers in Britain would have recorded utterances that could be related to sentences like *This book is different from that book* and *This book is different to that book*. A manual of 'faults' to be avoided by the public speaker would have listed the *different to* construction as one to be avoided. Linguists, however, would have observed and recorded utterances corresponding to sentences with the *different to* construction and would have brought them into their descriptions. They might also have sought to account for the rise of this construction by noting the similarity in meaning between X being 'different from' Y and X being 'opposed to' Y, or by observing the occurrence of *to* with adjectives like *opposite* and *opposed*. Change has not stopped there. In the 1990s linguists will record utterances related to sentences like *This book is different than that book*. They might bring this too into their descriptions, accounting for the construction by noting the connection between saying that X and Y are 'different' and that X and Y are 'to be compared'. The comparative construction makes use of *than* as in *X is smaller than Y*, and we note constructions like *other than* and *rather than*.

The *different than* construction is probably even less acceptable to the authors of public-speaking manuals than the *different to* one. Yet many speakers of English use both constructions, and in the course of time both may become acceptable even to the purist. If linguists declined to record such constructions they would not only be falsifying the facts of the language but also throwing away data that affords an insight into how a language functions as a system, and how such systems change.

We do not assert that linguists never come across 'incorrect' data – our previous discussion of slips of the tongue, the omission of words and so on illustrated that they do. We maintain, however, that 'correctness' is a notion relative to particular uses of language and to particular dialects or subdialects. The description of a language may concentrate on the literary dialect of the language or on some other dialect, but it is inappropriate to assert that the former deals with 'good' and the latter with 'bad' grammar.

Finally, let us say that the study of language can be different and exciting. No complete grammar of any language, be it a literary language or a dialect, has yet been written. Even the enormous amount of work done recently on the syntax of English, far from solving all the problems of English, has only served to increase the number of complexities that require investigation.

People with a little training in syntax (and in other branches of linguistics) will find much to occupy their attention. Let us recall that people have to be taught to observe; whether it be the doctor learning to observe and 'read' the human body; the artist learning to observe and 'read' great paintings; or the geologist and geomorphologist learning to observe and 'read' the landscape. At the very least, a knowledge of syntax should enable students to observe and 'read' the utterances they hear, opening their ears to a multitude of curiosities.

Part one

Constituent structure

1 Constituent structure

1.1 Determining constituent structure

The analysis of the structure of sentences is traditionally known as 'parsing'. Part of the *Oxford English Dictionary*'s definition of PARSE is: 'to resolve (a sentence etc.) into its component parts of speech and describe them grammatically'. In linguistic work each of the 'component parts' of a sentence is a 'constituent' and the whole procedure is 'constituent structure analysis'.

In this chapter we concentrate on the two closely related operations suggested by the quotation:

(1) the analysis of the sentence into its constituents;
(2) the grammatical description of these constituents.

We will expect the first operation to tell us how to break a sentence down into its constituent parts, and which strings of words are, and which are not, constituents. Or, seen the other way round, the description will tell us how words can combine to form larger constituents, and how these, in their turn, can form yet larger constituents until we have constructed a sentence.

The second operation will describe how constituents differ from each other, how each type is constructed, how they combine with each other, what order they can, or must, occur in, and so on. This will involve naming the different types of constituent so that we can identify them.

Let us, as an example, consider how we might describe the structure of the sentence:

1 The dog frightened the child

We will make three initial assumptions, all of them justified in due course. First, although we are considering only a single sentence, it is not the only sentence in the language, and we can, indeed must, assume that we can use our knowledge of other potential sentences to guide our analysis. The description we give to this sentence must be compatible with the analysis we would like to make of other sentences we might have chosen; our ultimate aim is the description not of this single sentence but of the language as a whole.

Secondly, we assume that the smallest constituents with which we are concerned are the five words represented in **1**. This assumption begs a number of questions. For one thing, it is clearly not quite true, since a word like *frightened* is recognizable as the 'past tense' form of the verb FRIGHTEN and is readily analysable into the smaller constituents *frighten* and *-ed*. The analysis is based on the analogy of comparable 'past tense' forms of other verbs: *kill: kill-ed*, *walk: walk-ed*, *cook: cook-ed*, and so on. The analysis of words introduces a number of complex issues which we can disregard for our present purposes but to which we will return in Part Two. However, although we will for the time being accept words as unanalysable wholes it will be helpful to introduce three conventions to distinguish between different uses of the term 'word' itself. The first is to use italics to quote actual word forms like *frightened* and *killed* when they are quoted in the text. The second convention is to use small capitals to refer to 'dictionary' or 'lexical' entries (the technical term is 'lexeme'). Thus FRIGHTEN is the lexeme common to all the variant word forms of FRIGHTEN: *frighten* and *frightened*, which we have already met, and the other regular forms of FRIGHTEN, *frightens* and *frightening*, which we will soon encounter. Our third notational convention arises from the observation that *frightened* is the 'past tense' form of FRIGHTEN. It will sometimes be helpful to use a grammatical description like this and when it is, we will annotate the grammatical category involved as a 'feature' subscripted to the relevant lexical item; thus *frightened*, 'the past tense form of FRIGHTEN', will, when necessary, be represented as FRIGHTEN$_{[past]}$; similarly *killed*, the past tense form of KILL, by KILL$_{[past]}$. If we need to refer in general terms to the 'past tense form of a verb', we can use the annotation V$_{[past]}$.

Our third assumption concerns the sentence. We will use the neutral term 'string' to refer to any sequence of constituents; so we can refer to *the dog*, *frightened the child*, or indeed the whole of **1** as strings with no commitment as to whether they do or do not form a constituent or any identification of the type of constituents they are. What entitles us to refer to the string **1** as a sentence, when the other strings mentioned do not seem to be sentences? Unfortunately, as with the word, there are considerable problems about the identification of sentences; to call a string a sentence implies that it has a certain sort of unity, but it is far from easy to describe exactly what sort of unity a string needs to have for it to be referred to as a sentence. We might regard the study of syntax as an attempt to answer just this question. For the time being we merely accept that **1** is a sentence; again our provisional justification is that it is supposed that we would all agree that **1** is indeed a sentence.

With these three assumptions in mind, let us contemplate the first operation noted at the beginning of the chapter: the analysis of the sentence:

2   The dog frightened the child

into its relevant parts, its constituents.

At an intuitive level *the dog*, *frightened* and *the child* appear to be relevant constituents in a way that strings like *frightened the* or *dog frightened* do not. Furthermore, again at an intuitive level, the strings *the dog* and *the child* seem to be constituents of the same type. We can back these intuitions by formal criteria if we consider the relationships between our sentence and other sentences in the language. Here we will use two types of criteria; one has to do with the internal structure of a constituent and the other with its distribution within the sentence. Both demonstrate that the strings we regard as constituents have a coherence which will justify their treatment as units.

We will first think about internal structure. Consider the strings *the dog* and *the child* and note that in both strings the article *the* occurs. Articles cannot co-occur with words like *frightened* (here, and throughout the book, the symbol * preceding a string indicates that it is not well formed):

3   *The dog the frightened the child

It must also be the initial word in its constituent:

4   *Dog the frightened child the

We also note that these strings can be substituted by a single word, and the sentence as a whole remains grammatical:

5a   *Fido* frightened *Charlie*
5b   *It* frightened *him*

Similarly, these constituents can be substituted by other, longer strings, which we intuitively recognize as 'expansions', and the sentence still remains grammatical:

6   *The big dog that lives across the road* frightened *the child next door*

Comparable substitutions and expansions are not possible for strings like *frightened the*. We can make similar observations about *frightened*. Since it is a single word, and we are treating words as the smallest constituents, we will say nothing about its internal structure, but it can certainly be substituted by various expansions:

7a   The dog *has frightened* the child
7b   The dog *may have frightened* the child

and we note that these expansions (*has*, *may have*) are impossible with constituents like *the child*:

8a   **The has child* frightened the dog
8b   **May have the child* frightened the dog

just as the expansions appropriate to constituents like *the child* are impossible with constituents like *frightened*:

9a   *The dog *big frightened* the child
9b   *The dog *frightened that lives next door* the child

So much for internal structure; constituents may be substitutable by single words (for example, *the dog*, *Fido*, *it*) or be appropriately expanded (for example, *the dog*, *the big dog*) and different constituents have different structural properties.

Now consider the distribution of constituents within the sentence. We need to know the range of environments in which a particular type of constituent can be found and whether it retains its integrity as a constituent in these other structural positions. Consider once more the strings *the dog* and *the child*. To begin with they are mutually substitutable:

10a The dog frightened the child
10b The child frightened the dog

but neither is substitutable for *frightened*. Next note that these strings retain their unity in sentences like those in **11**, all of which, it would probably be agreed, are systematically related to our original sentence **1**:

11a *The child* was frightened by *the dog*
11b It was *the dog* that frightened *the child*
11c What *the dog* did was frighten *the child*
11d What happened to *the child* was that *the dog* frightened it

Note also the corresponding question-and-answer sequence:

12a *What* frightened the child?
   The dog
12b *Who* did the dog frighten?
   The child

The constituents we are interested in retain their integrity as they are 'moved around' the sentence, as in **11**, and in related sentences, as in **12**. Note that the substitutions and expansions exemplified above in **5** and **6** show exactly the same integrity; that is, substitution of *Fido* or *the big dog that lives next door* for *the dog* in any of the examples in **11** or **12** still yields a grammatical sentence. There is no way in which arbitrary strings like *dog frightened* or *frightened the* show a comparable integrity.

The discussion shows, then, that there is some justification for regarding the constituents of our sentence as:

13 The dog – frightened – the child

Let us now turn to the second operation we noted at the beginning of the chapter, the grammatical description and naming of parts. We declared at the beginning of the chapter that the smallest constituents we would recognize for our present purposes would be the individual word forms. Traditionally the individual words have been classified as shown in **14**, as can be verified in any dictionary. We will accept this classification and return to justify it in more detail in a later chapter.

14   *frightened* is a V(erb)
    dog is a N(oun)
    child is a N(oun)
    the is an Art(icle)

What then of the larger constituents we identified? The discussion showed that constituents like *the dog* and *the child* are of the same type, and following accepted usage we will name these constituents Noun Phrases, abbreviated as NP. The choice of name is not accidental; the NP has an N as its principal constituent.

Summarizing, the whole string is a sentence with the structure shown in **15a**; each of the NPs has the structure shown in **15b**, and the individual words have been classified as in **16**:

15a	S:	NP V NP		(Sentence; Noun Phrase; Verb)
15b	NP:	Art N		(Article; Noun)

16	*child*:	N	(Noun)
	dog:	N	(Noun)
	frightened:	V	(Verb)
	the:	Art	(Article)

15 is a simple grammar of our sentence and **16** is a lexicon or dictionary. Together, albeit in a simple way, they meet the requirements with which we started the chapter:

(1)   the analysis of the sentence into its constituents – **15** tells us what the correct analysis of the sentence as a whole and of each of its parts should be;

(2)   the grammatical description of these constituents – **16** tells us the word class of each individual word, and **15** tells us how each word class functions in larger structures; articles precede nouns in noun phrases, noun phrases can occur as 'subject' and 'object'[1] of a sentence, and so on.

1.2   Representing and talking about constituent structure

There are a number of ways of representing this information about constituent structure. One is to indicate constituent structure by bracketing:

17   (((The) (dog)) (frightened) ((the) (child)))

There is a pair of brackets round each word, since each word is a constituent. Since the strings *the dog* and *the child* are also constituents, these are also enclosed by a pair of brackets. Since the sentence as a whole is a unit, there are brackets round the whole string. Since brackets come in pairs, there must always be as many right-facing opening brackets as there are left-facing closing brackets. Bracketing by itself shows the constituent structure but omits information about the type of constituent. This can be included by labelling the brackets with a subscript identifying the type of constituent, shown on the left of the opening bracket:

18 $_S(_{NP}(_{Art}(\text{The})\ _N(\text{dog}))_{VP}(\text{frightened})\ _{NP}(_{Art}(\text{the})$

$_N(\text{child})))$

Representations of this kind are called labelled and bracketed strings.

Sometimes such representations are not easy to read, especially if there is a good deal of structure to represent. An alternative representation, often preferred, is the 'tree diagram', illustrated in Figure 1.1.

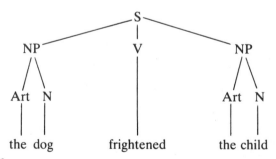

Figure 1.1

It is conventional to draw trees in the manner shown in Figure 1.1, with the 'branches' of the tree developing downwards, as it were, from the 'root' S. To complete the botanical metaphor, when no further branching is possible we have 'leaves' – in Figure 1.1 the individual words are the leaves of the tree. Yet another kind of representation, which is often convenient for those who use typewriters and word processors, is a 'vine diagram', as in Figure 1.2.

```
        S
            NP
                    Art         the
                    N           dog
                    V           frightened
                    NP
                    Art         the
                    N           child
```

Figure 1.2

It should be stressed that the vine diagram in Figure 1.2, the tree in Figure 1.1 and the labelled and bracketed string in **18** all convey exactly the same information. We will use all three kinds of representation, the choice on any particular occasion being determined by which is the clearest or most convenient. It may also be observed that it is sometimes convenient to show a partial structure; for instance, we might need to know that some string is an NP, but not be particularly interested in the internal structure of the NP and we could represent this in a structure like that in Figure 1.3.

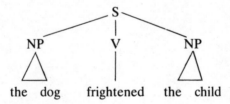

Figure 1.3

At this point it is convenient to introduce some vocabulary to talk about representations of this kind. We will introduce this with respect to the tree diagram, where the terminology is perhaps most clearly demonstrable, though it can be generalized to the other representations. Those places where the tree branches are nodes. To identify nodes we label them. We can thus refer to the 'rightmost NP node', the 'V node', and so on. Note that nodes do not have to branch; some do (the S and NP nodes in Figure 1.1), while others do not (the V node).

We can use this terminology to talk about some of the grammatical relations represented in the tree. First, the relation of dominance: a node dominates all the constituents that are traceable back to it. Thus in Figure 1.1, the first NP dominates the string *the dog*, but it does not dominate, say, *frightened*. A more particular notion is that of immediate dominance; a node A immediately dominates another node B if there are no other intermediate nodes. Thus S dominates everything in the sentence, indeed it must do so, but it immediately dominates only NP, V and NP. S dominates, but does not immediately dominate, Art + N.

The relation of constituency is a slightly different way of talking about the same configurations. Thus, *the* and *dog* are constituents of the leftmost NP, and, corresponding to the notion of immediate domination, Art and N are the immediate constituents of the leftmost NP. In this terminology, constituents are described as being 'in construction' with each other if they are immediate constituents of the same node; thus Art and N are in construction in the leftmost NP.

The relationship of order, or precedence, describes the order in which constituents can or must occur. Thus, within NPs, articles must precede nouns and within the sentence the NP which precedes the verb can be identified as the 'subject' and that which follows the verb as the 'object'.

'Family tree' terminology, which combines the relations of dominance, constituency and order, is often used to describe some of these relationships. In Figure 1.1, NP, V and NP are daughters of S, the leftmost NP being the left daughter, and the rightmost NP being the right daughter. In the same terms, S is the mother of NP, V and NP, the leftmost NP is the left sister of V (both are daughters of the same mother), and the rightmost NP is the right sister of V.

1.3 Hierarchical structure

We close this chapter by drawing attention to the hierarchical structure of the analysis in Figure 1.1; the sentence is analysed into its immediate constituents, each of these constituents into its immediate constituents, and so on. The hierarchical nature of the analysis illustrates what appears to be a universal principle of the organization of human languages, that they have hierarchical syntactic structures. It is not immediately obvious why this should be so, nor why this analysis is preferable to an analysis in terms of a single string (a 'string constituent analysis') as illustrated for sentence **1**, in Figure 1.4.

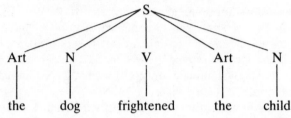

Figure 1.4

Let us compare Figures 1.1 and 1.4. First, Figure 1.4 does not indicate that the NP is a relevant sentence constituent, yet our previous discussion suggests it is an important constituent, in that a number of generalizations about syntactic structure can be more clearly formulated using such a constituent. Secondly, a hierarchical analysis shows that the relationship between any pair of constituents must be considered in terms of relationships established within the tree as a whole; mere contiguity is not necessarily a particularly interesting relationship.

Thus, in Figure 1.1, there is a close relationship between the contiguous items *the* and *dog*, they are constituents of NP, but there is no immediate relationship between *dog* and *frightened*, even though they are contiguous. Rather the V *frightened* has a relationship to the NP *the dog*, since both are constituents of S. This can be seen more clearly if we compare the relationships between the strings *the child* and *frightened* in the two sentences analysed in Figures 1.5 and 1.6.

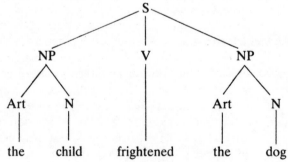

Figure 1.5

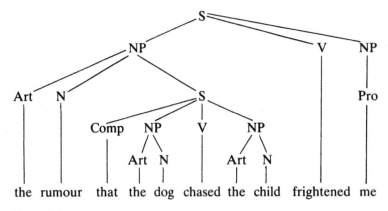

Figure 1.6

The string *the rumour that the dog chased the child* is an NP which
has the sentence *the dog chased the child* embedded in it.[2] In Figure
1.5 both *the child* and *frightened* are daughters of S. In traditional
terms *the child* is the 'subject' of the verb *frightened*; this sentence
would be used when the child in question 'did' the 'frightening'. In
Figure 1.6 *the child* is a daughter of the embedded S, and in
traditional terms the 'object' of the verb *chased* (it is 'the child' that
is 'chased'), and *frightened* is a daughter of the superordinate S.
Whereas in Figure 1.5 *the child* is the subject of *frightened*, in Figure
1.6 the subject of *frightened* is the NP *the rumour that the dog chased
the child*. The relationship between the contiguous items *the child*
and *frightened* is close in Figure 1.5, but remote in Figure 1.6.

Finally, if we adopt a hierarchical analysis we discover that 'the
same' constituents keep appearing at different places within
constituent structures. We have already observed this in the case of
the NP; we may now observe in Figure 1.6 that this is also true of
sentence structures, since one sentence of the structural form NP +
V + NP is embedded inside another sentence of precisely the same
form. This 'nesting' property of constituents is an important
characteristic of language, and one to which we shall return in
Chapter 9.

Technical terms

bracketing	leaves
branching	lexeme
constituent	lexical entry
constituent structure	mother of
construction	node
daughter of	parse
distribution	phrase
domination	root
expansion	sister of
hierarchical structure	string
immediate constituent	substitution
immediate domination	tree diagram
in construction with	vine diagram
internal structure	word class
labelled and bracketed string	word form
labelling	

Notes

1   The notions of 'subject' and 'object' are discussed in more detail in Chapter 19. For our immediate purposes we can consider the subject as the NP immediately preceding the verb and the object as the NP immediately following the verb.
2   NPs of this kind are discussed in more detail in Chapter 9.

2 Form classes

2.1 Form classes

The previous chapter discussed the sentence *The dog frightened the child* and assigned to it the constituent structure of Figure 2.1.

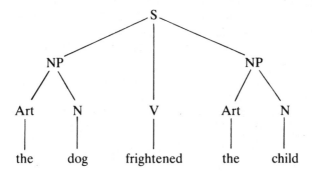

Figure 2.1

Many hundreds of sentences in English can be analysed in an analogous fashion, for example:

1a The dog chased the child
1b The cat killed a bird
1c A child hit the man
1d The dog caught a cat

In these sentences the words fall into groups that are mutually substitutable within the sentence structure shown in Figure 2.1, as summarized in Figure 2.2.

the	dog	frightened	the	dog
a	child	chased	a	child
	cat	killed		cat
	bird	hit		bird
		caught		

Figure 2.2

Selecting one word from each column yields a string which is an acceptable sentence of English. Tables like these, which may be familiar from foreign-language teaching manuals, are called substitution tables, since they use the principle of simple substitution. They are also very simple grammars.

A set of words like {*dog, child, cat, man, bird*} where the individual words are mutually substitutable is known as a word class or, since words are also the items we find in a dictionary or lexicon, as a 'lexical class', a usage we will prefer. Curly brackets, { . . . }, are used to indicate set, or class, membership. Our analysis has established three lexical classes: the class {*the, a*}, the class {*dog, child, man, cat, bird*} and the class {*frightened, chased, killed, caught, hit*}. We have named them, following traditional usage, Art(icle), N(oun) and V(erb).

Lexical classes are not the only classes needed in a grammar. In the preceding chapter we saw that strings of words like *the dog* and *the child* also need to be accounted for. We identified them as Noun Phrases (NP) and will refer to categories like NP as 'phrasal classes'. The general term 'form class' will be used to cover both lexical (or word) classes and phrasal classes. A substitution table can accommodate information about form classes in general, including both lexical and phrasal classes, as in Figure 2.3.

	S			
NP		V	NP	
Art	N		Art	N
the	dog	frightened	the	dog
a	child	chased	a	child
	cat	killed		cat
	bird	hit		bird
		caught		

Figure 2.3

We saw in Chapter 1 that there are two important and closely related points about the constituent structure of form classes:

(1)   the membership or the internal structure of the class;
(2)   the distribution of the class in other constituents.

With respect to the first point, as far as lexical classes are concerned, we assigned {*the a*} to the class Art(icle), {*dog, child, cat, bird*} to the class N(oun) and {*frightened, chased, killed, caught, hit*} to the class V(erb). In Chapter 1 we decided that we are not at present concerned with the internal structure of words; we did, however, observe that a form like *frightened* is the 'past tense form of the verb FRIGHTEN' and annotated this by showing 'past' as a 'feature' of the item FRIGHTEN: FRIGHTEN$_{[past]}$. We can now make the more general point that particular lexical classes can be associated with particular 'grammatical categories'. In English, the grammatical category of 'tense' is uniquely associated with verbs and, as we will see in Part Two, it has the two terms 'past' and 'present'. For our immediate purposes we record this association with the notation in **2a**; the alternation is exemplified in **2b**:

2a   V[tense: past, present]
2b   The dog frightens the child   FRIGHTEN$_{[pres]}$

     The dog frightened the child   FRIGHTEN$_{[past]}$

From these examples, a preliminary hypothesis would be that with FRIGHTEN 'present' and 'past' can be associated with the word fragments -*s* and -*ed*, an alternation that is also found with other verbs; for example, among the members of our class of verbs we find CHASE: *chases, chased* and KILL: *kills, killed*. However, the position is not always as simple as this, as other members of our class of verbs illustrate; thus CATCH: *catches, caught* and HIT: *hits, hit*. All verbs have 'past tense' forms but the way tense is 'realized' is not uniform, as the examples illustrate. It is because of complications of this kind that we determined that at this point we would consider the word as the minimal unit of analysis and not concern ourselves with its internal structure. We return to consider this question in detail in Part Two. For our present purposes it is sufficient to note that particular grammatical categories can be associated with particular word classes.

Just as verbs are associated with the category of tense, so nouns are associated with the grammatical category of 'number', with the two terms 'singular' and 'plural', as illustrated in **3**:

3a   N[number: sing, pl]

3b   The dog frightened the children DOG$_{[sing]}$ CHILD$_{[pl]}$

   The dogs frightened the child   DOG$_{[pl]}$ CHILD$_{[sing]}$

3b shows that nouns show number alternation in a variety of ways. DOG: *dog, dogs* illustrates the 'regular' pattern, but other members of the class of nouns have a different way of marking plural: CHILD: *child, children*; MAN: *man, men*. As before, we will merely note here that nouns are associated with the category of number, annotate this where appropriate as in the annotations in **3** and leave matters of their internal structure to Part Two.

We now turn to the question of distribution. By the distribution of an item, we mean the set of environments in which it occurs. In sentence **1** in Chapter 1 the distribution of *frightened* is as shown in **4a**, the sign __ indicating the place within the sentence, the environment, in which this item occurs. Since all the verbs in **1** occur in this or a comparable environment a more economical, and revealing, description can be made by describing the relevant environment not in terms of other individual words, but in terms of class membership. So we can say that the distribution of V is as shown in **4b**:

4a   The dog __ the child

4b $_S(NP \underline{\quad} NP)$

That is, V occurs in sentences with an NP as right sister and another as left sister. Since *frightened* is a V, this means that it occurs in just this environment.

The distribution of *the* in the data is the two environments shown in **5a** and **5b**. More economically, *the* is a member of the class Art and the distribution of Art is as shown in **5c**, that is, articles precede nouns in NPs:

5a   __ dog frightened the child

5b   The dog frightened __ child

5c $_{NP}(\underline{\quad} N)$

In the case of the phrasal class NP, it would be absurd and cumbersome to state its membership in terms of strings of individual words; the class NP consists of the strings {*the dog, the cat, the bird* . . .}, and so on. Instead we can describe its internal structure in terms of other form classes – the NP consists of strings of the form Art + N – and leave a specification of what these classes contain to our description of the membership of Art and N.

We now have elementary grammatical descriptions of these various classes expressed in terms of their internal structure and their distribution within other structures. **6a** shows the internal structure and distribution of the class of Noun Phrases. **6b–d** describe the three lexical classes Art, N and V; here instead of a description of internal structure we note the association between a lexical class and a particular grammatical category:

6a A Noun Phrase (NP) contains a noun which may optionally be preceded by an article, that is, $_{NP}((Art)\ N)$

It occurs in the environments: $_S(\underline{\quad}\ V\ NP)$ and $_S(NP\ V\ \underline{\quad})$

6b An Art(icle) occurs in the environment: $_{NP}(\underline{\quad}\ N)$

(that is, it occurs in Noun Phrases preceding a noun)
Members include: {*the, a*}

6c A N(oun) is associated with the grammatical category of number: N[number: sing, pl]
It occurs in the environment: $_{NP}(Art\ \underline{\quad})$

(that is, it occurs in Noun Phrases following an article)
Members include: {*dog, child, cat, man, bird*}

6d A V(erb) is associated with the grammatical category of tense: V[tense: past, present]
It occurs in the environment: $_S(NP\ \underline{\quad}\ NP)$

(that is, it occurs in Sentences preceded and followed by a Noun Phrase)
Members include: {*frightened, chased, killed, caught, hit*}

2.1 Widening the data base

Lexical classes contain words. Other form classes, however, may contain as members not only single words, but also strings of words and indeed other form classes. Consider the membership of the class NP. Let us first widen our data base to include sentences like:

7a   The dog frightened the child
7b   Fido frightened the child
7c   The child frightened Fido
7d   John frightened Fido

These data introduce a new lexical class, with the membership {*Fido, John*}. We call this class Proper Names (PN). The distribution of PN is different from that of N in that members of this class may not be preceded by an Art *(*the Fido*). We have already assigned strings Art + N to a class labelled NP. We must now consider whether the class PN is itself a member of the class NP, or whether PN and NP are quite separate classes. If PN and NP are considered quite separate classes, the analyses of **7a** and **7b** are as shown in Figures 2.4 and 2.5.

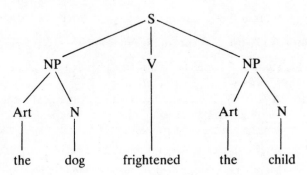

Figure 2.4

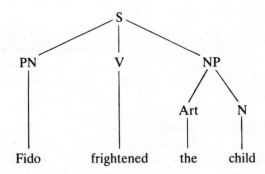

Figure 2.5

In these analyses the two sentences appear to be quite different since they do not have the same structure at any level, as can be seen by comparing the immediate constituents of S in each case:

8a NP V NP (Figure 2.4)
8b PN V NP (Figure 2.5)

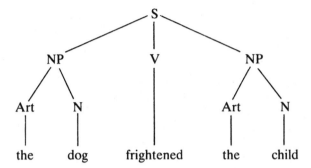

Figure 2.6

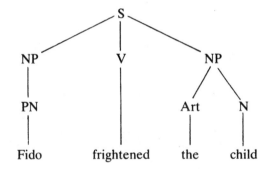

Figure 2.7

If, on the other hand, PN is considered a subclass of NP, the analysis is as shown in Figures 2.6 and 2.7. With these analyses the two sentences have the same structure at the most 'fundamental' level since the immediate constituents of S are, in both cases:

9 NP V NP

The two sentences differ only in the internal structure of the initial NP. This solution seems the more satisfactory on an intuitive basis, and formal evidence supports it. Before looking at this evidence, let us widen the data base a little further to include the following sentences:

10a   The boy yawned
10b   The dog slept
10c   Fido yawned
10d   John slept

As before, we consider that strings like {*the dog, the boy*} have the structure Art + N and are members of the class NP. {*Fido, John*} are once more members of the class PN.

{*Yawned, slept*} also form a substitution class. In terms of their 'internal structure' these items are verbs because, just like FRIGHTEN, and so on, they vary for the category of tense: YAWN$_{[pres]}$: *yawns*; YAWN$_{[past]}$: *yawned*; SLEEP$_{[pres]}$: *sleeps*; SLEEP$_{[past]}$: *slept*. Their distribution within the sentence, however, is different. As **11a** and **11b** show, verbs like FRIGHTEN must be followed by an NP, whereas verbs like YAWN cannot be followed by an NP (**11c** and **11d**):

11a   *Fido frightened
11b   Fido frightened the boy
11c   The dog yawned
11d   *The dog yawned the boy

The traditional labels for these subclasses of verb are 'transitive' (FRIGHTEN, and so on) and 'intransitive' (YAWN, and so on). We will adopt these labels, abbreviating them as VT and VI.

Using these two new subclasses of verb, VT and VI, if we analyse NP and PN as distinct classes, we end up with six distinct sentence types:

12a   NP VI   (sentences **10a** and **10b**)
12b   PN VI   (sentences **10c** and **10d**)
12c   NP VT NP   (sentence **2**)
12d   NP VT PN   (sentence **7a**)
12e   PN VT NP   (sentence **7b**)
12f   PN VT PN   (sentence **7c**)

whereas if we take PN as a subclass of NP we need account for only two types of sentence:

13a S: NP VI
13b S: NP VT NP

The distinction between Art + N and PN is now a matter of the NP. This leads to a more economical description, particularly if we seek to extend our data base still further, as we will.

This solution also makes possible a more economical statement of the distribution of our two verb classes. If NP and PN are distinct classes, then we must describe the distribution of our verbs in some such terms as:

14 VI occurs in the environments: NP __ #; PN __ #
VT occurs in the environments: NP __ NP; NP __ PN; PN __ NP; PN __ PN

(The symbol # indicates a constituent boundary – in terms of the immediate discussion, the sentence boundary. So the notation NP __ # says that VI must be preceded by an NP, and cannot be followed by another constituent.)

However, if we consider PN as a subclass of NP, a more economical statement results:

15 VI occurs in the environment NP __ #
VT occurs in the environment NP __ NP

The evidence we have considered has been entirely based on the substitutability of PN for strings Art + N. The external distribution of PN is also the same as that of strings Art + N, as can be determined by the appropriate substitutions in sentences like **11** and **12** discussed in the previous chapter. All this strongly suggests that PN and Art + N form a single class, NP, and we consider them as such.

Let us now look again at the statements made in **13** and **15**. By the same kind of argument, we might propose that VI and VT + NP themselves constitute a form class; many analysts would indeed adopt such a position and argue for a VP (Verb Phrase) constituent. We have already noted that both VT and VI are verbs in the sense that both are associated with the category of tense. Furthermore, using the sort of argument adopted earlier, introducing a VP will mean that at the most fundamental level all our sentences have the same structure, as shown in Figures 2.8 and 2.9. (Structure below the NP level is not shown since it is irrelevant to the argument.)

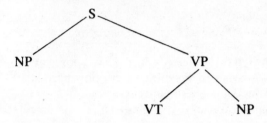

Figure 2.8

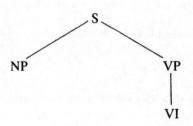

Figure 2.9

At the 'deepest' level, all the sentences are now analysed as having the common structure:

16   S: NP VP

rather than as being of two distinct structures, as in **13**.

This analysis can be supported by distributional evidence of the kind we have used earlier in the chapter, but superficially evidence for a VP is not so strong as it is for the NP. For instance, although we do find sentences like:

17   The cat chased the bird and the dog did so too
        (that is, the dog (chased the bird) too)

where *did so* might be thought of as a substitution for the VP *chased the bird*; we also find sentences like:

18a   The cat chased the bird and the dog the rat
         (that is, the dog (chased) the rat)
18b   The cat chased and the dog caught the bird
         (that is, the cat chased (the bird))

where constituents other than the VP are involved. Evidence in favour of identifying a constituent of the VP type is less conclusive than that leading us to recognize the NP. We will nevertheless recognize the VP as a constituent for two reasons; it allows us to offer all our sentences the same structure at the 'deepest' level (S: NP VP) and it will simplify our description of the relevant environments for verb subclassification.

The grammar and lexicon we developed in Chapter 1 (see page 16) can now be revised as in **19**. As before, the rules for constituent structures are separated from the lexicon. Generalizations about the grammatical categories that can be associated with word forms are noted in the lexicon:

19a *Constituent structures:*[1]
  S: NP VP
  VP: VI
    VT NP
  NP: Art N
    PN

19b *Lexicon*:

a	Art	Fido	PN
bird	N	frightened	VT
boy	N	hit	VT
cat	N	John	PN
caught	VT	killed	VT
chased	VT	slept	VI
child	N	the	Art
dog	N	yawned	VI

To conclude, we will introduce one further notational amendment. Earlier in the chapter we noted that the difference between intransitive verbs (VI) and transitive verbs (VT) can be summarized in the formula shown in **15**. Given that we now recognize a VP constituent, this can be reformulated as:

20 VI occurs in the environment $_{VP}(\text{—} \#)$

  VT occurs in the environment $_{VP}(\text{—} NP)$

That is, within the VP, transitive verbs (VT) require to be followed by an NP and intransitive verbs (VI) cannot be followed by another constituent. **20** suggests that instead of distinguishing between transitive and intransitive verbs by the label VT and VI, we could use the general form class label (V) together with the distributional environments themselves. The relationship between the old and the new notation is shown in **21**:

21   *old*   *new*
    transitive verbs: TV   V, __ NP
    intransitive verbs: IV   V, __ #

For reasons which will become apparent the new notation is more flexible, and we will use it hereafter. The necessary changes to the lexicon are shown in **23b** below.

This change has consequences for the constituent structure rules also. In particular, the two rules of **19a** (repeated below for convenience):

    19a   VP: VI
             VT NP

can be replaced by the single rule:

    22   VP: V (NP)

That is, the VP has V as an obligatory constituent, optionally followed by an NP. If nothing follows the verb, then we will need to select for the V node an intransitive verb (that is, V, __ #); and if V is followed by NP, then we will need to select a transitive verb (that is, V, __ NP). It may also be noted that the trees produced by the new rules will be slightly different, as can be seen by comparing Figures 2.8 and 2.9 (derived according to the 'old' rules in **19a**) with Figures 2.10 and 2.11 (derived according to the 'new' rules in **23a**).

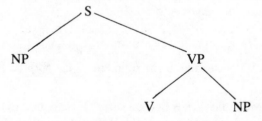

Figure 2.10

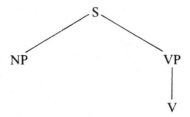

Figure 2.11

The revised rules are:

23a *Constituent structures*:
S: NP VP
VP: V   (NP)
NP   Art N
       PN

23b *Lexicon* (except for the verb entries, shown below, this remains as in **19b**):
caught   V, __ NP
chased   V, __ NP
frightened V, __ NP
hit   V, __ NP
killed   V, __ NP
slept   V, __ #
yawned   V, __ #

Technical terms

distribution	part of speech
environment	phrasal class
form class	substitution table
grammatical category	tense (past, present)
lexical class	term (in a grammatical category)
number (singular, plural)	word class

Note

1   In this chapter we will not be concerned with the formation rules for (singular and plural) nouns, or (past and present tense) verbs and we have consequently ignored this issue in the constituent structure and lexical rules in **20** and elsewhere.

Exercises

(1)   Examine the following tree diagram and answer the questions:

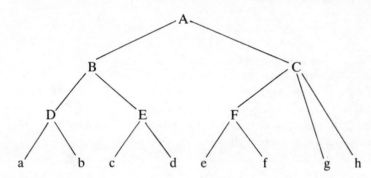

Tree diagram 1

    (a)   Which of the following are constituents of A? For each case of a constituent, what is the mother?

        (i)   c + d   (v)   c + d + e + f

        (ii)   g + h   (vi)   D + E

        (iii)   a + b + c   (vii)   E + C

        (iv)   a + b + c + d   (viii)   F + g + h

    (b)   What are the immediate constituents of: (i) C; (ii) B?
    (c)   What do the following immediately dominate? (i) A; (ii) F.
    (d)   What are the sisters of g?
    (e)   What is the mother of E?

(2)   Draw constituent structure trees for the following sentences:

The cat caught the rat
The cat ate the rat under the table
The cat was sick
The cat slept

(a) Write a grammar and lexicon which will generate your sentences.

(b) Write two more sentences that your grammar will generate.

(3) Examine the following structure and answer the questions:

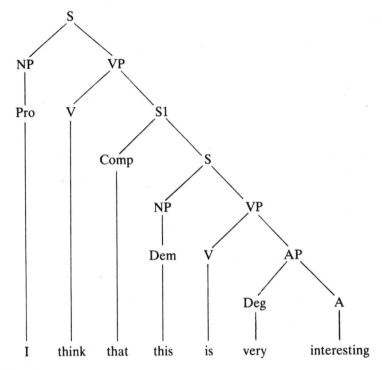

Tree diagram 2

Notes on the class names:

Pro(noun): in English items like *I, you, he, she* and *it*.

S1: the structure dominating an embedded sentence (see Chapter 9).

Comp(lementizer): a class of items including *that* which introduce embedded sentences (see Chapter 9).

Dem(onstrative): in English items like *this* and *that*.

AP: Adjective Phrase (see Chapter 6).

A(djective): in English items like *red, tall* and *interesting*, often found in NPs as 'noun modifiers' – *red hat, tall boy*.

Deg(ree word): in English items like *very, quite* and *rather*, often used as 'adjective modifiers' – *rather tall*.

(a)   Identify two phrasal nodes.
(b)   Identify two lexical categories.
(c)   Identify two branching nodes.
(d)   Identify two non-branching nodes.
(e)   What does AP immediately dominate?
(f)   What does AP dominate?
(g)   What is the mother of Dem?
(h)   What is the left sister of A?
(i)   Does V have a left sister?

(4)   Consider the following examples. Which do you find acceptable? Sort the verbs into classes on the basis of your judgements:

   (i)   The flour scattered over the floor
   (ii)   The child scattered the flour over the floor
   (iii)   The apple scattered over the floor
   (iv)   The child scattered the apple over the floor
   (v)   The child scattered the apples over the floor
   (vi)   The apples scattered over the floor
   (vii)   Sue and Harry met at Durham
   (viii) Sue met at Durham
   (ix)   Sue met Harry at Durham
   (x)   Children gathered in the playground
   (xi)   A crowd gathered in the square
   (xii)   Liz, Harry, Helen and Gordon gathered at the farmhouse
   (xiii) Water gathers in one corner of the garden
   (xiv)   Stones gather in this corner of the garden
   (xv)   We gathered water in a bucket
   (xvi)   The parents gathered the children in the playground
   (xvii) We gather stones in this corner of the garden

3 Constituent structure grammar

3.1 A simple grammar

In Chapter 1 we said that two of the tasks of a grammar are to provide a systematic account of the constituent structure of sentences and to account for the distribution of forms into classes. In this chapter we produce a formal and explicit grammar for the data discussed so far. To begin with, it is convenient to summarize our description.[1]

A: Constituent structures. The constituent structures discussed in the previous chapters are:

1 S: NP VP
   VP: V   (NP)
   NP: Art N
        PN

B: Lexical class membership. The lexicon introduced at the end of the previous chapter was:

2 a   Art   Fido   PN
   bird   N   frightened V, __ NP
   boy   N   hit   V, __ NP
   cat   N   John   PN
   caught   V, __ NP   killed   V, __ NP
   chased   V, __ NP   slept   V, __ #
   child   N   the   Art
   dog   N   yawned   V, __ #

This presentation shows the class (Art, N, PN, and so on) to which particular words belong. For convenience, and to follow traditional dictionaries, it has been arranged alphabetically, though a list arranged by some other principle, or even an unordered list, would serve our purpose equally well. We can also observe that this is not the only way in which the description could be arranged. It could have been organized to show the membership of individual word classes:

3   Art: {the, a}
   N: {bird, dog, child, boy, cat}
   PN: {Fido, John}
   VT: {frightened, chased, killed, caught}
   VI: {yawned, slept}

The description in **1** and **2** (or **3**) is itself a grammar in that it constitutes, as required, a systematic account of the language. We shall, however, further formalize our grammar, by using the following symbols:

symbol	*interpreted as*
$\rightarrow$	'consists of', 'has the constituents', 'is to be expanded as'
{X, Y} or $\begin{Bmatrix} X \\ Y \end{Bmatrix}$	'either X or Y, but not both'
X (Y)	'X is obligatory, and may be optionally followed by Y; X and Y must occur in the order specified'

The first symbol is used in rules like:

4   S $\rightarrow$ NP VP

Rules of this sort, known as 'rewrite rules', show constituency. For our purposes we will further stipulate that they also show the order of the constituents they introduce; that is, the constituents introduced on the right-hand side of a rule must occur in the order specified. We can now interpret **4**, in ordinary language, as: 'The sentence consists of the constituent NP followed, in that order, by the constituent VP.'

In rewrite rules, in order to avoid ambiguity, there must be only a single symbol on the left-hand side of the arrow; the right-hand side of the arrow may have one or more symbols. If the left-hand side of the arrow is not restricted to a single symbol it is unclear exactly what is a constituent of what. For instance, in:

5a S   → A B
5b A B → X Y Z

we do not know whether **5b** is to be interpreted as 'X + Y is an expansion of A and Z an expansion of B', as in Figure 3.1a, or as 'X is an expansion of A and Y + Z is an expansion of B', as in Figure 3.1b.

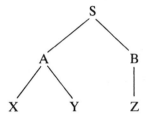

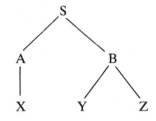

Figure 3.1a   *Figure 3.1b*

If we want the analysis of Figure 3.1a, the rules should be:

6 S → A B
   A → X Y
   B → Z

Or if we want the analysis in Figure 3.1b, the rules should be:

7 S → A B
   A → X
   B → Y Z

The rules must lead to an explicit and unambiguous account of constituent structure. For this reason we must only ever expand one symbol at a time, and hence only one symbol may be on the left-hand side of the arrow.

We have already noted that the constituents introduced on the right-hand side of the rule are considered by convention to be ordered. Thus the rule:

8 A → X Y

means that A is to be expanded into two constituents, X followed by

Y in that order. If the constituents may be in either order, the rule states this explicitly:

9   A → $\left\{\begin{array}{l} X\ Y \\ Y\ X \end{array}\right\}$

We have already seen the use of 'curly brackets' to indicate set or class membership (see page 24). Hence we introduce the further convention that when this notation occurs on the right-hand side of a rule, one and only one member of the set must be chosen. So in **9** A can be expanded either as X + Y or as Y + Z. The notation in effect collapses the two rules:

10   A → X Y
         A → Y X

into the single rule **9**. We will use the notation in rules like:

11   NP → $\left\{\begin{array}{l} Art\ N \\ PN \end{array}\right\}$

which can be read as: 'An NP consists of either Art + N or PN.'

The final notation introduces optional items:

12   A → X (Y)

This means that A can be developed either as X or as X + Y. This notation, like the last, is, in effect, a means of collapsing two rules into a single rule; **13a** can be seen as collapsing the two rules in **13b**:

13a   VP → V (NP)
13b   VP → V NP
          VP → V

Using these conventions, we can write our constituent structure rules like this:

14   *Constituent structure rules*:
14.1   S   → NP VP
14.2   VP → V (NP)
14.3   NP → $\left\{\begin{array}{l} Art\ N \\ PN \end{array}\right\}$

(The rules numbers are there only to identify the rules in the discussion in section 3.2 below.)

A few more technical terms will be useful to this point. The symbol S is the initial symbol. It is initial because S is the root of any sentence tree, and hence, as we shall see in section 3.2, the derivation of any sentence must start with this symbol. The initial symbol is distinguished as the only symbol that occurs only on the left-hand side of a rule. In this grammar the symbols {Art, N, PN, V} are terminal symbols since there are no constituent structure rules to develop them further. Terminal symbols only occur on the right-hand side of a rule. The symbols {VP, NP} are non-terminal symbols. Non-terminal symbols can be further developed by the rules of the grammar and can occur on either the left- or the right-hand side of a rule.

These rules define structure like those in Figure 3.2, that is, trees with no lexical items in them.

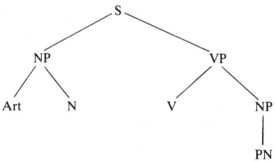

Figure 3.2

To derive an actual sentence we clearly need a lexicon, as in **3** above, together with a rule to insert lexical items into trees:

15 *Lexical rule*:

For each terminal symbol of the constituent structure rules, select from the lexicon a word

(1) that is described as being a member of the class of the terminal symbol;

(2) whose categorization environment matches that of the terminal symbol;

and attach this word as a daughter of the relevant symbol.

The application of this rule to the structure in Figure 3.2 will yield the lexicalized tree of Figure 3.3.

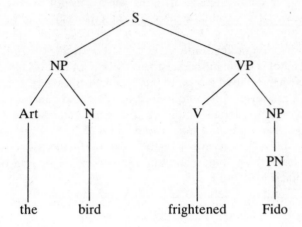

Figure 3.3

3.2   Generating and parsing sentences

A grammar, lexical rule and lexicon such as that above can be used as the basis of a set of explicit rules to produce a sentence (a 'sentence generator') or to analyse some given sentence (a 'sentence parser'). To see how this may be, let us start with an informal account of sentence generation. We will assume the following informal rules:

16   *Sentence generating rules:*

    (1)   Start with the initial symbol.

    (2)   For every node X which is not a terminal symbol, find a grammar rule with X as the left-hand symbol and a category or categories as the right-hand symbol(s) (for example, X → Y Z) and develop a partial tree with X as the mother and the right-hand symbols as ordered daughters.

    (3)   Apply rule (2) until all branches end in terminal symbols.

    (4)   Attach a lexical item to each terminal symbol in accordance with the lexical rule.

(5) Apply rule (4) until every terminal symbol is replaced by a lexical item.

Let us see how this works. Rule (1) tells us to start with S, the initial symbol. Rules (2) and (3) require us to expand non-terminal symbols until there are none left. S is a non-terminal symbol, so we must find a grammar rule with S as the left-hand symbol – rule **14.1** is the only candidate. We thus derive the partial tree of Figure 3.4.

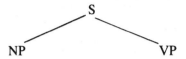

Figure 3.4

VP is not a terminal symbol, so we must find a grammar rule to develop it: **14.2**. If we choose the optional NP allowed for in this rule, we develop the structure of Figure 3.5.

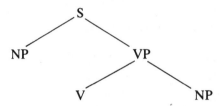

Figure 3.5

NP is not a terminal symbol either, so these too must be developed. Choosing different expansions for each NP we can develop the structure of Figure 3.6.

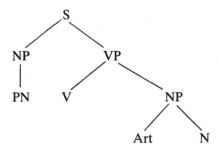

Figure 3.6

All the symbols are now terminal symbols, so we proceed to rule (4) and insert from our lexicon words with the appropriate class membership and, in the case of V, a word that occurs in the specified environment (that is, ___ NP). When we have applied rule (4) to every terminal symbol (and always providing that the grammar is correct and that we have operated the generating rules correctly) we will have a grammatical sentence together with its labelled and bracketed analysis. In this instance, as shown in Figure 3.7, this is the case.

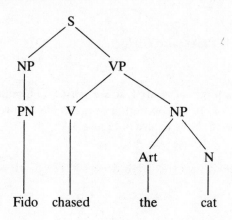

Figure 3.7

Having used the grammar as the basis of a 'generator', we will now use it as the basis of a sentence 'parser'.

17   *Sentence parsing rules:*

  (1) Determine from the lexicon the form class of every word and develop a partial tree for each word where the form class label dominates the word.

  (2) Find a grammar rule with X as the left-hand symbol and a category or categories as the right-hand symbol(s) (for example, X → Y Z) and where the right-hand symbol(s) match some sequence of categories in the structure so far and develop a partial tree with X as the mother and the right-hand symbols as ordered daughters.

  (3) Continue rule (2) until the tree is rooted in S and there are no unattached items.

Consider, for example, the analysis of:

18 The cat frightened the bird

The lexicon assigns these words to the classes shown in Figure 3.8. Inspection of the constituent structure rules tells us that the sequence Art + N constitutes an NP (rule **14.3**). Incorporating the information, we get the structure of Figure 3.9.

Figure 3.8

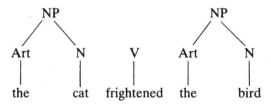

Figure 3.9

Repeating rules (2) and (3) we find that V + NP constitutes a VP (rule **14.2**) and that NP + VP constitutes an S (rule **14.1**). Incorporating this information yields the tree in Figure 3.10. Since this is rooted in S and there are no unattached items, the parse is concluded. Once again we have a labelled and bracketed analysis of a sentence, as shown in Figure 3.10.

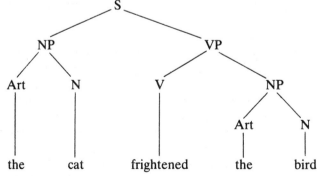

Figure 3.10

3.3   Generative grammar

It will be sensible at this point to distinguish two senses of the lexeme GENERATE. We used GENERATE-1 in **16** in the previous section to describe an algorithm, or set of rules, which will 'generate', or produce, sentences. In this use 'generate' is in contrast to 'parse', or 'analyse'.

There is another, more abstract sense of GENERATE, GENERATE-2, which is used in the term 'generative grammar'. The grammars we have been describing can be thought of as a set of statements or rules that relate a sentence to its labelled and bracketed description. GENERATE-2 refers to the relationship between a grammar and the set of sentences it accounts for. A generative grammar in this sense doesn't GENERATE-1 anything; it is, in principle, neutral as between the production (or generation in the sense of GENERATE-1) and the analysis (or parsing) of a sentence. The grammar in **14** above is indeed neutral in this respect, as can be seen from the fact that we have called upon the identical grammar in both our sentence generator (**16**) and our sentence parser (**17**).

A generative grammar in this sense has a number of properties. To begin with, although we constructed the grammar on the basis of the analysis of a small set of sentences, it will in fact account for large numbers of sentences other than those on which it was immediately constructed. In other words, it can predict that many sentences that we haven't looked at are grammatical and assign descriptions to them. If we were to enlarge our lexicon to three or four times the size it is, it would make predictions about the well-formedness of a very large number of sentences. Indeed, if we incorporate rules of the kind that we will look at in Chapter 9, we will see that out of a finite, and quite small, set of rules we can construct a grammar that will account for an infinite set of sentences.

A mathematical analogy is appropriate. The *Oxford Advanced Learners Dictionary* defines SQUARE ROOT as 'a number greater than 0, which when multiplied by itself gives a particular specified number'. The definition describes the relationship between, or generates, an infinity of pairs of numbers: a number and its square root. The definition is not a rule that tells you either how to produce square roots, or how to determine the square root of any given number (a number of different algorithms for either operation are available).

Technical terms

category	lexical insertion
constituent structure rules	lexical rule
expansion	non-terminal symbol
generative grammar	partial tree
grammatical	rewrite rule
initial symbol	terminal symbol

Note

1 As in the previous chapter we are disregarding issues concerned with the internal structure of words.

Exercises

(1) *Some verb classes in English*

(a) The following sentences exemplify three different sentence structures, and hence three different subclasses of verb:

   (i)   The man seemed angry
  (ii)   The man laughed
 (iii)   The man terrified the children
 (iv)   The children cried
  (v)   The woman telephoned the policeman
 (vi)   The policeman looked strong

The relevant environments for the subclassification of the verbs are shown below. Which verbs occur in which environments?

The verbs   . . .   occur in the environment __ Adj
The verbs   . . .   occur in the environment __ NP
The verbs   . . .   occur in the environment __ #

(The environment __ # means the verb occurs with no following constituent.)

(b) Draw a tree diagram for each sentence type. Use the class labels VCop (Copulative verb), VT (Transitive verb) and VI (Intransitive verb) for the three classes of verb identified above.

(c)   Now consider the following additional data:

(vii)   The man ran away
(viii)   The man hid under the hedge
(ix)   The policeman looked down
(x)   The policeman saw the man
(xi)   The policeman caught the man
(xii)   The woman was happy
(xiii)   The policeman stood near the playground

These data introduce two new sentence types and hence two new verb subclasses (and also include further examples of structures we have already analysed). What are the environments for these two new verb classes? Use the additional constituent labels PP (Prepositional Phrase) and Part(icle), and use the labels VbPP and VbPart for the two new classes of verb. A Prepositional Phrase has the constituents Prep(osition) + NP. The class Prep includes items like {*under, near, in, on*}. The NP can be any NP as described earlier.

(d)   Example **14** in this chapter presented a grammar for a restricted set of English sentences. Extend this grammar to include the data from this exercise.

(2)   *Parsing and generating sentences*

For each of the sentences (vii)–(xiii) in exercise (1) above:

(a)   Generate the sentence using the sentence generating rules in section 3.2 (**16**) and show how the analysis develops by drawing a series of partial trees as in the examples in Figures 3.4–3.7.

(b)   Parse the sentence using the parsing rules in section 3.2 (**17**) and show how the parse develops by drawing a series of partial trees as in the examples in Figures 3.8–3.10.

4 Formal grammars

Grammars of the sort discussed so far are referred to as 'formal' grammars. Formal here can be taken in two senses.

In one sense the grammar is formal in that it is concerned with the distribution of forms, but not with the sense of individual forms, nor with the meaning of whole sentences, nor with whether any appropriate context of use can be found for the sentence. It is concerned only with the distribution of forms. Form classes are established in terms of their distribution – items with the same distribution are placed in the same form class. In this sense 'formal' may be opposed to 'notional'. A notional description would include in the same class items held to have a common element of meaning, but not necessarily with the same distribution.

The distinction between a formal and a notional approach can be illustrated by considering the following data from the African language Akan, from central and southern Ghana:

1a	Kofi ware	Kofi is tall
1b	Kofi reware	Kofi is getting tall
1c	Kofi aware	Kofi has grown tall
2a	Kookoo no bere	The cocoa is ripe
2b	Kookoo no rebere	The cocoa is ripening
2c	Kookoo no abere	The cocoa has got ripe
3a	Kofi kasa	Kofi speaks
3b	Kofi rekasa	Kofi is speaking
3c	Kofi akasa	Kofi has spoken
4a	Kofi yɛ kɛseɛ	Kofi is big
4b	Kofi reyɛ kɛseɛ	Kofi is getting big
4c	Kofi ayɛ kɛseɛ	Kofi has become big

Sentence sets **1** to **3** contain the verbs WARE 'to be or become tall', BERE 'to be or become ripe or red' and KASA 'to speak'. Set **4** has a verb Yɛ 'to be or become' followed by an adjective KɛSEɛ 'big'. We can identify the verbs in formal terms as those forms that can be inflected by various verbal affixes; the **a** sentences contain the simple verb stem, the **b** sentences the prefix *re-*, the **c** sentences the prefix *a-*.[1] By contrast, adjectives like KɛSEɛ are invariant, so there are no sentences like:

5   *Kofi kɛseɛ
    *Kofi rekɛseɛ
    *Kofi akɛseɛ

Furthermore, adjectives must be preceded by the 'copula'[2] verb Yɛ, 'to be or become', whereas verbs, like WARE or BERE, cannot co-occur with Yɛ, so we do not find:

6   *Kofi yɛ ware
    *Kookoo no yɛ bere

In formal terms items like WARE 'to be tall' or BERE 'to be red' are clearly verbs, just as KASA 'to speak' is a verb. Grouping WARE 'to be tall' and KɛSEɛ 'big' into the same class falsifies the facts of the language. Both are 'descriptive' words, but their grammatical behaviour is different, and the grammar should be based on grammatical considerations (like the ability to bear verbal affixes) rather than notional considerations (like the fact that they are descriptive words).

We can make the same point by considering the following English sentences:

7   John talks; John is talking
8   The fruit ripens; The fruit is ripening
9   The fruit is ripe; The fruit is getting ripe

TALK and RIPEN in **7** and **8** are clearly verbs (they occur in the verbal forms *ripens, is ripening*, and so on); equally clearly RIPE in **9** is an adjective (it occurs with the copula BE and in constructions with the verb GET). We cannot use the verb RIPEN with the syntax of an adjective, nor the adjective RIPE with the syntax of a verb, as can be seen by comparing **8** and **9** with the ungrammatical:

10   *The fruit ripes; *The fruit is riping
11   *The fruit is ripen; *The fruit is getting ripen

The fact that RIPE and RIPEN are lexically related, though true, is irrelevant; RIPE is an adjective and RIPEN a verb. In attempting to describe the grammar of a language, formal criteria are to be preferred to notional criteria. Members of a formally established form class may have a common notional element; indeed, this is often the case and is no surprise if we hold that language is a system for communicating meanings. On the other hand, the principles behind the establishment of formal and notional classes are quite different, and formal criteria are in general preferable.

The second sense of formal implies that the grammar should be formalized, that is, presented in terms of a set of formal rules, like those of the previous chapter, explicitly and economically. It must be clear just what data are accounted for and how they are being accounted for, just what assumptions are made about the nature of the language and just what claims about the structure of the language are presented. In this sense formal is opposed to informal.

Formal in the first sense does not necessarily exclude considerations of meaning; this would be impossible and undesirable. Ostentatious attempts to expel considerations of meaning have usually allowed meaning to creep surreptitiously back under some other guise. We can see how meaning is smuggled in if we consider the sort of problem sometimes presented for analysis to beginning linguistics students. Such problems often present data from a little-known language which can sometimes be analysed without knowing the meaning of the sentences, rather like a puzzle from a Sunday newspaper. Here is an example from Scots Gaelic (we have omitted glosses to demonstrate a formal analysis):

12 Bha an cù dubh
13 Bha an cat bàn
14 Bha Calum mór
15 Bha an cù sgìth
16 Bha Calum sgìth
17 Bha Màiri beag
18 Bha an gille mór
19 Bha an cù beag
20 Bha Màiri bàn
21 Bha an gille beag
22 Bha an cat mór
23 Bha Màiri beag

We are provided with the additional information that these strings are all sentences, and that no other word order is possible for these sentences – the following, for example, are impossible:

24   *An cat dubh bha
25   *Bha cat an dubh
26   *Bha dubh an cat

We are also told that strings like:

27   *Bha an Calum sgìth
28   *Bha cat dubh

are not found.

It is possible to write a grammar for these data without knowing what the sentences mean, using only the techniques of expansion and substitution. Thus, we allocate {*dubh, sgìth, beag*} to the same form class since they are all mutually substitutable following *bha an cù* (12, 15, 19). {*mór, beag*} are mutually substitutable in 18 and 21, and {*beag, bàn*} are substitutable in 17 and 20. Since these classes have overlapping membership we assume that they are all members of the same class, to which we will give the arbitrary label A. If a Gaelic speaker were handy we could test this supposition by inquiring whether a string such as:

29   Bha an cù mór

which we do not find in our data, but which this analysis predicts, is well formed. (It is.)

Next we note that our data include a class of words {*cù, gille, cat*} that only occur after *an*, and we see from the ungrammaticality of 28 that at least one member of this class cannot appear without a preceding *an*; let us assume this is typical of the class, which we give the arbitrary label B.

In our data {*Calum, Màiri*} are never preceded by *an*, and 27 shows that *Calum* at least may not be preceded by *an*. We will assume that this is also true of *Màiri* and give this class the arbitrary label C. This leaves only *bha* and *an* unaccounted for. The evidence suggests these must be considered separate one-member classes, D and E. So much for simple substitution. We can summarize our findings in substitution tables, one for each string type, Figures 4.1 and 4.2.

D	E	B	A
bha	an	cù cat gille	dubh bàn sgìth beag mór

Figure 4.1

D	C	A
bha	Calum Màiri	dubh bàn sgìth beag mór

Figure 4.2

At this point we note that strings of the form E + B appear substitutable for members of the class C. This suggests a new form class, F, which can be expanded as either E + B or C. This too we can represent in the substitution table, Figure 4.3.

S			
D	F		A
	E	B	
bha	an	cù cat gille	dubh bàn sgìth beag
	C		mór
	Calum Màiri		

Figure 4.3

Alternatively, we could write a little grammar for our data:

30   *Constituent structure rules*:
S → D F A
F → $\begin{Bmatrix} E\ B \\ C \end{Bmatrix}$

Lexicon:
bha D
an E

and so on.

At this point we must give up our pretence. If we had glossed the sentences:

31a   The dog was black (= **12**)
31b   The cat was white (= **13**)
31c   Calum was big (= **14**)

and so on (and reference to the lexicon in Figure 4.4 will yield glosses for the other examples), the reader would quickly have identified the class arbitrarily labelled A as a class of Adjectives, B as a class of Nouns, C as a class of Proper Nouns, D as a copular verb and E as an article. Using these more familiar class names we could write the grammar and lexicon of Figure 4.4.

Constituent structure rules:
S   → V NP Adj
NP → $\begin{Bmatrix} \text{Art N} \\ \text{PN} \end{Bmatrix}$

Lexicon:
an   Art 'the'
bàn Adj 'white'
beag Adj 'small'
bha Vcop 'was'
Calum PN 'Calum'
cat N 'cat'
cù   N 'dog'
dubh Adj 'black'
gille N 'boy'
Màiri PN 'Maire'
mór Adj 'big'
Figure 4.4   sgìth Adj 'tired'

Exercises like this with or without glosses are useful. They encourage a formal (rather than a notional) approach to description; they illustrate the principles of distributional analysis; and they can be used to practise writing formal grammars. They also draw the student's attention to the ways in which languages can differ with respect to such features as constituent order within the sentence or class membership; note the difference in constituent order between English:

32   (subject + verb + complement)[3]

and Gaelic:

33   (verb + subject + complement)

In the Akan data at the beginning of the chapter we saw that the class Verb in Akan includes items that translate as Adjectives in English. The exercises also illustrate, albeit in an oversimplified way, an approach to language analysis; sentences with similar structure are gathered together so that they may be compared directly and the likenesses and differences between them clearly observed.

Such exercises are, however, artificial. The data have been carefully selected and arranged; and it is here that meaning has surreptitiously crept in. A random sample of data from a native speaker of a language speaking naturally would not look anything like the data we have examined; it would be impossible to make a formal grammar on the basis of a dozen or so utterances collected at random.

Lexicon for the Gaelic data in **12–23**

an	Art	'the'	dubh	Adj	'black'
bàn	Adj	'white'	gille	N	'boy'
beag	Adj	'small'	Màiri	PN	'Mairi'
bha	Vcop	'was'	mór	Adj	'big'
Calum	PN	'Calum'	sgìth	Adj	'tired'
cù	N	'dog'			

Sentences **12–23** translate as:

12 The dog was black
13 The cat was white
14 Calum was big

and so on.

Technical terms

formal (of forms) vs notional
formal (formalized) vs informal

Notes

1 This is not the whole story since tonal distinctions are also involved, and these are not marked. However, this account is adequate for our purposes.
2 Copula verbs are those which are followed by an NP or Adjective which usually constitutes a 'description' of the subject NP. In English copula verbs include BE, GET and BECOME, as in the examples. For further discussion see Chapter 5.
3 For our present purposes we can consider a complement to be the NP or Adjective that follows the copula verb, as in examples **12** or **31a**. They are discussed in more detail in Chapter 5.

Exercises

(1)   The data in this exercise are from Scottish Gaelic.

(i)	Chunnaic mi an cù	I saw the dog
(ii)	Bhuail e an gille	He struck the boy
(iii)	Ghlac Calum breac	Calum caught a trout
(iv)	Reic Calum an cù	Calum sold the dog
(v)	Sgrìobh mi litir	I wrote a letter
(vi)	Ghlac Calum an cù	Calum caught the dog
(vii)	Bhuail Tearlach an gille	Charlie struck the boy
(viii)	Chunnaic an cù Calum	The dog saw Calum
(ix)	Bhàsaich Tearlach	Charlie died
(x)	Fhuair Tearlach cù	Charlie got a dog
(xi)	Sheinn mi	I sang
(xii)	Bhàsaich an cù	The dog died
(xiii)	Chunnaic Calum cù	Calum saw a dog

(a) Group the words into classes. Use the class names Art(icle), N(oun), PN (Proper Noun), VT (Transitive verb), VI (Intransitive verb), Pro(noun).

(b) Find an appropriate translation meaning for each word.

(c) Write a grammar for these data and incorporate it into the grammar given in the text in Figure 4.4.

(2) In the sentences below, also from Scottish Gaelic, there is an additional constituent not present in the corresponding sentences in the previous exercise. Let us refer to this as a Prepositional Phrase (PP). What are the constituents of the PP? Use the class name Prep(osition) in addition to the class names already available to you. Enlarge the grammar you wrote for the previous exercise to accommodate these new data.

(i) Bhuail Tearlach an gille le bata
Charlie struck the boy with a stick

(ii) Ghlac Calum breac ans an linne seo
Calum caught a trout in this pool

(iii) Chunnaic mi an cù aig an dorus
I saw a dog at the door

(iv) Sgrìobh mi litir gu Calum
I wrote a letter to Calum

(v) Bhàsaich Tearlach anns an Eadailt
Charlie died in Italy

(3) The following data are from Kwahu, an Akan language from Ghana.

(i) ɔkyerɛkyerɛfoɔ no rekasa — The teacher is speaking
(ii) abɔfora no regoro — The child is playing
(iii) Amma regoro — Amma is playing
(iv) Kofi rehwɛ ɔkyerɛkyerɛfoɔ no — Kofi is looking at the teacher
(v) ɔkyerɛkyerɛfoɔ no reboa Amma — The teacher is helping Amma
(vi) ɔkyerɛkyerɛfoɔ no reboro abɔfora no — The teacher is beating the child
(vii) abɔfora no resu — The child is crying
(viii) Amma reboa abɔfora no — Amma is helping the child

(a) Group the words into classes. Use the class names Art(icle), N(oun), PN (Proper Noun), VT (Transitive verb), VI (Intransitive verb).

(b) Find an appropriate translation meaning for each word based on the English gloss. Since we are assuming that words are the smallest constituents of interest to us, you will have to identify a word like *regoro* as a member of the class VI and give it a gloss like 'is playing'.

(c) There are two types of Noun Phrase (NP) shown in the data. What are the constituents of these NPs?

(d) Write a grammar for these data.

(e) Using your grammar, draw tree diagrams to represent the grammatical structure of sentences (i) and (vi).

5 Verbs and nouns

In this chapter we will look at some of the considerations that are important in establishing subcategories of verbs and nouns.

5.1 Some verb classes in English

We have seen in an earlier chapter that each of the major lexical categories has a corresponding phrasal category with the lexical category as its principal constituent or head.[1] In these terms, the verb is the head of the phrasal category VP.

The relationship between the head of a phrasal category and its sisters is particularly important because lexical classes are categorized into subclasses on the basis of the number and nature of their sisters within the phrase. We will refer to this kind of categorization as '(strict) subcategorization'.

Verbs have traditionally been subcategorized on the basis of the number and nature of their sisters within the VP, often referred to as the 'complement(s)' of the verb. Note that it is the verb's sisters that are criterial for strict subcategorization. Constituents that precede the VP, most crucially the 'subject' NP, are non-criterial; in English all sentences must have a 'subject' NP so its presence cannot be critical for subcategorization, and in the kind of tree that we have been drawing, the subject NP is not a sister of the verb. Similarly, constituents that follow the verb but are not sisters of the verb within the VP are not criterial either, as we shall see when we discuss adverbs in Chapter 7. The position is illustrated in Figure 5.1. GIVE is subcategorized to occur with two object NPs (it is a 'ditransitive' verb in terms of the classification in subsection 5.1d below) and these are shown as sisters of the verb within the VP; neither the subject NP nor the optional adverbial PP is a subclassifier, and neither is a sister of the verb.

There are some more examples in **1** below. The constituents in small capitals are sisters of the verb within the VP (that is,

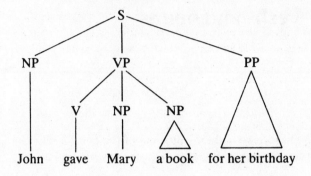

subject NP   the verb – and its sisters   optional adverbial
within the VP

Figure 5.1

complements of the verb), and hence relevant to subcategorization, and the italicized items are adverbials, not sisters of the verb within the VP (and not complements of the verb), and hence not relevant to subcategorization:

1a   Mary coughed *loudly*
1b   John read A BOOK – *in bed* – *last night*
1c   Harry put – A VASE OF FLOWERS – ON THE MANTELPIECE – *yesterday* – *to celebrate his wife's birthday*

We discuss adverbial 'modifiers' in more detail in Chapter 7.

Some traditionally recognized verb classes include the following:

5.1a   'Copular or 'linking' verbs

Within the VP these occur in the environments:

2a $VP(- \begin{Bmatrix} NP \\ AP \\ PP \end{Bmatrix})$

2b   John is a soldier   (__ NP)
2c   John is strong   (__ AP)
2d   John is in bed   (__ PP)

The 'copula' BE,[2] as in the examples, is the prime exemplar of these verbs and, as the examples demonstrate, it may be followed by an AP, NP, or PP. Other copular verbs include BECOME, LOOK and SEEM, though these do not always occur so readily in all of the environments shown in **2a**; thus BECOME co-occurs readily with an NP or an Adj, but hardly with a PP:

3a He became a general
3b He became miserable
3c *He became in France

In English, if a copula is followed by an NP then the NP generally agrees in number with the subject NP of the sentence:

4a He is a soldier
4b They are soldiers
4c *They are a soldier. *He is soldiers

There are some exceptions to this generalization, particularly when the NP to the right of BE contains a 'collective' noun: *They are a crowd of lazy idlers*; *They are the best regiment in the army*.

In some languages, like French, adjectives vary in form, 'agreeing' with the Noun they modify in gender (for example, masculine or feminine) and number (that is, singular or plural); this is illustrated in **5a–c**. In such languages, adjectives in constructions involving copula verbs usually also agree in number and gender with the subject NP, as illustrated in **5d–e**:

5a	le petit garçon	'the small boy'	(all masc sing)
5b	la petite fille	'the small girl'	(all fem sing)
5c	les petites filles	'the small girls'	(all fem pl)
5d	le garçon est petit	'the boy is small'	(masc sing)
5e	les filles sont petites	'the girls are small'	(fem pl)

Since only copular verbs are followed by either an NP, an AP, or a PP we can treat these three categories in this case as members of a single form class, defined by the environment V_{cop} __ . We will call this form class, again following traditional terminology, Pred(icate). This means we must change the statement at the head of this section to read, 'these occur in the environment shown in **6a**'. **6b** is a grammar rule to introduce the category Pred:

6a $VP(\text{—}\;Pred)$

6b $Pred \rightarrow \left\{ \begin{array}{l} NP \\ AP \\ PP \end{array} \right\}$

The category Pred offers a unique environment for the classification of copular verbs. It also enables us to identify which NPs are 'predicate NPs', information we need, in English, to ensure that predicate NPs agree in number with the subject of the sentence, and in other languages to make the correct statements about the agreement of adjectives. An exercise at the end of this chapter shows that we can use this category elsewhere too.

5.1b *'Intransitive' verbs*

Within the VP these occur as the sole constituent of the VP:

7a $VP(\text{—})$

7b   The women $VP(\text{wept})$

7c   The children cried

7d   *The children cried their toys

7e   *The soldiers died their country

7f   The men wept bitterly

Intransitive verbs cannot be followed by an NP, as examples **7d** and **7e** show, but may be followed by an optional adverb, as in **7f**. The adverb is, of course, not a sister of the verb within VP. Further intransitive verbs are BREATHE, TALK and WORK.[3]

5.1c *'Transitive' verbs*

These occur within the VP in the environment:

8a $VP(\text{—}\;NP)$

8b   The dog $VP(\text{bit}\;\text{–}\;\text{the man})$

8c   The child thrashed the dog

Verbs like BITE and THRASH are traditionally called transitive verbs because in a typical case 'the action of the verb' is considered to 'pass over' from the 'agent' subject to the 'patient' object.[4] Transitive verbs cannot typically occur without a following NP:

9a *The dog bit
9b *The child thrashed

With all true transitive verbs, for any sentence of the form:

10a $_S$(NP $_{VP}$(V NP))
10b The dog bit the man

there are corresponding sentences of the form:

11a The man was bitten by the dog
11b What the dog did to the man was bite him
11c What happened to the man was that the dog bit him

Such sentences are impossible with copular verbs, even though superficially they may seem to have a similar NP + V + NP structure at some level (another reason for introducing a Pred category):

12a He became a soldier
12b *A soldier was become by him
12c *What happened to the soldier was that the man became him

Other transitive verbs include KILL, COOK and FIND.

5.1d 'Di-transitive' verbs[5]

These occur within the VP in the environment:

13a $_{VP}$(— NP NP)
13b John $_{VP}$(gave – Mary – the book)
13c Harriet taught the children Italian

These verbs are called 'di-transitive' since they are typically followed by two NPs. Characteristically, sentences of the form illustrated in **13** have corresponding sentences where the two NPs are reversed in order, the second occurring in a preposition phrase, typically with *to*:

> **14a**　John gave Mary the book
> **14b**　John gave the book to Mary

Like sentences containing transitive verbs, sentences like those in **14a** and **14b** have 'passive' counterparts, except that in this case either object NP (the NP immediately following the verb) can become the subject of the corresponding 'passive' sentence: *Mary* in **14a** : **15a** and *the book* in **14b** : **15b**):

> **15a**　Mary was given the book by John
> **15b**　The book was given to Mary by John

Other di-transitive verbs include OFFER, THROW and SELL.

5.1e　*'Intransitive locative' verbs*[6]

These occur in the environment:

> **16a**　$_{VP}(\text{— PP})$
> **16b**　The lamp $_{VP}(\text{stood – on the table})$
> **16c**　The gun leant against the wall

Most verbs of this class require to be followed by a PP:

> **17a**　*The lamp stood
> **17b**　*The gun leant

The PP typically indicates a location, hence the name for this class of verbs. Other intransitive locative verbs are HANG, SIT and SLUMP.

5.1f　*'Transitive locative' verbs*

These occur in the environment:

> **18a**　$_{VP}(\text{— NP PP})$

18b John $_{VP}$(stood – the lamp – on the table)

18c Mary leant the gun against the wall

Frequently, as in the examples given, these verbs correspond to the verbs found as intransitive locative verbs, except for the object NP immediately following the verb. These verbs resemble transitive verbs in that there are corresponding sentences like:

19a The gun was leant against the wall by Mary
19b What happened to the gun was that Mary leant it against the wall

and so on, in a manner analogous to transitive verbs. They differ from simple transitive verbs in that, typically, they require to be followed by a PP as well as an NP. We find no sentences:

20 *John stood the lamp

and so on. These verbs differ from di-transitive verbs in that they cannot be followed by two NPs:

21a John stood the lamp on the table
21b *John stood the table the lamp

Other transitive locative verbs are PUT, LAY and HANG.

Constituent structure rules for the six verb classes

We have looked at six different verb classes, each distinguished in terms of the environments in which members of the class occur. These classes are summarized in **22**:

22a $VP \rightarrow V_{cop}$ Pred (see **5**: V_{cop} = cop vb (BE)

22b $VP \rightarrow V_i$ (see **7**: V_i = intrans vb (WEEP)

22c $VP \rightarrow V_t$ NP (see **8**: V_t = trans vb (BITE)

22d $VP \rightarrow V_{dt}$ NP NP (see **13**: V_{dt} = di-trans vb (GIVE)

22e $VP \rightarrow V_{il}$ PP (see **16**: V_{il} = intrans loc vb (STAND)

22f $VP \rightarrow V_{tl}$ NP PP (see **18**: V_{tl} = trans loc vb (STAND)

In terms of the discussion in Chapter 2 the rules can be simplified by discarding the subscripts and collapsing the six rules of **22** into the single rule **23**:

$$\textbf{23} \quad VP \rightarrow V\left(\left\{ \begin{matrix} \text{Pred} \\ \text{(NP)} \ \left(\left\{\begin{matrix}\text{PP} \\ \text{NP}\end{matrix}\right\}\right) \end{matrix}\right\}\right)$$

Recall that, by our conventions, items curly-bracketed together are alternatives and items in ordinary parentheses are optional, so **23** generates the strings: V; V + Pred; V + NP; V + PP; V + NP + NP; V + NP + PP – which is just the set of environments described in **22**. Example lexical entries are shown in Figure 5.2, where the rules discussed in this section are summarized.

Constituent structure rules:

$$S \ \rightarrow NP \ VP$$

$$VP \ \rightarrow V\left(\left\{ \begin{matrix} \text{Pred} \\ \text{(NP)} \ \left(\left\{\begin{matrix}\text{PP} \\ \text{NP}\end{matrix}\right\}\right) \end{matrix}\right\}\right)$$

$$\text{Pred} \rightarrow \left\{ \begin{matrix} \text{NP} \\ \text{Adj} \\ \text{PP} \end{matrix} \right\}$$

$$NP \ \rightarrow Det \ N$$

$$AP \ \rightarrow (Int) \ Adj$$

$$PP \ \rightarrow P \ NP$$

Lexicon:

BE	V,	__ Pred
WEEP	V,	__ #
BITE	V,	__ NP
GIVE	V,	__ NP NP
STAND	V,	__ (NP) PP

Figure 5.2

5.2 Some noun classes in English

In the preceding section we looked at the strict subcategorization of verbs, that is, their subcategorization in terms of their sisters within the VP. In this section we will look at some subcategories of nouns. As in the previous section, our purpose is to account for distributional restrictions in terms of a set of syntactic subclasses, but this time we will approach the question of subcategorization from a different perspective. Instead of considering the kinds of sisters that a noun can have within the NP we will be concerned much more with what seem to be inherent properties of the noun itself. For this reason we will refer to this kind of subcategorization as 'inherent subcategorization'. Inherent subcategorization is illustrated in **24**, where some noun subclasses are characterized in terms of a set of 'syntactic features':

24a [+−anim(ate)] distinguishes between 'animate' and 'inanimate' objects; MAN and DOG are [+anim(ate)] and BEAUTY and OIL are [−anim(ate)]

24b [+−hum(an)] distinguishes between 'human' and 'non-human' animates; MAN is [+hum(an)] and DOG is [−hum(an)]

24c [+−male] distinguishes between 'male' and 'female' animates; MAN is [+male] and WOMAN is [−male]

24d [+−conc(rete)] distinguishes between 'concrete' and 'abstract' nouns; DOG is [+conc(rete)] and BEAUTY is [−conc(rete)]

24e [+−c(oun)t] distinguishes between 'count' and 'mass' nouns; count nouns are typically those nouns that are used to refer to discrete objects that can, in a literal sense, be counted (*one chair, two chairs*, and so on); mass nouns are typically those nouns that are used to refer to non-discrete objects, like OIL, BUTTER and CHEESE, that cannot be counted (**one butter, *two butters*, and so on)

24f [+−com(mon)] distinguishes between 'proper' and 'common' nouns; proper nouns like JOHN or FIDO, typically the names of individuals, are [−com(mon)], whereas nouns like MAN or DOG, that can be applied to classes of individuals, are common nouns (+com(mon)]

It seems most suitable to regard a subcategorization of this kind as part of the lexical specification of an item. **25** shows some nouns characterized in these terms:

25a MAN   N; [+conc, +ct, +anim, +hum, +male, + com]

25b WOMAN   N; [+conc, +ct, +anim, +hum, −male, +com]

25c JOHN   N; [+conc, +ct, +anim, +hum, +male, −com]

25d BEAUTY   N; [−conc, −ct, +com, −anim]

25e TRUTH   N; [−conc, +ct, +com, −anim]

25f OIL   N; [+conc, −ct, +com, −anim]

25g DOG   N; [+conc, +ct, +anim, −hum, ±male, + com]

25h FIDO   N; [+conc, +ct, +anim, −hum, −com]

Note that for any particular lexeme we have given only one specification. In some cases the items in question have more than one possible use. Thus MAN in the sense specified indicates 'individual human male'; there is another sense of MAN as 'mankind'; this use is [−ct] and is not accounted for here. In the entry for DOG we have specified [+ −male] to indicate the sense where DOG is used to refer to a canine irrespective of sex. Another sense of DOG would need to be specified as [+male] in contrast to BITCH [−male]. Similarly, although OIL is most usually a mass noun, as in *Would you like some oil?*, it can, like most other mass nouns, also be used in a count sense, as in *Our grocer stocks two oils, olive and sunflower*. In such a sentence *oils* has the sense 'kind(s) of oil'. We discuss cases like this in more detail in Chapter 16. For the present we assume that OIL is a mass noun.

There are different kinds of relationships between the features. Some of them 'cross-classify'; JOHN and FIDO are both [−com], and MAN and DOG are both [+com]; JOHN and MAN are both [+hum] and FIDO and DOG are both [−hum]; similarly BEAUTY is [−conc, −ct] but TRUTH is [−conc, +ct], OIL is [+conc, −ct] and MAN is [+conc, +ct]. Others are 'hierarchical'; the distinction [+ −hum] is contingent on the prior choice of [+anim], as is [+ −male], since sex is only distinguished in animates.

Inherent subcategorization typically manifests itself in terms of restrictions on some grammatical processes, like pronominalization, or, more interestingly, in terms of co-occurrence restrictions relating to grammatical categories.

With respect to pronominalization, we may observe that the pronoun typically used for [−hum] nouns is *it* whereas the pronoun for [+hum] nouns is *he* or *she* depending on whether the noun in question is [+male] or [−male].

With respect to grammatical categories, we have already noted that nouns are associated with the category of number and its terms singular and plural. Most nouns have both a singular and a plural form, but some subclasses of noun typically occur only in the singular (or if they occur in the plural they have a different sense): proper nouns (*Fido* but not *Fidos*); mass nouns (*oil* but not in the relevant sense *oils*); and most abstract nouns (*beauty* but not in the relevant sense *beauties*). There are also restrictions with respect to the category of definiteness. Proper nouns are often thought of as 'inherently' definite, and, as we have already seen, they do not usually co-occur with an article (*Fido* but not in the relevant sense *the Fido*, *a Fido*, and so on). More striking is the complex web of co-occurrence restrictions affecting definiteness, as reflected in articles, and number, with count, [+ct], and mass, [−ct], nouns. Some of these are illustrated in **26a**.[7] The reader is invited to test the validity of the restrictions illustrated by inserting each of the NPs into the sentence frame of **26b**; only those sentences containing the unstarred forms (*I am going out to buy oil*, but not *I am going out to buy chair*) will be found to be grammatical:

26a		[+ct]	[−ct]
	singular	the chair	the oil
		a chair	*a oil
		*sm chair	sm oil
		*chair	oil
	plural	the chairs	*the oils
		*a chairs	*a oils
		sm chairs	*sm oils
		chairs	*oils

26b I am going out to buy ___

We can use this information to control lexical insertion in a way exactly parallel to that used for the insertion of verbs and discussed at the end of the preceding section. Suppose that the following general convention attaches to the lexicalization of the N node within an NP (these rules only account for proper nouns and the data in **26**):

27   *Lexicalization of NP*:

N[−com] may be inserted to N within the NP providing

(1)   N is [−pl]
(2)   There is no Art

(that is, proper nouns only occur in the singular and cannot co-occur with an article)

N[−ct] may be inserted to N within the NP providing

(1)   N is [−pl]
(2)   Art, if present, is not *a*

(that is, mass nouns (N[−ct]) only occur in singular NPs and may co-occur with an article, but not *a*)

N[+ct] may be inserted to N within NP providing
(1)   If N is [−pl]; Art is present, but not *sm*
(2)   If N is [+pl]; Art, if present, is not *a*

(that is, count nouns (N[+ct]) in singular NPs must co-occur with an article (but not with *sm*) and in plural NPs may co-occur with an article, but not with *a*)

Thus, given the three trees in Figure 5.3, the rules ensure that only a mass noun can be inserted into Figure 5.3a (*sm oil*, *sm chair, *sm Fido); that only a count noun can be inserted into Figure 5.3b (*chairs*, *oils, *Fidos); and that a mass or a proper noun can be inserted to Figure 5.3c (*oil*, *Fido*, *chair).

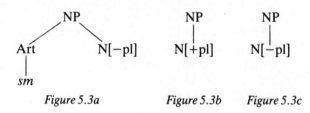

Figure 5.3a   Figure 5.3b   Figure 5.3c

We have looked at two kinds of subcategorization: 'strict subcategorization' in section 5.1 and 'inherent subcategorization' in section 5.2. Strict subcategorization primarily concerns co-occurrence restrictions between a lexical head and its sisters within the corresponding phrasal category; intransitive verbs do not occur with a following NP (*Fido yawned* but not **Fido yawned the child*), whereas transitive verbs must be followed by an NP (*Fido chased the child* and not **Fido chased*). Inherent subcategorization typically involves restrictions on particular grammatical processes; proper nouns do not typically occur with articles (*Fido* but not usually **the Fido*) or in the plural (*Fido* but not usually **Fidos*).

It is, however, important to note that although we have illustrated strict subcategorization with verbs and inherent subcategorization with nouns, both kinds of subcategorization apply equally to both categories. So, for example, nouns can be strictly subcategorized, by their sisters, into those that do, **28b**, and those that do not, **28c**, occur with a complement sentence (complement sentences are briefly discussed in Chapter 9):

28a	NP →	N	(S)
28b	RUMOUR	N,	__ S
	IDEA	N,	__ S
28c	RUMOUR	N,	__ #
	MAN	N,	__ #
	CLOUD	N,	__ #

28d The rumour $_S$(that the world is about to end)

   *The man $_S$(that the world is about to end)

Verbs can be inherently subcategorized in terms of the grammatical categories of tense and aspect, a matter to which we return briefly in Chapter 16.

5.3 Selection restrictions

This section examines yet another, rather different type of co-occurrence restriction between verbs and NPs, 'selection restrictions'. They can be illustrated by the following:

29a The man admired the picture
29b *The picture admired the man

30a   The picture frightened the man
30b   *The man frightened the picture

Both ADMIRE and FRIGHTEN are transitive verbs and in all four sentences the verb is duly followed by an NP; in so far as they follow all the rules of grammar we have looked at so far they seem to be 'grammatical'. However, whereas the **a** sentences seem to be perfectly acceptable, the **b** sentences seem to be 'semantically' deviant.

We might explain the semantic 'deviance' in some such terms as the following. Only animates can 'admire' things, so ADMIRE requires an animate subject expression. Conversely, since one cannot 'frighten' things, FRIGHTEN must have an animate object expression. Framing these observations as a 'selection restriction' we can say that ADMIRE 'selects' an animate subject expression, and FRIGHTEN 'selects' an animate object expression.

Before considering how we might account for selection, it is important to observe that selection statements such as those in the previous paragraph rely on an intuition of what is the 'normal' or 'literal' use of language, and they beg an important question. Is a sentence like:

31   Sincerity admires the young poet

'unacceptable', since ADMIRE here has an abstract subject, or is the sentence quite acceptable, although involving the 'figurative' or 'metaphorical' use of language?[8] Traditional grammars of Indo-European and other languages sometimes recognize this problem by giving a passing mention to various kinds of figurative language. In doing so they usually assume that the reader knows the difference between the literal and figurative use of language and makes allowances accordingly: implying that we can distinguish 'normal' states of affairs and a literal use of language from 'abnormal' states of affairs and figurative language. It is not at all clear just how this might be done, nor even, if it can be done, whether it is to be considered a specifically linguistic ability (like knowing that in English transitive verbs require to be followed by an 'object' NP), or whether it rests on our general knowledge of the world, or the way in which we choose to conceptualize the world. A thorough account of such matters is beyond our scope; the essential thing for the reader is to recognize that deep questions lie behind any attempt to include any information about selection restrictions in a grammar. However, supposing that we can indeed somehow identify a 'literal' use of language and that we will restrict our description to this sort of language, how might we take some account of such information in the grammar?

In the case of FRIGHTEN and ADMIRE the necessary information, as we have seen, is that the subject of ADMIRE and the object of FRIGHTEN should be animate. In the previous section we established a feature categorization for nouns which involved features like [±anim(ate)], so an immediate suggestion would be that we should use this characterization to specify a selection restriction for FRIGHTEN and ADMIRE. ADMIRE can be inserted into a structure of the form:

32 $_{NP}(\ .\ .\ N[+anim]\ .\ .\ )$ __ NP

32 is a 'selection frame'. As stated it is oversimplified, but it is intended to indicate that the subject NP for ADMIRE must contain an anim(ate) head noun, whatever other constituents there may be (see Chapter 8 for discussion of the term 'head noun'). There are no restrictions on the object NP. A similar selection frame for FRIGHTEN is:

33 NP __ $_{NP}(\ .\ .\ N[+anim]\ .\ .\ )$

Selection information could be added to other specifications in the lexicon; so for ADMIRE and FRIGHTEN we could have:

34a	ADMIRE	V	(syntactic category)
		__ NP	(strict subcategorization)
		(. .N[+anim]. .) __ NP	(selection frame)
34b	FRIGHTEN	V	
		__ NP	
		NP __ (. .N[+anim. .])	

As before, V indicates that the items are members of the syntactic category V(erb), and __ NP that they belong to the subcategory of transitive verbs. The third specification is the selection restriction. Note that whereas information about strict subcategorization only includes sister constituents within the VP, selection restrictions must also include information about the subject, and indeed may have to include still other constituents of the sentence as a whole not relevant to strict subcategorization.

We suggested above that we might use the noun 'syntactic features' discussed in the previous section for the selection frames of verbs. **35** below suggests some selection restrictions based on the feature set illustrated in **24**:

> **35a** [±hum(an)]: MARRY only co-occurs with human nouns, since animals do not 'marry' (in a literal use of language) (see **36a**)
>
> **35b** [±male]: PREGNANT co-occurs with female animates and not with males (see **36b**)
>
> **35c** [±conc(rete)]: FALL requires a concrete subject noun, since abstracts cannot 'fall' (see **36c**)
>
> **35d** [±c(oun)t]: FLOW co-occurs with a mass rather than a count subject noun; we find *The oil flowed over the floor* but not **The chair flowed over the floor* (see **36d**)
>
> **35e** [±com(mon)]: verbs of 'naming' typically require a proper noun: *Call me Ahab*

These can be the basis of lexical entries:

> **36a** MARRY   V   (see **35a** and note 3)
>   __ NP
> $NP^{(.\ .N[+hum,\ \alpha male].\ .)}$ __ $_{NP}(.\ .N[+hum,\ -\alpha male].\ .)$
> (αmale = either +male or −male; −αmale = the opposite value)
>
> **36b** PREGNANT A   (see **35b**)
>   Cop __
> $_{NP}(.\ .N[-male].\ .)$ Cop __
>
> **36c** FALL   V   (see **35c**)
>   __ #
> $_{NP}(.\ .N[+conc).\ .)$ __
>
> **36d** FLOW   V   (see **35d**)
>   __ PP
> $_{NP}(.\ .N[-ct].\ .)$ __ $_{PP}(.\ .N[conc].\ .)$

Such descriptions account for the acceptability or otherwise of:

37a The man/oil/dog fell
37b *Beauty fell
　　　(non-concrete subject)
37c The woman/dog is pregnant
37d *The man/John is pregnant
　　　(non-female subject)
37e *The dog prayed
　　　(non-human subject)
37f *The dog flowed over the beauty
　　　(count subject; non-concrete N in PP)

The examples show the sort of judgements that formally stated selection restrictions force on us, and bring us back to a question mentioned at the beginning of the section – is 'figurative language' to be considered in some way 'deviant'? It has been suggested that what we recognize as 'metaphorical language' is language that 'breaks' a selection restriction. But since so much of our 'ordinary' use of language is 'metaphorical' we might question the validity of such an account – it is far from clear where, or how, to draw the boundary. We now return to the question of whether it is appropriate to use the same set of features to control both grammatical co-occurrence restrictions, like those illustrated in **26**, and selectional co-occurrence, illustrated in **37**? It does not seem appropriate for two main reasons, both to do with the fact that selection restrictions appear more a matter of semantic compatibility between lexical items than of the grammaticality of sentences as such.

The first is that there is no reason to expect the semantic and syntactic characterization of some item to be congruent. In setting up a set of syntactic features, we would be wisest to pay attention to syntactic facts. This can be illustrated with the category ($\pm$ct] in English. Our initial characterization of the distinction was semantic – as between 'discrete' and 'non-discrete' objects. This characterization holds rather generally but not universally. Some nouns, like GRAPE, PLUM and PEAR, are normally [+ct]; others, like GRAPEFRUIT and APPLE, may be either [+ct] or [−ct], as can be verified by checking the nouns in NPs on the lines of **26b**. I could inquire of a guest:

38   Would you like some (sm) grapefruit?

but hardly:

39   *Would you like some (sm) plum?

even though what was being offered was similar – in the one case a plate of segmented grapefruit and in the other a plate of stewed plums.

The categorization of nouns as [+ −ct] is not only to some degree idiosyncratic within a language; it is also idiosyncratic between languages. This point, the mismatch between a syntactic and a semantic characterization, can be made even more clearly by reference to a language that has a grammatical category of 'gender'. In French, for example, all nouns are categorized as being in one of two classes (with a few exceptions which may be in both classes) which are usually given the names 'masculine' and 'feminine'. The grammar needs to know the gender of a noun in order that appropriate grammatical rules can be applied: for example, the rules of 'concord' that ensure that a masculine noun co-occurs with the masculine form of the article, *le, un*, and so on, and a feminine noun co-occurs with a feminine form of the article, *la, une*, and so on. Gender distinctions in French are not typically a semantic matter, since all nouns are assigned to one gender class or the other (cf. *le stylo* 'the pen', but *la table* 'the table') even when the notion of sex is irrelevant. We could handle this by a syntactic feature [±masculine], but that feature would hardly be appropriate for stating selection restrictions. For the correct selection restriction of an adjective like ENCEINTE 'pregnant', for example, we need to known the sex of the referent, not the grammatical gender of the noun. This is particularly clear in the case of those nouns that are masculine in gender but may be used to refer to individuals of either sex, like *le docteur* 'doctor'.

This question also has marginal relevance in English. Some kinds of object, like a 'ship' and a 'car', are often pronominalized with *she*, rather than *it*, and conversely a 'baby' is often referred to as *it*.

The second reason is that a complete specification of the semantic selection restrictions of some item clearly cannot be handled by syntactic features alone. Consider the verb EAT. In its literal sense this means 'consume as food'. The object NP might be specified as [+conc] since we normally eat 'things'. But clearly not all 'things' are 'edible'. We might then suppose that we should add a feature [+edible]. If we do, this is clearly not a syntactic feature in the sense discussed, since it has no relevance at all for any grammatical process, syntactic co-occurrence restriction, and so on. And even a feature like [+edible] does not solve all our semantic problems; what is to be classed as [+edible] depends on what is 'doing the eating'. Humans do not normally eat wood, coal, carrion, or clothes – but termites, fires, crows and clothes-moth caterpillars do! Even a man might on occasion be said to *eat his hat* – though this might be considered 'figurative' language.

Technical terms

complement	linking verb
copula	locative verb
copular verb	object
cross-classification	predicate
di-transitive verb	selection frame
feature	selection restriction
indirect object	strict subcategorization
inherent subcategorization	strict subcategorization frame
intransitive locative verb	subject
intransitive verb	transitive locative verb
lexicalization	transitive verb

Notes

1 In Chapter 2 (example **6d**) we noted that the verb word is associated with the grammatical category of tense – [tense: past, present]. Tense will not be our concern in this chapter. We return to the question in Chapter 16.

2 It will be recalled that we introduced the convention of referring to the dictionary or lexical entry of a particular item by the use of small capitals (see the discussion in Chapter 1, example **1**). Thus BE is the lexical entry relating the various forms of BE: *be, am, is, are, was, were, being, been.*

3 Many English verbs can occur in more than one environment. These examples can also occur transitively: *breathe the mountain air, talk rubbish, work a mine.* We are only concerned with the intransitive usage here.

4 The grammar discussed in the preceding chapter, and elaborated at the end of this chapter, can be used to give a formal definition to the terms 'subject' and 'object'. The subject NP is that NP which is immediately dominated by S; the object is that NP immediately dominated by VP. In these terms the NP

dominated by Pred which occurs after the copula verb BE discussed in 1–7 is not an object NP – in traditional terms it is referred to as a 'predicative complement'. Notions such as subject, object and complement are discussed in more detail in Chapter 19. The notions 'agent' and 'patient' are discussed in detail in Chapter 18.

5   In terms of our previous definition of object, such verbs may be said to have two objects – hence the description 'di-transitive'. The two objects are usually distinguished as the 'indirect object', the first of the two NPs in the structure shown, and the 'direct object', the second of the two NPs. In sentences with only one object, like **11**, this is called the direct object.

6   These verbs are intransitive because in terms of the definition of object in note 4 there is no NP in the VP.

7   The item shown as *sm* represents the orthographic word *some* which has a pronunciation /sm/. This item is to be distinguished from other words *some*, as for example in the phrase *Some chicken, some neck*; *some* here cannot be pronounced /sm/.

8   If *Sincerity* is a girl's name, the sentence is perfectly well formed in terms of the selection restriction stated above, and is non-figurative. We also exclude the case where the sentence occurs in some allegorical tale; this is usually said to involve 'personification'.

Exercises

(1)   *Subclassifying verbs*
      The text of this chapter distinguished six verb classes. To which of these classes do the following verbs belong? Note that some belong to more than one class. For each verb draw up a lexical entry like that shown in example **22** on page 67.

      ANTAGONIZE, APPEAR, ARRIVE, BECOME, CRY, DIE, EAT, FIND, GIVE, GROW, GROWL, HANG, LIE, LIVE, LOCK, PASS, PUZZLE, REMAIN, SEEM, SEND, SHOOT, SING, SMELL, SPREAD, WRITE

(2)   *More subclasses of verb*
      Consider the following sentences:

      (i)   The girls made John happy (NP V NP Adj)
      (ii)   The committee elected John chairman (NP V NP NP)
      (iii) The committee gave John a cheque (NP V NP NP)

      (a)   Using the same sorts of criteria that you used to distinguish between copular and transitive verbs, distinguish between the three apparently similar sentence types (in particular think of syntactically related sentences – *The committee gave John a cheque: The committee gave a cheque to John*).

(b) To which of the verb classes you establish do the following belong?

CHOOSE, CONSIDER, GIVE, IMAGINE, MAKE, OFFER, PRESENT, SHOW, THINK, VOTE

(3) *Selection restrictions*
You are probably familiar with playground jingles like:

> One fine day in the middle of the night
> Two dead men got up to fight,
> One blind man to see fair play,
> Two dumb men to shout, 'Hooray.'
> Back to back they faced each other,
> Drew their swords and shot each other.

Would you wish to consider such jingles as 'ungrammatical'? If not, how could you handle a linguistic description of the obviously anomalous nature of such jingles?

6 Adjectives and prepositions

Our discussion hitherto has centred on the two major lexical categories of Noun and Verb, and the corresponding phrasal categories Noun Phrase (NP) and Verb Phrase (VP). In this chapter we will look at two other major form classes, Adjectives and Prepositions, and the corresponding phrasal categories.

6.1 Adjectives and adjective phrases

Consider the NPs in **1a** and **1b**:

1a	a	long	story
1b	an	old	man
1c	Det	A	N

It is fairly uncontroversial to suppose that they can be described by a string of categories shown in **1c**: {*a, an*} are Det(erminers),[1] {*story, man*} are N(ouns), and {*long, old*} are members of a new class – A(djectives).

For reasons which we will justify as this chapter proceeds, but which will be essentially the same kinds of argument as were used in Chapter 2 to support the analysis of an intransitive verb as a minimal VP, we will suppose that in examples like these an A(djective) is the sole constituent of the corresponding phrasal category AP (Adjective Phrase). As we shall see, APs share the same general characteristics as the other phrasal categories we have introduced, NP and VP; the head[2] of the phrasal category, which is obligatory, is the lexical category from which the phrasal category takes its name. This implies a constituent structure for **1a** as in Figure 6.1.

In Chapter 2 we noted that a grammatical description of a form class involved a description of (1) its distribution in other structures and (2), in the case of a phrasal category, its internal structure or, in the case of a word class, its association with grammatical categories.

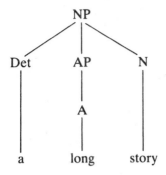

Figure 6.1

Adjectives, and hence Adjective Phrases, are usually defined in terms of four criteria.[3] Two of these, illustrated in **2** and **3** below, involve the distribution of AP within other categories, and two, illustrated in **4-6**, the internal structure of the category itself.

Adjective Phrases, and hence adjectives, can occur within the NP as an optional 'premodifier'[4] of the head noun, as shown in **2**:

2a	NP(Det	AP(—)	N)
2b	that	*old*	man
2c	that	*strong*	cider
2d	those	*very tall*	trees

They can also occur after the verb BE in descriptive sentences attributing a 'quality' to the subject NP, as in **3**:

3a	S(NP	VP(BE	AP(—))
3b	that man	is	*old*
3c	that cider	is	*quite strong*
3d	those trees	are	*extremely tall*

As for the internal structure of the AP, we have already seen in some of the examples above that an adjective within an Adjective Phrase can itself be preceded by an optional modifier taken from a class we will call 'Int(ensifiers)' and including {*very, quite, rather, amazingly* . . .} as in **4**:

4a		AP(Int	Adj)	
4b	that	(very	old)	man

4c	that	(rather	strong)	cider
4d	an	(extraordinarily	long)	story

Finally adjectives can be associated with the grammatical category of [degree] with the terms [ord(inary), comp(arative) and sup(erlative)]. Some adjective words, as illustrated in **5**, show this grammatical category by changes in their form, and since we are treating words as the smallest unit with which we are concerned, we will, as before, note these facts about the internal structure of words with a feature annotation on the class label; note that for convenience we will only annotate the comparative and superlative forms. Other adjectives form their comparative and superlative forms by using the intensifiers *more* and *most*, as illustrated in **5d**:

5a	Adj:	old; strong; tall; pretty
5b	$Adj_{[comp]}$:	older; stronger; taller; prettier
5c	$Adj_{[sup]}$:	oldest; strongest; tallest; prettiest
5d	AP(more/most A):	more (most) beautiful
		more (most) boring

The rules **6a** and **6b** below summarize the distribution of AP, and hence of A; rule **6c** shows the internal structure of the AP and **6d** records the fact that adjectives are associated with the category of degree:

6a	VP → BE (AP)
6b	NP → Det (AP) N
6c	AP → (Int) A
6d	A[degree: ord, comp, sup]

6.2   Prepositions and prepositional phrases

Let us now turn our attention to the NPs in **7**:

7a	a	long	story	about	an	old	man
	the		house	across	the		road
	an	old	mill	by	a		stream
7b	Det	AP	N	P	Det	AP	N

As with **1**, the word string can be categorized in terms of the class labels shown below the words. This time note the new class P(reposition), which includes the members {*about, across, by* . . .}. Once again, and for reasons which will become clear, we will consider this new class to be the head of the corresponding phrasal category, PP. In terms of our present assumptions about constituent structure this implies a constituent structure analysis like that shown in Figure 6.2. This figure shows a very 'flat' structure in that the mother NP dominates a number of daughters of various kinds. In Chapter 8 we will return to the question and propose a more hierarchical structure.

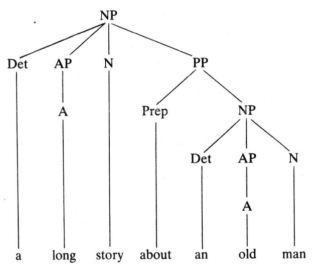

Figure 6.2

Three of the major word classes we have examined so far have been associated with a grammatical category: N with [number: sing, pl], V with [tense: past, pres] and A with [degree: ord, comp, sup]. P(repositions), by contrast, are invariant. The corresponding phrasal category, however, does have internal structure, as shown in Figure 6.2. The most frequent complement for a preposition is an NP, as can be verified by what we know about NPs, and as illustrated in **8**:

8a $_{PP}$(Prep   NP)

8b	about	politics	(NP = N)
8c	under	the sea	(NP = Det N)
8d	with	a powerful engine	(NP = Det AP N)

There are other possible internal structures for PP, but we will ignore them in this chapter.

In terms of its distribution in other structures PP is extremely versatile, and we will mention here only three of the many environments in which it can occur. As we saw in **7**, a PP can occur as an optional 'postmodifier' of the head noun in an NP:

9a $_{NP}$(Det   N $_{PP}$(—))

9b	a	scandal	about politics
9c	a	city	under the sea
9d	a	car	with a powerful engine

Like the AP, it can occur after the verb BE, this time typically to describe a location:

10a $_{S}$(NP $_{VP}$(BE $_{PP}$(—))

10b	he	is	in bed
10c	the mouse	is	under the chair

It also occurs as an obligatory constituent after some verbs like PUT, as we saw in Chapter 5, subsections 5.1e and 5.1f:

11a $_{S}$(NP $_{VP}$(V   NP $_{PP}$(—))

11b	she	put	the lamp	in the window
11c	he	laid	the flowers	on the table

12a–c describe part of the distributional range of PP and **12d** describes the internal structure of PP:

12a	VP → BE PP
12b	VP → V NP PP
12c	NP → (Det) (AP) N (PP)
12d	PP → P NP

Technical terms

degree (with the terms ordinary, comparative and superlative)
intensifier

Notes

1 Hitherto we have described items like {*a, the*} as Art(icles). Here we categorize
   Art as a subclass of a larger class of Det(erminers). In addition to the subclass
   Art, Det also includes as subclasses Dem(onstratives) like {*this, that, these,
   those*} and Quant(ifiers) like {*all, few, many*}.
2 The notion 'head' will be explored in more detail in Chapters 8 and 17. For our
   immediate purposes, and with respect to phrasal categories, we can think of the
   head as being the obligatory constituent common to all instances of a particular
   phrasal category. Thus, for example, all NPs will contain an N head and may
   contain other material, perhaps an article or an adjective. See also note 4.
3 This applies to 'central' adjectives. There are other classes of adjectives which do
   not meet all of these criteria but we will not be concerned with them here. See
   Quirk *et al.*, 1972, ch. 7.
4 Modifiers are generally optional constituents which are syntactically dependent
   on some head. In Noun Phrases an Adjective Phrase is usually an optional
   modifier of the obligatory head Noun. As the names suggest, a 'premodifier'
   precedes the head, as in **2**, and a 'postmodifier' follows it, as in example **9a** above.
   For further details see Chapters 8 and 17.

Exercises

(1) *The structure of the NP in English*
   There are restrictions on the possible order of constituents in
   English NPs. Thus we find NPs like *all their old cotton dresses,
   a lovely pale blue silk shirt, five worn-out jumpers*, but not NPs
   like **their all old cotton dresses, *a pale lovely silk blue shirt*.

   (a) Construct twenty NPs each of not more than six words
       using as 'head noun' one of the following: *dress, shirt,
       jumper, sock, petticoat, apron, blouse*, and as 'pre-
       modifiers' of the head noun appropriate items from the
       following list:

       a, all, big, blue, cotton, few, five, her, lovely, my, new,
       old, pale, quite, red, silk, small, some, spectacular,
       splendid, the, two, very, woollen, worn-out, your

(The notions 'head noun' and 'premodifiers' are discussed further in Chapter 8; in NPs of the sort you are
asked to consider, the head noun is always the final, and
obligatory, constituent, which may be preceded by a
number of optional premodifiers.)

(b)   Assign each word above to one of the form classes:

Quant(ifier) *all, several* . . .   Num(eral) *five, two* . . .
Art(icle) *a, the* . . .   Adj(ective) *blue, red* . . .
Poss(essive) *my, your* . . .   Int(ensifier) *very, pale* . . .

(c)   There are ordering restrictions on the adjectives – thus
old blue dress but not **blue old dress*. Assign adjectives
to 'order classes' labelled Adj1, Adj2, and so on. (Can
you make any semantic generalizations about these
order classes?)

(d)   There are also co-occurrence restrictions on the quantifiers – thus *all their socks*, but not **several their socks*.
Assign quantifiers to one of the two subclasses Quant1
and Quant2.

(e)   Write formulae to show possible orders of elements in
the NP (and to exclude impossible orders): for example,
all blue dresses (Quant Adj N), *all dresses* (Quant N). Try
to collapse the formulae into a single general statement
using brackets for 'optional' constituents: for example,
(Quant) (Adj) N – which will cover the examples above;
the N is an obligatory constituent and so is unbracketed.
You will need to add a note about the difference between
singular and plural head nouns – to account for the fact
that we find *a* with singular NPs (*a red sock*, **a red socks*)
and *all* with plural NPs (*all red socks*, **all red sock*), and
so on.

odifies; thus the scope of
clear sentence *The woman*
onal constituents; this is
closing the adverbial PP
he modifier can, to some
ces it. In the case of **15** the
he nuclear sentence, so its

he constituent *The woman*
seful distinction between
s. Nuclear constituents of
immediately dominated by
re non-nuclear. Nuclear
sentence to be accepted as
classification. Non-nuclear
ly, modifiers. Frequently,
in a separate sentence, as
deriving from an expansion
he expansion of S are non-

sic' and simplest sentence
sentences is not, however,
n between nuclear and non-
tter of optionality. We saw,
at the NP that immediately
ory; both *He stood the lamp*
table are grammatical. It is,
cessary strict subcategoriza-
onal but nuclear constituents
WALK:

clear but not obligatory; **17**

ned to school

like READ and WRITE which

7   Optional constituents

7.1   Optional constituents

In Chapter 5 we noted that the subject NP is non-distinctive for purposes of verb subclassification; since all sentences require a subject NP, only what follows the verb can be distinctive. Let us now consider some other constituents that are non-distinctive for the purpose of verb subclassification. Consider these sentences:

1   The woman wept in the bathroom
2   The dog bit the man in the bathroom
3   John gave Mary the book in the bathroom
4   John stood on the table in the bathroom
5   John stood the gun against the wall in the bathroom

We can analyse each of these sentences as having a constituent *in the bathroom* in construction with one of our example sentences from Chapter 5.[1] In categorial terms *in the bathroom* is a prepositional phrase. Traditionally the function of constituents of this kind has been referred to as 'adverbial' – in this instance, since they indicate where the action took place, as 'place adverbials'.

There are a number of things we should observe about adverbial constituents in deciding their constituent structure. First, in each case *in the bathroom* is an optional constituent; without it, an acceptable sentence remains. By contrast, we cannot leave out the constituent immediately following the verb. We can have:

6   The dog bit the man

but not:

7   *The dog bit in the bathroom

Secondly, the constituent *in the bathroom* is not criterial for verb

subclassification; since it occurs with all the verb class
it cannot be criterial. Finally, sentences like those in
be paraphrased by two sentences, one containing
predication and the other the place adverbial, for exa

8   The women wept. This happened in the bath
9   John stood the gun against the wall. This ha
    bathroom

We cannot find sentences resembling 8 and 9 which
any of the other constituents in 1–5:

10   *The dog bit. This happened to the man

This last characteristic of constituents like *in th*
particularly valuable when we contrast them witl
similar constituents like *against the wall* and *on the tab*
4 and 5. The following are acceptable:

11   John stood on the table. This happened in tl
12   John stood the gun against the wall. This ha
     bathroom

but the following are nonsense:

13   *John stood. This happened on the table
14   *John stood the gun. This happened against

In Chapter 5 we observed that the constituents cri
subclassification are those constituents that are sis
daughters of VP with V. This suggests that we shoul
adverbial constituents as constituents of some node c
For the present we will assign to them the constiti
shown in Figure 7.1.

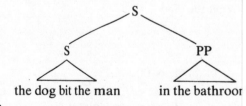

Figure 7.1

to the constituents which the modif
the modifier *in the bathroom* in **1** is tl
wept. Syntactically, modifiers are
shown in the first rule in **15** by
constituent in brackets. The scope
degree, be shown by the rule that int
adverbial PP is introduced as a siste
scope is the nuclear sentence as a wl

    The previous paragraph referred
wept as 'nuclear'. We can draw
'nuclear' and 'non-nuclear' constit
the sentence are NP + VP and all th:
VP. Other sentence constituent
constituents are either obligatory fo
grammatical, or criterial for verb
constituents are optional and, typ
non-nuclear constituents can be pl:
illustrated by **8** and **9**. In these terms
of VP are nuclear, PPs deriving fro
nuclear.

    Nuclear sentences are the most
types in the language. Defining nucl
entirely straightforward. The distinc
nuclear constituents is not a simple
for instance, in the previous chapte
follows a verb like STAND is not obli
on the table and *The lamp stood on*
however, nuclear, as it is part of the
tion frame. Other verb classes with o
include 'verbs of motion' like RUN a

16   John is running
17   John is running to school

where the *to school* constituent is
cannot be paraphrased by:

18   *John is running. This hap

Another similar case involves ver
take an optional object NP:

19 John is reading
20 John is reading a book

The constituent *a book* can hardly occur in a distinct sentence on the model of **8** or **9**. Furthermore, it makes no sense to say that *a book* 'modifies' *John is reading* in a comparable fashion to the way *in the bathroom* modifies *the woman wept* in the sentence *The woman wept in the bathroom.*

7.3 Adverbs and adverbials

The traditional category of Adverb is very mixed, and we have not used the term in this chapter. Instead we have distinguished between the grammatical category of a constituent like *in the bathroom* – it is a PP – and its function as an 'adverbial of place'. The reason for making this distinction between category and function can be seen if we consider two questions. Are there other types of constituent that function as adverbials of place? Are there other types of adverbial in addition to adverbials of place? The answer to both questions is yes.

First, consider other adverbials of place:

21a The dog bit the man *in the bathroom*
21b The dog bit the man *where it hurt*
21c The dog bit the man *upstairs*

In terms of their internal constituent structure, *in the bathroom, upstairs* and *where it hurt* all clearly belong to different categories. We have already seen that *in the bathroom* is a PP. *Where it hurts* is a form of subordinate sentence. *Upstairs* and other items like *downstairs, here* and *there* we will consider to be members of the category 'Adverb', more specifically the subcategory of 'Adverbs of Place'.

They all, however, have the same external distribution in that they are mutually substitutable. They will all answer place interrogative sentences of the form:

22a Where did the dog bite the man?
22b Upstairs/in the bathroom/where it hurt, and so on

And they all have the same syntactic function as modifiers to the nucleus *the dog bit the man*. We will refer to this function as 'adverbial'.

Adverbials of time, as the name suggests, locate events, and so on, in time:

23a   John has lived in London *for twenty years*
23b   John visited the country *whenever he could*
23c   The dog bit the man *yesterday*

As before, PPs (*for twenty years*), subordinate sentences (*whenever he could*) and time adverbs (*yesterday*) can all have an adverbial function. Sentences with adverbials of time correspond to interrogative sentences with *when, how long*, and so on:

24a   How long has John lived in London?
24b   Twenty years

25a   When did the dog bite the man?
25b   Yesterday/whenever he could

Adverbials of place and time are usually considered to be sentence modifiers. They occur most frequently sentence finally, as in the examples we have been examining, but by a process we can refer to as 'adverb fronting' can usually occur at the beginning of the sentence as well:[2]

26a   Yesterday the dog bit the man
26b   For twenty years John has lived in London

A sentence may have both adverbials – time most naturally following rather than preceding place (though both orders may occur):

27a   The dog bit the man upstairs yesterday
27b   The dog bit the man yesterday upstairs

Adverbials of manner, as their name suggests, indicate the manner in which the event described by the verb is carried out:

28a   The dog bit the man *viciously*
28b   The man beat the dog *with apparent enjoyment*

Once again we find prepositional phrases and manner adverbs. Manner adverbs are the items that most readily spring to mind as examples of the class adverb, especially those formed by the suffixation of *-ly* to a corresponding adjective form:

29a happy: happily
29b vicious: viciously

In these cases there is typically a paraphrase *in an [Adj] manner*:

30a The man beat the dog viciously
30b The man beat the dog in a vicious manner

Manner adverbs correspond to *how* in interrogative sentences:

31a How did the man beat the dog?
31b Viciously/with apparent enjoyment, and so on

Manner adverbs most naturally immediately follow the VP, preceding other adverbs:

32a The man beat the dog viciously in the garden yesterday
32b ?The man beat the dog yesterday in the garden viciously

Further, manner adverbs, unlike other adverbs, occur readily within the verb constituent:

33a The man viciously beat the dog
33b The man is viciously beating the dog
33c *The man is in the garden beating the dog

We began this section by distinguishing between category and function. The distinction between adverb and adverbial should now be clear; adverb is the name of a category, and adverbial the name of a function. Adverbs typically have an adverbial function. PPs may have an adverbial function, but are not adverbs.

We also noted that adverbs are modifiers and that to some extent the scope of the modification can be caught in constituent structure representations. We have already seen that time and place adverbials may be seen as sentence modifiers. By contrast, the behaviour illustrated in **32** and **33** leads us to suggest that manner adverbials are VP modifiers. This can be captured in constituent structure diagrams of the kind shown in Figure 7.3, which also illustrates the fact that the same category, PP, can occur in a variety of functions – as the strict subcategorizer of a verb, as a VP adverbial and as a sentence adverbial.

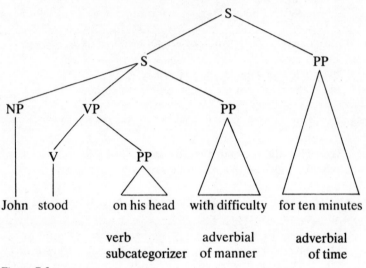

Figure 7.3

Technical terms

adverb   modifier
adverbial   nuclear constituent
grammatical function   scope
head

Notes

1   Some of these sentences are ambiguous. For example, **2** could be analysed as either of:

   (1)   The dog – bit – the man – in the bathroom
   (2)   The dog – bit – the man in the bathroom

   In (1) the constituent *in the bathroom* indicates where the man was bitten, and can be related to sentences like:

(3)   It was in the bathroom that the dog bit the man
      Where the dog bit the man was in the bathroom
      Where did the dog bite the man? In the bathroom

In sentence (2) the constituent *the man in the bathroom* is an NP. This sentence is related to other sentences like:

(4)   It was the man in the bathroom that the dog bit
      Who did the dog bite? The man in the bathroom

We are immediately concerned with the first of these analyses, that is, (1). We will return to the other analysis. We may also observe that constituents like *in the bathroom* do not typically occur in sentences with copular verbs:

(5)   *John is tall in the bathroom

This is why such sentences are not included in **1–5**.
2   We return to the derivations involving the 'alternative' placements of adverbs in Chapter 9.

Exercises

(1)   *Optional and obligatory constituents*
      The text suggests that obligatory constituents are always nuclear, but that nuclear constituents are not always obligatory. It is further suggested that nuclear constituents are important for the strict subcategorization of verbs. In the sentences below the relevant constituents have been separated by strokes. Which of them would you consider to be obligatory and which non-obligatory, and which nuclear and which non-nuclear? You should give reasons to support your decisions; these may be based on the unacceptability of some sentence if a constituent is omitted, considerations that arise from strict subcategorization, considerations relating to possible transformations of the sentences in question, and so on.

      (i)   I/agree/with John
      (ii)   I/went/to the cinema/ with John/ yesterday
      (iii) The fifteenth Music Festival/will be held/in the Assembly Rooms/in May 1990
      (iv)   John/went/to Bristol/in 1982
      (v)   Harriet/always/plays/with a rubber duck/in the bath
      (vi)   Mary/will write/a letter/to mother/for you
      (vii) Harriet/is/in the bath

    (viii)   They/elected/Charlie/president
    (ix)   We/sent/a parcel/to Mary/for Christmas
    (x)   We/pierced/the membrane/with a needle
    (xi)   They/thought/Charlie/foolish

8 Intermediate levels of structure

8.1 Intermediate levels of structure

Hitherto we have been largely concerned with the major lexical categories of N(oun), V(erb), A(djective) and P(reposition) and the phrasal categories that correspond to them, NP, VP, AP and PP. We have also been interested in the functional relationship between the lexical category, the head of the corresponding phrasal structure and other constituents within the phrasal category, modifiers of the head. In this chapter we shall be concerned with two issues: first, whether it is helpful to identify categories intermediate between the lexical and the phrasal; and second, whether we can usefully identify a more elaborated system of functional relationships.

In Chapter 6 we saw that a string like **1a** can be described by the string of categories shown in **1b**, where the A(djective) *juicy* is the sole constituent of the corresponding phrasal category AP (Adjective Phrase):

1a That juicy apple
1b Det AP N

What constituent structure should we asign to the string? We will consider three possibilities.

One is the 'flat' structure of Figure 8.1, where all three constituents are sisters.

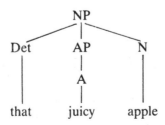

Figure 8.1

The second is the structure of Figure 8.2 in which *that* and *juicy* are sisters (we provisionally label the mother category 'Y').

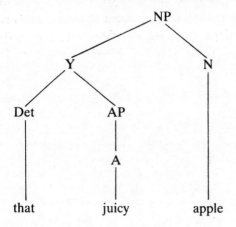

Figure 8.2

The third is a structure where *juicy* and *apple* are sisters as in Figure 8.3 (the mother is provisionally labelled 'X').

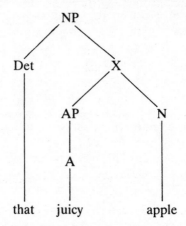

Figure 8.3

In choosing between these structures we return to the issues of bracketing (that is, the identification of constituents) and labelling (that is, their naming) that we discussed in Chapters 1 and 2.

We will consider first the question of constituency. In previous chapters we have applied several tests for constituency. Here we will consider two; constituents can be substituted by a proform and constituents can be conjoined.

Consider proforms first. There are two proforms typically associated with the NP: pronouns (*he, she, it, they*, and so on) and the proform *one*. We will illustrate their distribution by a slightly more elaborate NP, *that tall young man with fair hair*; the head noun, *man*, co-occurs with a determiner, *that*, two premodifying adjectives, *tall* and *young*, and a postmodifying PP, *with fair hair*. A pronoun can substitute for the whole NP, as **2c** shows, but it cannot substitute for a sub-part of the NP, as can be seen from the fact that pronouns do not co-occur with articles (**2d**), adjectives (**2e** and **2f**), or post-nominal PPs (**2g**). It might indeed be more accurate to call them 'proNPs' rather than 'pronouns':

2a		That tall young man with fair hair stole the peach
2b	Q:	Who stole the peach?
2c	A:	He (sc *that tall young man with fair hair*) did
2d		*that he (*he = tall young man with fair hair*)
2e		*that tall he (*he = young man with fair hair*)
2f		*that tall young he (*he = man with fair hair*)
2g		*that he with fair hair (*he = tall young man*)

One, by contrast, is the proform for the head N and for subconstituents of the NP which include the head noun and its associated AP and PP modifiers but exclude an article. Thus, *one* in **3** cannot substitute for the whole NP (**3c**) but can substitute for the head noun (**3h**), the head noun and one (**3g**) or more (**3f**) adjective(s) and the head noun and a following PP (**3d** and **3e**):

3a		That tall young man with fair hair stole the peach
3b	Q:	Who stole the peach?
3c	A:	*One (sc *that tall young man with fair hair*) did
3d		that one (*one = tall young man with fair hair*)
3e		that tall one (*one = young man with fair hair*)
3f		that tall young one (*one = man with fair hair*)
3g		that one with fair hair (*one = tall young man*)
3h		that tall young one with fair hair (one = *man*)

If only constituents can be substituted by a proform, then it seems that we will need to postulate a structure for our NP as shown in Figure 8.4.

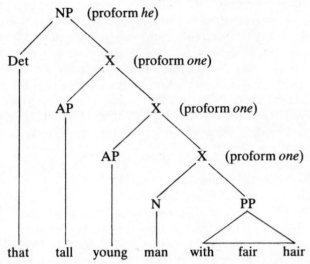

Figure 8.4

If we apply these tests to the structures shown in Figures 8.1–8.3, only 8.3 passes. The flat structure of Figure 8.1 must fail as it has no internal structure at all. Figure 8.2 fails because it does not have the relevant structure; there is no proform for the string Det + Adj, the constituent 'Y' of the figure. The structure in Figure 8.3, however, passes since the string *juicy apple*, 'X' in the figure, is substitutable by the proform *one*:

4 Q: Who wants one of these juicy apples?
     A: I'd like that one (that is, that juicy apple)

The structure of Figure 8.4 is, of course, only a more elaborate version of Figure 8.3.

The co-ordination test is more ambiguous. Strings of Adj + N (that is, 'X' of Figure 8.3) can be readily co-ordinated as shown in **5a**, with the structure shown in the vine diagram **5b**:

5a Those juicy apples and ripe pears

5b NP

Det	those
X	
X	
adj	juicy
N	apples
conjunction	and
X	
adj	ripe
N	pears

If we now turn to the structure of Figure 8.2 we find that strings of Det + Adj can also conjoin, as **6** illustrates:

6a *Those French* and *these English* apples
6b NP

Y	
Y	
Det	those
AP	French
conjunction	and
Y	
Det	these
AP	English
N	apples

However, in so far as 'X' passes more constituency tests than 'Y' it seems that Figure 8.3 offers a better analysis, and it is indeed the one we shall prefer. Furthermore, as we shall see, functional considerations offer further substantial reasons for preferring this structure.

However, before turning to functional considerations, we should consider what kind of a constituent 'X' is, and hence what label we should attach to it. If we are restricted to only lexical and phrasal categories, 'X' must be either an NP or an N. If it is an NP, we will have the analysis illustrated in Figure 8.5 together with rules that would generate the structure.

The difficulty with this solution is that while the rules correctly generate legitimate strings like **1a**, there is, unfortunately, nothing to stop the repeated application of rule 8.5.i which will generate impossible strings with repeated determiners like:

7 *the a that those juicy apples

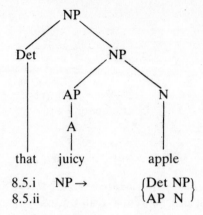

Figure 8.5

This suggests that 'X' is not a whole NP, but rather that part of an NP that lacks a determiner. Is it then a Noun? Clearly it contains an N, *apples*, but what then of *juicy*, the modifying adjective? In this case 'X' seems to be more than an N but less than an NP. It seems that 'X' is a category intermediate between the N and the NP. It is more than a Noun in that it permits a modifying AP, but less than an NP since we want it to exclude the determiner. There is no traditional label for an intermediate category of this type, but it is now customary to refer to an intermediate constituent of this type as 'N-bar', or N1. Figure 8.6 shows this structure.

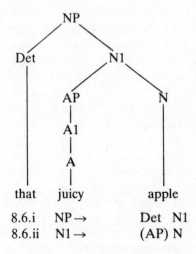

Figure 8.6

For a reason which will appear immediately, we will make one further modification to this structure, as shown in Figure 8.7; the difference between the two structures lies in the iteration of the N1 node in Figure 8.7.

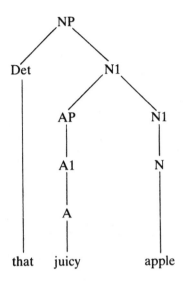

Figure 8.7

The point of the elaborated structure of Figure 8.7 is twofold. First, it enables us to capture more accurately the distributional properties of certain items like the determiners (they are daughters of NP and sisters of N1) and distinguish between pronouns, *he, she,* and so on, and the proform *one* (the pronouns will substitute for an NP; *one* substitutes for N or N1).[1]

Secondly, we can use the structures to capture an array of functional relationships between the lexical head of a phrasal category and other phrasal constituents. We will distinguish between four importantly different types of constituent:

(1) The lexical category itself, the *head* of the phrasal category, which is the daughter of the intermediate N1 node (*apples* in Figure 8.7).

(2) The head may itself have sisters, and when it does we will call them the *complements* of the lexical node. In fact there is no example of a complement in the structure shown in Figure 8.7, but we will meet complements shortly.

(3)   Constituents like the determiner, which are daughters of the
phrasal node and sisters of an intermediate node N1: we will
call these items *specifiers* (*that* in Figure 8.7).
(4)   Constituents like the AP which are daughters of an intermediate N1 node and sisters of another intermediate N1 node:
we will call these items *modifiers* (*juicy* in Figure 8.7).

It should now be clear why we elaborated the structure of
Figure 8.6 to that of Figure 8.7; in 8.6 the modifying AP *juicy* is
shown as a sister of the lexical head, which implies that it is a
complement of the head, whereas in 8.7 it is correctly shown as a
modifier of the head.

Figure 8.8 shows these functional relationships in a schematic
form. Note that the tree illustrated is not a proper constituent
structure tree, since functional relations should not be used as labels
in a constituent structure tree. Rather it attempts to illustrate the
typical structural configurations of various functional relations and
for this reason the functional relations are shown in brackets. Note
that the dominating category is shown as XP; X is intended to
represent any of the major categories N, V, A, or P, and hence XP
as the corresponding phrasal category.[2]

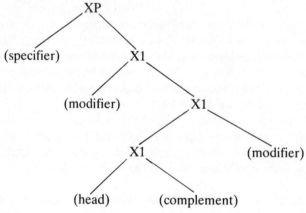

Figure 8.8

Constituent structure representations constructed along the lines
outlined in the previous paragraphs are a version of what is known
as 'X-bar' syntax. In X-bar syntax the major lexical categories (in
our case X = N, V, A and P) are basic categories in the sense that

they themselves have no constituent structure in the syntax – and we have always considered the individual noun or adjective word as the smallest category the syntax is concerned with.[3] Corresponding to each of the major lexical categories is a phrasal category of the same type, the lexical category being the head, or principal constituent, of the phrasal category; that is, an N is the head of an NP, and V is the head of a VP, and so on. Furthermore, the phrasal category is the 'maximal projection' of the lexical category in the sense that it is the largest category of which the corresponding lexical category is the head. If you like, there is nothing noun-like smaller than an N and nothing noun-like bigger than an NP. We have supposed that categories intermediate between the lexical and the phrasal are X1 categories and, as Figure 8.8 suggests, there may be any number of these. We will label them all X1, and assume that X1 may iterate as often as is required.

To summarize, a phrasal structure (XP) is the maximal projection of its head, the corresponding lexical category. There may be any number of intermediate categories (X1). XP may have as its daughter a specifier; the lexical head may have complements as its sisters. The intermediate X1 categories dominate modifiers. These relationships are summarized (together with a number of alternative notational conventional conventions) in Figure 8.9, and Figure 8.10 is an annotated diagram of the NP *that young man with fair hair*.

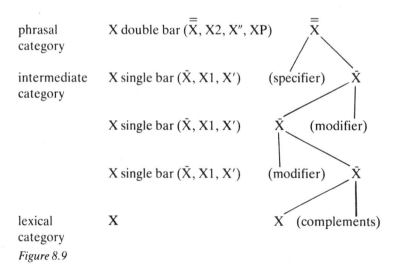

phrasal category	X double bar ($\overline{\overline{X}}$, X2, X″, XP)	
intermediate category	X single bar ($\bar{X}$, X1, X′)	(specifier)
	X single bar ($\bar{X}$, X1, X′)	(modifier)
	X single bar ($\bar{X}$, X1, X′)	(modifier)
lexical category	X	(complements)

Figure 8.9

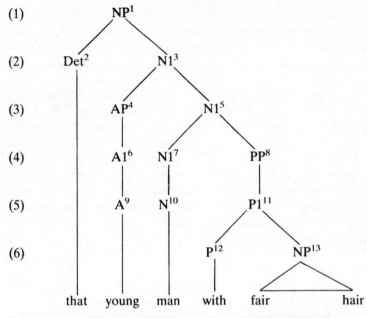

(the annotations are purely for identification)

	category	dominates the word string	functional relation to head
(1)	NP^1	*that young man with fair hair*	maximal projection of N^{10}
(2)	Det^2	*that*	**specifier of NP^1**
	N1^3	*young man with fair hair*	head of NP^1
(3)	AP^4	*young*	modifier of N1^5
	N1^5	*man with fair hair*	head of N1^3
(4)	A1^6	*young*	head of AP^4
	N1^7	*man*	head of N1^5
	PP^8	*with fair hair*	modifier of N1^7
(5)	A^9	*young*	head of A1^6 so head of AP^4
	N^{10}	*man*	head of N1^7 so head of NP^1
	P1^{11}	*with fair hair*	head of PP^8
(6)	P^{12}	*with*	head of P1^{11}
	NP^{13}	*fair hair*	complement of P^{12}

Figure 8.10

8.2 The specifiers, modifiers and complements of the major categories

We will conclude this chapter by summarizing the constituency structure of each of the major categories of English. For each of the major lexical categories N, V, P and A, the maximal projection is the corresponding phrase NP, VP, PP, or AP. There are also intermediate levels of structure N1, V1, P1 and A1. The maximal projection, the phrasal category, will not iterate. It will have an X1 daughter as head, and may also have a specifier daughter. The lexical category will be the head daughter of an X1 node and will not iterate either. It may have complements as sisters and if it does will be subcategorized by its complements. The intermediate category, X1, may iterate, but need not. It may dominate another X1 and its sisters, and in this case the sisters will be 'modifiers'. The relevant structural relationships were illustrated in Figure 8.8.

8.2a Noun phrases

The head must be a lexical N.

NP Specifiers include articles (*a, the*), demonstratives (*this, that.* . .) and quantifiers (*all, some.* . .).

NP Modifiers include Adjective Phrases (*those* BORING *arguments*), relative clauses (*those boring arguments* THAT WE USED TO HAVE WHEN WE WERE STUDENTS) and certain Prepositional Phrases, typically those with locative and temporal senses (*those boring arguments* IN THE BAR; *those stimulating discussions* AFTER MIDNIGHT).

NP Complements are those categories that subcategorize the head including S1 (*the rumour* THAT THE POUND IS ABOUT TO FALL; *the question* WHETHER THIS IS ALL COMPREHENSIBLE) and PPs (*an argument* ABOUT LINGUISTICS). Many nouns, of course, cannot occur with complements (*girl, boy* . . .).

8.2b Adjective phrases[4]

The head must be a lexical A.

AP Specifiers include degree words (VERY *clever*; QUITE *silly* . . .) and perhaps some articles (THAT *fond of Mary*).

AP Modifiers include certain kinds of Prepositional Phrases, typically, as with NP modifiers, locative and temporal expressions (*anxious about the children* ON BONFIRE NIGHT).

AP Complements are those categories that subcategorize the head including S1 (*glad* THAT THE POUND IS ABOUT TO RISE; *unsure* WHETHER THIS IS ALL COMPREHENSIBLE) and PPs (*averse* TO FISH; *fond* OF MARY). Many adjectives, of course, require no complement (*red, fast*).

8.2c   *Prepositional phrases*[5]

The head must be a lexical P.

PP Specifiers include degree words (RIGHT *against the garden fence*; ALMOST *in the garden next door*).

PP Modifiers are rather infrequent, but include certain kinds of Adverbials (ALMOST CERTAINLY *in the wrong*) and PPs (*out of touch* IN SOME WAYS).

PP Complements are those categories that subcategorize the head. Most obvious are NPs (*after* DINNER; *under* THE BED), but we can also consider S1 (*after* HE HAS HAD HIS DINNER), PPs (*out* OF THE WINDOW; *down* AMONG THE DEAD MEN) and, of course, 'nothing at all' (I'll see you AFTER; *he went* OUT).

8.2d   *Verb phrases*[6]

The head must be a lexical V.

VP Specifiers are the perfect (*have*) and progressive (*be*) auxiliaries (HAS BEEN *seen by the police*).

VP Modifiers include 'manner adverbials' (*answered the questions* QUICKLY) and PPs (*answered the questions* WITH SKILL; *cut the meat* WITH A KNIFE).

VP Complements are those categories that subcategorize the head including 'nothing at all' (that is, intransitive verbs) (*laughed*), NPs (*ate* HIS DINNER), PPs (*argue* ABOUT LINGUISTICS, *rely* ON MARY), S1 (*complain* THAT THE POUND IS ABOUT TO FALL, *ask* WHETHER THIS IS ALL COMPREHENSIBLE), and so on.

Figure 8.11 illustrates these relationships within the VP.

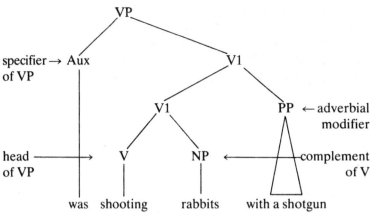

Figure 8.11

Technical terms

complement	phrasal category
co-ordination	proform
head	specifier
lexical category	X-bar
modifier	

Notes

1 The situation is actually somewhat more complicated than this, but this formulation will serve our immediate purposes.
2 The ordering relations shown are those of English, where determiners are indeed 'at the front' of the NP, complements follow the head, and modifiers either precede the head (adjectives) or follow it (prepositional phrases). The general schema, however, is intended to be applicable to any language, including those where the ordering relations may be different. See, for example, the discussion on ordering relations in Chapter 17.
3 The question of the internal structure of words is one we turn to in Part Two.
4 See Chapter 6, section 6.1.
5 See Chapter 6, section 6.2.
6 For an extensive discussion of some verb subclasses see Chapter 5, section 5.1.

Exercises

In the text we have assumed an X-bar scheme of the following kind:

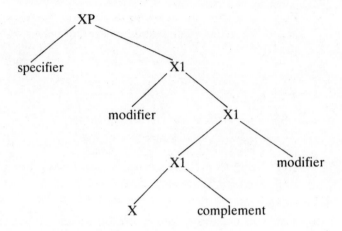

X1 can reiterate as often as you want, but X (the head of the construction) and XP cannot. An XP structure need not include a specifier, modifier, or complement, but must have an X head. So, for example, in the NP: ALL THOSE WONDERFUL OLD *anecdotes* ABOUT OUR HOLIDAYS LAST SUMMER IN ITALY only the head N *anecdotes* is obligatory (cf. *I find anecdotes really boring*)

(1) (a) What is the structure of the following NPs (ignore all other structure)?

     (i)   *Most old people* can't stand *the cold winters*
    (ii)   *My mother* refused to believe *the spicy rumour that Kim and Shane were having an affair*
    (iii) *The local police* are supposed to investigate *all reports of break-ins*
    (iv)   *Children* like *sweets*
    (v)   *I* admire *her*
    (vi)   *Kim* can't stand *whisky*
   (vii)   *Young children* are supposed to like *fizzy drinks*

    (b) In the following NPs which of the PPs would you consider to be 'complements' and which 'modifiers' and why?

- (i) arguments about linguistics
- (ii) arguments in the bar
- (iii) gifts to charity at Christmas
- (iv) the girls in trousers near the window

(c) Can you make any generalization about the relative ordering of specifiers, modifiers and complements within the NP?

(2) (a) What is the structure of the following APs (ignore all other structure)?

- (i) John is *frightfully clever at linguistics*
- (ii) John isn't *that clever at linguistics*
- (iii) Charlie is *so clever with his hands*
- (iv) I am *very excited indeed about your new poem*
- (v) I am *frightened in the dark*
- (vi) I am *frightened of spiders in the dark*

(b) Can you make any generalization about the relative ordering of specifiers, modifiers and complements within the AP?

(3) (a) What is the structure of the following PPs (ignore all other structure)?

- (i) The ball rolled *right across the table* and *almost into the pocket*
- (ii) Kim will go *into the garden shed* whenever Shane comes *out of the house*
- (iii) Kim will go *in* whenever Shane comes *out*
- (iv) The man *over the road* seems to go *down to the pub* every evening *when his brother comes home*
- (v) The beetle crawled *right down into the crack*

(b) Can you make any generalization about the relative ordering of specifiers, modifiers and complements within the PP?

(4) What is the structure of the VPs in the following? Which of the PP constituents that follow the verb are 'complements', which are 'modifiers' within the VP, and which are 'sentence adverbials'? How would you know? Some of the sentences may be ambiguous!

(i)   He laughed lightly and ran quickly into the house
(ii) Kim was talking to Shane about linguistics in the library at midnight
(iii) Shane goes to church with Kim on Sundays in the winter
(iv) Kim decided on the boat with no difficulty
(v)   Harry frequently complained to Mary that he felt ill
(vi) Williams shot Harold in the eye with an arrow
(vii) Harold fell off his horse in agony
(viii) It served Harold right

9 Embedding, recursion and ambiguity

9.1 Embedding and recursion

When a phrasal or sentential constituent is completely contained within another phrasal or sentential constituent it is said to be embedded. Here are some examples; only the bracketing of the subordinate or embedded category and the matrix or containing category is shown (for example, in **1a** the PP *over the river* is embedded in the NP *the bridge over the river* which is a constituent of the PP *by the bridge over the river* which is itself embedded in the NP *the house by the bridge over the river*):

1a $_{NP}$(the house $_{PP}$(by $_{NP}$the bridge $_{PP}$(over the river)))

1b $_{NP}$(The rumour $_S$(that Charlie married Mary)) is untrue

1c $_S$(Fred believes $_S$(that Charlie married Mary))

1d $_{NP}$(a book $_S$(which I bought yesterday))

Consider first the derivation of an NP like **1a**, the structure of which is shown in Figure 9.1. It can be derived by the rules in **2**:[1]

2a NP → Det N (PP)
2b PP → Prep NP

We first use rule **2a**. Suppose we choose the option of introducing a PP constituent. We now expand the PP constituent by rule **2b**, which introduces another NP. We must now return to **2a** to expand this NP and this can produce another PP, which in turn will produce another NP, and so on. The process of 'cycling' through rules over and over again is called recursion and it is necessary for NPs like **1a**.

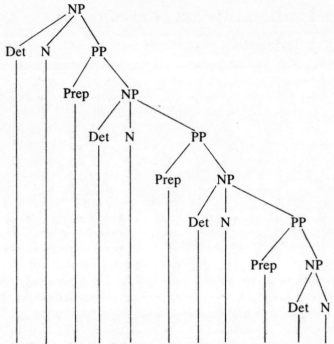

the house by the bridge over   the river beyond the town

Figure 9.1

Consider next the NP *the rumour that Charlie married Mary* in **1b**, which we will suppose to have the structure shown in Figure 9.2 (and using the X-bar notation developed in Chapter 8). Here the

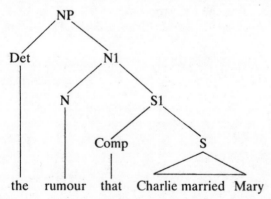

Figure 9.2

sentence *Charlie married Mary*, the internal structure of which is not shown as it is irrelevant to the point at issue, is embedded as the complement of the noun RUMOUR. Note that the complement sentence (the embedded sentence) is preceded by a 'Comp-(lementizer)', *that*, so called because its function is to indicate that the subordinate or embedded sentence structure immediately following is a 'complement' of the head noun.

The examples in 1 illustrate two types of complementation: Noun complementation, as in **1b**, where the embedded sentence is the complement of the noun RUMOUR; and Verb complementation, as in **1c**, where the embedded sentence is the complement of the verb BELIEVE. Not all nouns co-occur with complement sentences:

3   $*_{NP}$(The house $_{S1}$(that Charlie married Mary)) is unsafe

so we will need to indicate in the lexicon which nouns can take complements by including an appropriate subcategorization frame in the lexical specification of nouns like RUMOUR, STORY, FACT and INSINUATION, as follows:

4   RUMOUR: N; __ S1

where the strict subcategorization frame __ S1 indicates that RUMOUR can take a complement sentence.

Similarly, not all verbs co-occur with a complement sentence; we do not find:

5   *John killed $_{S1}$(that Charlie is married)

For those verbs that do take complement sentences, like BELIEVE, EXPECT, THINK, and SUPPOSE, we can, once again, indicate this fact in the lexical specification:

6   BELIEVE: V; __ S1

The subject of verb complementation in English is complex and we do not consider it in this book. Those interested in pursuing the subject are referred to the books in 'Further reading' on page 372.

9.2   Attachment and ambiguity

Consider the following two sentences:

7a   The hunter shot the rabbits with a catapult
7b   The nun pitied the man with a wooden leg

Although superficially rather similar, the two sentences have radically different interpretations. The most natural interpretation of **7a** is that the PP *with a catapult* has an 'instrumental' function, an understanding that can be related to a loose paraphrase like:

8   The hunter used a catapult to shoot the rabbits

The apparently similar PP *with a wooden leg* in **7b** cannot reasonably be understood in this way; it is difficult to make sense of:

9   ?The nun used a wooden leg to pity the man

In this case the most sensible interpretation is that the PP is a constituent of the NP *the man with a wooden leg*, serving as a 'modifier' of the noun *man*. In informal terms, it specifies a property of 'the man'. In this case the sentence can be related to a loose paraphrase like:

10   The nun pitied the man who had a wooden leg

A comparable paraphrase related to **7a** can only make sense in a fairy-story world where rabbits could possess catapults:

11   ?The hunter shot the rabbit who had a catapult

The difference between the PPs can be captured in a syntactic analysis, by showing them with different 'attachments', the different attachments corresponding to different semantic interpretations. For the instrumental relationship of **7a** the PP is attached as a daughter of the VP *shot the rabbit* as in Figure 9.3. The postmodifier relationship of **7b** is captured by attaching the PP as a modifier of MAN, as in Figure 9.4.

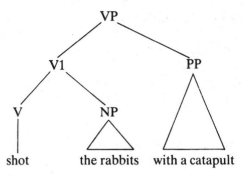

Figure 9.3

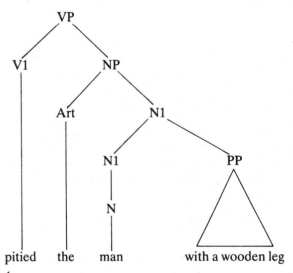

Figure 9.4

It is perhaps inevitable that different PP attachments like those illustrated yield ambiguities. So a sentence like **12**:

12 The policeman watched the man with the telescope

is ambiguous as between an instrumental reading, shown schematic-ally in **13** (see also Figure 9.3):

13 S

    NP   the policeman
    VP

        V1

           V   watched
           NP   the man
        PP   with the telescope

and a postmodifier interpretation, shown schematically in **14** (see also Figure 9.4):

14 S

    NP   the policeman
    VP

        V   watched
        NP   the man with the telescope

These two interpretations do not exhaust possible PP attachments. The sentence:

15   The policeman watched the man in the woods

has a NP postmodifier interpretation related to the paraphrase:

16   The policeman watched the man who was in the woods

which will have an analysis like **14**. There is another interpretation where *in the woods* can be understood as a place adverbial, describing where the event as a whole took place. In this interpretation the 'locative' PP modifies the entire sentence. We can show this interpretation by attaching the PP to S1, as in Figure 9.5.

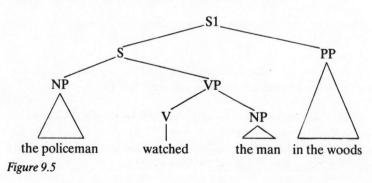

Figure 9.5

We now have three different PP analyses. The syntactic difference lies in the differing attachments of the PP. In **17a** we assume the PP *in the woods* is a sentence adverbial (cf. *where they buried the body was in the woods*). Here the PP modifies the sentence as a whole and so we analyse it as a daughter of S1 and sister of S (see Figure 9.5):

17a They buried the body *in the woods*
17b S1

| S | they buried the body |
| PP | in the woods |

In **18a** the instrumental PP, *with a catapult*, is analysed as a modifier of V1, *broke the window*, so it is a daughter of VP and sister of V1 (see Figure 9.3):

18a He broke the window *with a catapult*
18b S

NP
VP

| V1 | broke the window |
| PP | with a catapult |

In **19a** the PP is a postmodifier of *man* within the NP *the man with a wooden leg* (see Figure 9.2):

19a I saw the man *with a wooden leg*
19b S

NP			I
VP			
	V1		
		V	saw
		NP	
			Art	the
			N1	man
			PP	with a wooden leg

We noted at the end of Chapter 1 that all languages appear to have hierarchical structure. In this chapter we have looked at embedding and attachment, both issues that are intimately bound up with the question of hierarchical structure. If, as suggested in

Chapter 1, hierarchical structure is a necessary feature of human language, then perhaps embedding is too. It is then an interesting speculation that if all languages raise the same kind of attachment issues as English does, then syntactic ambiguity is a necessary, perhaps a defining, feature of human language.

Technical terms

attachment
complement
embedding
noun (verb) complementation
recursion

Note

1   These rules follow the simpler conventions we introduced in early chapters. A more sophisticated X-bar treatment would require rules like this:

(1)   NP → Art N1
(2)   N1 → N1 PP
           N
(3)   PP → P1
(4)   P1 → P   NP

The simpler rules are used for ease of exposition.

Exercises

(1)   *Verbs with sentential complements*
Many verbs can have sentences as complements:

(i)   I think *that Edinburgh is a lovely city*
(ii)   I asked *whether Charlie was at home*
(iii)   I told Mary *that I loved her*

that is the complementizer for 'embedded declarative sentences' and *whether* for 'embedded yes–no interrogative sentences'. Assume that lexical entries for such verbs are of the form:

THINK: V, __ S1
TELL: V, __ NP S1
ASK: V, __ S1 (qu)

Write lexical entries along these lines for the following:

AGREE, ARGUE, ASSUME, ASSURE, DENY, EXPECT, FORETELL, HEAR, INQUIRE, KNOW, PERSUADE, PREDICT, PROMISE, SAY, SUPPOSE, TELL, WONDER

(2) *Attachment and ambiguity*
  (a) The following sentences are ambiguous:

  (i) John saw the man with a telescope
  (ii) John saw the man in the park

  Explain the ambiguity clearly (a paraphrase for each interpretation would be sufficient) and draw a phrase marker for each interpretation (making it quite clear which interpretation is intended to apply to which paraphrase). Your phrase marker should use a notation which consistently distinguishes XP, X1 and X for every phrasal category (see Chapter 8).

  (b) In how many ways are the following sentences ambiguous?

  (i) John saw the man with a telescope in his hand
  (ii) John saw the man with a telescope in the park

  (c) Are the following ambiguous? If not, how do you account for this?

  (i) John shot the rabbit with a gun
  (ii) John shot the rabbit with a furry tail

(3) *More ambiguities*
  The following sentences are all ambiguous in one way or another:

  (i) My brother teaches history in a school for young boys and girls of wealthy parents
  (ii) The bride and groom left early last night
  (iii) He greeted the girl with a smile
  (iv) We would like to attract more intelligent students
  (v) I bought an old French dictionary
  (vi) They decided on the boat

  (a) Show the ambiguity by drawing appropriate tree diagrams.

(b)   Can you think of paraphrases that resolve the ambiguities one way or the other? How commonly do you think that strings like those illustrated are in fact ambiguous in the everyday use of language?

10 Relations between sentences

10.1 Introduction

The preceding discussion of constituent structure has concentrated on examples and types of construction taken in isolation. Any human language contains many different constructions; using examples from English, we will see that instead of filing a given construction separately in its own pigeonhole, we should establish and make explicit its relationships with other constructions. The essential point is that the constructions of a given language do not make up an unconnected list but form a network of inter-connections.

Some interconnections are straightforward, as in the constructions in **1** and **2** (cf. the discussion of adverbs and their position in Chapter 7, section 7.3):

1 The dog was sleeping under the tree
2 Under the tree the dog was sleeping

1 and **2** describe the same situation, differing only with respect to the constituent at the front of the sentence. **1** has a neutral order of constituents, but in **2** the PP *under the tree* is in first position, thereby enjoying prominence over the other constituents. Why the speaker might wish to make it prominent is not important for present purposes (but see the discussion in Chapter 20). We need only note that the structure of **1**, which is neutral, can be taken as basic, and the structure of **2**, which is not neutral, can be considered as derived from the structure of **1**. We can interpret 'derivation' literally, and assume that the structure of **2** is derived by taking the structure of **1**, detaching the PP *under the tree* and moving it to the front of the sentence. Since the PP functions as an adverb (modifying *The dog was sleeping*), the movement of the PP, or alternatively the relevant rule in our description, is known as adverb fronting.

The above account of the relationship between the structure of **1** and the structure of **2** embodies a rather traditional approach. It is traditional in that grammars of languages written for foreign learners have always talked about moving words or phrases from one position to another, and it is traditional in that over the last twenty-five years many textbooks on syntax, and many descriptions of specific languages, have adopted it.

10.2   Active and passive

Not all pairs of constructions enjoy such a straightforward relationship as **1** and **2**. Consider **3** and **4**:

3   The cat has eaten the mouse
4   The mouse has been eaten by the cat

The semantic relationship lies primarily in the fact that both sentences share the same 'agent' (*the cat*), responsible for the action described by the verb, and the same 'patient' (*the mouse*), affected by the action described by the verb. (Notions like 'agent' and 'patient' are discussed more fully in Chapter 18, section 18.2.) One could say that **3** describes the situation from the cat's point of view, and **4** describes the same situation from the point of view of the mouse. (We will discuss these questions in due course; for the moment all that need be said is that whatever NP is in first position in the sentence is prominent and sets the perspective.) For present purposes, the relevant semantic relationship is that in both sentences the cat does the eating and the mouse is eaten. This is reflected in the traditional description of sentences like **3** as 'active' (agent subject) and **4** as 'passive' (patient subject).

   3 and **4** are considered to be related with respect to constituent structure. In broad outline, the relationship consists of the following three components:

(1)   The NP (*the mouse*) that is the object of the verb in **3** 'becomes' the subject of the verb in **4**.
(2)   Correspondingly, the NP (*the cat*) that is the subject in **3** has the preposition *by* adjoined to it to form the Prepositional Phrase (PP) *by the cat*, and this now follows the verb.
(3)   In **3** the verbal constituent *has eaten* consists of the auxiliary

verb *has* followed by the past participle *eaten*. In the passive sentence the verb is changed by the addition of *been*, a form of the verb BE, which is added immediately after (and as a right sister to) the auxiliary verb. We call this form of the verb BE the 'passive auxiliary'.

The active–passive relationship can be generalized to any sentence containing a transitive verb. Without going into the exact details, let us say that, in any active sentence, the main verb is replaced by BE or GET[1] and the passive participle form of the main verb; *eaten* in **3** is replaced by *was eaten*. Further examples are *bite* in **5**, replaced by *be bitten* (or *get bitten*) in **6**, and *reading* in **7**, replaced by *being read* in **8**:

5   The dog will bite the cat
6   The cat will be bitten by the dog
7   The commuter is reading the newspaper
8   The newspaper is being read by the commuter

Whatever the form of the main verb – just the stem (see page 175) as in **5** (*bite*) or the *-ing* form as in **7** (*reading*) – it is replaced by the corresponding form of the passive auxiliary verb, *be* in **6** and *being* in **8**. Continuing the parallel, if an active sentence, such as *The students have written the essays*, contains an *-ed/-en* form (the past participle)[2] of the main verb (here *written*), the corresponding passive sentence contains the *-en* form of BE (the passive participle): *The essays have been written by the students*.

Above we outlined three steps by which we might proceed from an active sentence to a passive sentence. It must be emphasized that the steps apply, not to particular examples, but to the active construction and the passive construction in general, provided step (3) is amended to take account of the comments in the preceding paragraph. A set of explicit rules could be provided to describe the relationship but they will not be introduced here because they would require the discussion of various problems concerning auxiliary verbs that are not essential for present purposes.

Before we move on to other constructions, two important points must be made. The first concerns the direction of the relationship between the active and passive constructions, and indeed between any two constructions. We have talked about the steps by which we can move from the active to the passive construction. Why not move in the opposite direction, from passive to active construction? The difficulty is that the passive construction is more restricted than the active. Subject NPs in active sentences correspond to *by* + NP in passives, and this is quite general, but not all *by* + NP phrases in passives correspond to subject NPs; *The car was left by the monument* does not correspond to *The monument left the car*. There are verbs, such as RESEMBLE, WEIGH (FIVE STONES) and COST (TEN POUNDS), which do not occur in passive sentences. If we took the passive as basic, we would need to work out a method of including these verbs in the description; but if the active is basic, we can simply say that these particular verbs cut off the route to the passive.

The second point concerns the rules. Chapters 3 and 4 introduced the idea of expressing descriptions of constituent structure in the form of rules which first specify what the largest constituents in a sentence are – that is, what constituents they contain – and then specify in turn what these smaller constituents consist of, and so on down to the level of words. These rules handle active sentences only. Other rules could be written to specify the structure of passive sentences, but this would result in two sets of rules that indeed generate active and passive structures but fail to express the relationship between them. The steps (1)–(3) described above are components of what is called a transformational rule, the name deriving from the notion that the structure of active sentences is transformed into the structure of passive sentences, and formal grammars incorporating such rules are called transformational grammars.

It is worthwhile mentioning that the above approach to relationships between constructions is essentially that developed by Chomsky and his predecessor, Zellig Harris (Lyons (1977b) offers a brief, clear introduction to Chomsky's work). From about 1952 to 1975 their transformational method had no rivals, but other approaches are now available. One alternative model regards the various constructions as described separately by their own sets of rules, and the trick is to specify that if a grammar contains one set of rules, it also contains another set. That is, there is no question of one construction being derived from another by the movement of constituents. A second approach likewise describes each construction separately but handles in the lexicon the relationship between constructions, emphasizing the role played by individual verbs or groups of verbs in permitting particular relationships. The relationships themselves are described with respect to grammatical functions, which are discussed in Chapter 19. For present purposes, however, it is not necessary to say anything in detail about transformational rules and transformational grammars. The essential idea is that there are systematic relationships between different constructions in any language – we will call them transformational relationships – and that the relationships must be described.

10.3   Declaratives and interrogatives

It will be useful to examine other constructions that are related, concentrating on the relationship between declarative and interrogative constructions, as in **9** and **10**. (The label 'declarative' relates to the function of the construction in expressing a declaration by the speaker – both the active and passive examples discussed above are declarative. 'Interrogative' relates to the typical function of expressing a question.)

9a   The cat will catch the mouse
9b   The cat is catching the mouse
9c   The cat has caught the mouse

10a   Will the cat catch the mouse?
10b   Is the cat catching the mouse?
10c   Has the cat caught the mouse?

9a corresponds to **10a**, **9b** to **10b**, **9c** to **10c**. As with the active and passive sentences, we can ask what steps will take us from the declarative to the interrogative construction. For **9** and **10** the answer is straightforward; take the declarative sentence, locate the auxiliary verb (*will, is, has*) and move it to the front of the sentence. This simple procedure applies to passive sentences too, which, as mentioned above, are a type of declarative sentence. See **11** and **12**:

11a   The mouse will be caught by the cat
11b   The mouse is being caught by the cat
11c   The mouse has been caught by the cat

12a   Will the mouse be caught by the cat?
12b   Is the mouse being caught by the cat?
12c   Has the mouse been caught by the cat?

The procedure takes the subject NP and the auxiliary verb and inverts them; this gives it the name 'subject–aux inversion'.

So far we have not looked at any of the simplest examples of active declarative sentences in English, such as *The cat caught the mouse*. The difficulty is that this simple type of declarative sentence requires a more complex procedure, because, although it does not contain an auxiliary verb but only the main verb *caught*, the corresponding interrogative sentence does contain an auxiliary verb, *did: Did the cat catch the mouse?* Where does the auxiliary verb DO come from? The obvious solution is to introduce DO as one of the steps by which we proceed from the declarative to the interrogative construction; that is, if a given example does not contain an auxiliary verb, introduce the auxiliary verb DO, making sure that it has the same tense as the main verb in the declarative sentence, as in *caught* and *did* (*catch*). For present tense, singular and plural will also have to be correctly specified, given that *Does the cat catch mice?* is correct in standard English, while *Does the cats catch mice?* is not. (The latter requirement leads to complexities which will be ignored here.)

Introducing DO as part of the transformational rule relating declarative and interrogative sentences was said above to be the obvious solution, but this example allows another solution, which is mentioned here merely to indicate how intricate a detailed and explicit analysis of English can be. A non-obvious solution is to have the auxiliary verb DO in the structure of declarative sentences that do not contain any other auxiliary, that is, to impose a restriction that all declarative sentences must contain an auxiliary, either DO on its own, or other auxiliaries, singly or in combination: *will* (*catch*), *will be* (*catching*), *will have been* (*catching*). A sentence such as *The cat does catch mice* is correct provided *does* carries emphatic stress. With this analysis, the step from declarative to interrogative structure is the simple one of moving the auxiliary verb to the front of the sentence, but another rule must be devised to delete DO whenever it follows the subject NP but does not carry emphatic stress. We do not have to explore the complex question of balancing one analysis against the other. The important point is that most problems in syntactic description allow more than one solution and that the obvious solution is not necessarily the best one.

Just as we silently assumed that the active construction should be the starting-point of the relationship between active and passive, so we have assumed that the declarative construction should be the starting-point of the relationship between declarative and interrogative. One reason is that declarative sentences are more frequent than interrogative ones and consequently it is the word order of declarative sentences that is more frequent and typical. A second reason is that constituents that are closely related occupy adjacent positions in declaratives but are separated by other constituents in interrogatives. Compare *The cat is chasing the mouse*, where *is* and *chasing* are adjacent and *is* requires an *-ing* form, with *Is the cat chasing the mouse?*, where the two words are separated by *the cat*. With such examples, the construction where the related constituents are adjacent is taken as basic. A third reason is that, at least on one analysis, the interrogative requires the insertion of the auxiliary verb DO, which is missing from the declarative.

The interrogative construction exemplified in **12** is called the *yes–no* interrogative, because its typical function is to ask questions that can be answered with *yes* or *no*. English possesses another type of interrogative construction, called the *wh* (pronounced 'double-u aitch') interrogative because it contains words beginning (in the written language) with *wh*: *who*, *what*, *where*, *why*, *when*. The list includes *how*, as in *How did you do that?*, although patently it does not begin with *wh*. (Note that other languages too have different constructions corresponding to the English ones.) Examples of the English *wh* construction are given in **13**:

13a What is the cat chasing?
13b Who has the cat bitten?
13c Where will the cat catch the mouse?
13d How will the cat catch the mouse?

What are the declarative sentences corresponding to **13**? On the assumption that the interrogative pronouns *who*, and so on, have non-interrogative counterparts, such as *someone*, the required examples are those in **14**:

14a The cat is chasing something
14b The cat has bitten someone
14c The cat will catch the mouse somewhere
14d The cat will catch the mouse somehow

Comparing **14a** and **13a**, we see that the route from the declarative to the interrogative involves three steps:

(1)   Replace the indefinite pronoun *something*, and so on, with the appropriate interrogative pronoun, here *what*.
(2)   Move the auxiliary verb to the front of the sentence.
(3)   Move the *wh* pronoun to the front of the sentence.

Applied to **14a**, step (1) replaces *something* with *what*. Step (2) moves *is* to the front of the sentence. Step (3) moves *what* to the front of the sentence, which means putting it to the left of *is*, which became the front constituent on Step (2). One property of this procedure, perhaps obvious but none the less significant, is that the rule for *yes–no* interrogatives – move the auxiliary verb to the front – is re-employed. A detailed exploration of transformational grammar would reveal the value of rules (or principles) that apply widely; for this introduction it is sufficient to say that two constructions, the two types of interrogative, which are alike semantically in that they both typically express questions, are also alike syntactically, in that they share the operation of subject–aux inversion.

10.4   *Wh* movement and relative clauses

Step (3) above moves the *wh* word to the front of the sentence. The corresponding transformational rule in full-scale descriptions of English is called *wh* movement, and we will apply that label here. One of the interesting properties of subject–aux inversion is that it applies to both *yes–no* and *wh* interrogatives. Similarly, *wh* movement applies to different constructions, constructions that are further apart than the two types of interrogative.

Consider the example in **15**:

15   I like that pullover. Moira gave me that pullover

Assuming that the speaker is using the phrase *that pullover* to refer to one and the same article of clothing, the sentences in **15** can be combined into one by a procedure that is, or at any rate used to be, taught in schools. It consists of taking the second sentence or clause, replacing *that pullover* by *which*, putting *which* at the front of the sentence and embedding the sentence inside the first sentence, to obtain *I like that pullover which Moira gave me*. That is, NPs containing relative clauses exemplify embedding, as discussed in Chapter 9.

Note the syntactic parallel between the *wh* interrogative and the relative clause. In both constructions a word or phrase is replaced by a *wh* word and the *wh* word is moved to the front. While the semantic parallels between the two types of interrogative are obvious, clear parallels are lacking between the *wh* interrogative and the relative clause. Rather, a parallel could be sought in the nature of *wh* words but the analysis would have to be developed and defended and would take us too far from the topic of this chapter.

What arguments support this relationship between ordinary declarative clauses and relative clauses? Compare **16** and **17**:

16 Moira gave me that pullover
17 (the pullover) which Moira gave me

Ignoring the phrase in brackets at the beginning of **17**, we see that **16** and **17** both contain the lexical items MOIRA, GIVE, I. They differ in that **17** has *which*, whereas **16** has *that pullover*, but the conventions of English syntax dictate that *which* relates to the bracketed phrase *the pullover* in **17** and is to be understood as the object of *gave*. The conventions can be expressed as follows. (We are not claiming that speakers of English could describe the procedure or even that they all follow it when interpreting utterances. **18** is simply part of our description.)

18 GIVE requires three Noun Phrases: a subject (the giver), a direct object (the thing given), and an indirect object (the recipient).
In the clause *which Moira gave me* we can identify a subject (*Moira*) and a recipient (*me*). Of the three required Noun Phrases, the direct object is missing. It is this Noun Phrase that has been replaced by *which*.

So far constituents have been described as moved to the front of sentences, but we have said nothing about constituent structure, in particular about the hierarchical arrangements of constituents, the representation of those arrangements by trees and where the moved constituents are to be attached. Suppose that the constituent structure of **9a**, *The cat will catch the mouse*, is as shown in Figure 10.1.

When we talk of *will* being moved to the front of the sentence, what this means is that it is detached from Aux, moved to the front

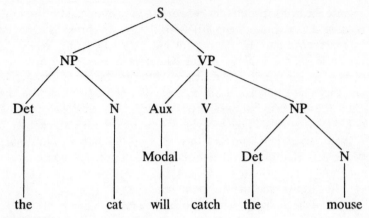

Figure 10.1

and reattached – to what? Not the NP node, because the resulting arrangement, as in Figure 10.2, would be claiming that *will* is part of the NP, which is nonsense. It could be attached to S, as in Figure 10.3, but many analysts nowadays use the extra node called Comp (COMP in earlier analyses), for Complementizer which was introduced in Chapter 9. There, the Comp node was used for the conjunctions at the front of subordinate clauses, but the analysis extends to relative clauses. Although relative pronouns like *which* in **17** belong to the core of the clause, they have a function in common with words like *before*, *because* and *when*; they signal that the clause is a special type of clause, a subordinate clause, with a

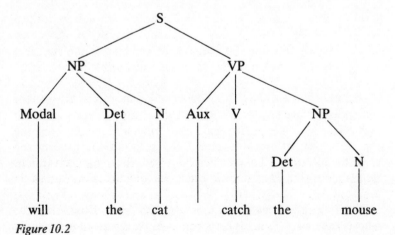

Figure 10.2

special relationship to other clauses in the sentence. The structure of **17** is thus as shown in Figure 10.4.

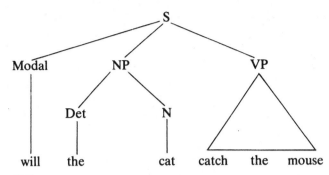

Figure 10.3

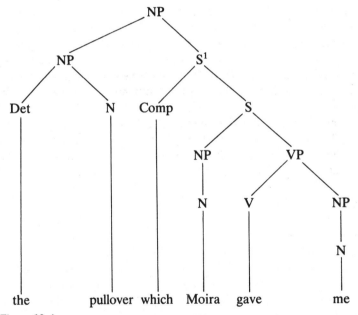

Figure 10.4

That is, *wh* movement detaches the *wh* word, moves it to the front of the sentence and attaches it to Comp. Now we can return to the analysis of *Will the cat catch the mouse*? Like *which*, *before*, and so on, *will* signals that the clause is a special type of clause. As it happens, the clause is not subordinate to another clause but is a main clause, but *will* is at the front, signalling that the clause is interrogative, and this fact is captured by attaching *will* to Comp, as in Figure 10.5. (Interestingly, written English possesses a conditional construction in which an auxiliary verb is at the front of a subordinate clause and, like *if*, signals that the clause is subordinate and expresses a condition, as in **19**:

19a   Had he helped, we would have finished sooner
19b   Should this be impossible, contact us at this number

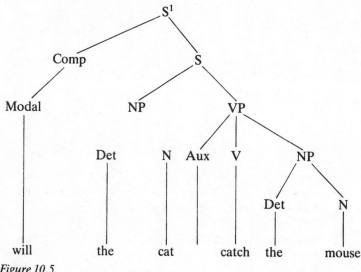

Figure 10.5

This chapter began with the active and passive constructions and the relationship between them, but the constituent structure of the passive has not been diagrammed. To conclude this section, the structure of **4** is given in Figure 10.6. The important points to note are that *by* + NP is a prepositional phrase, and that the structure under Aux is only a place-holder. We need the auxiliary verbs *has* and *been* and the main verb *eaten*, but we do not have the scope to go into the question of what structure should be assigned to *has been eaten by the cat*. Let us say only that a favourite contender is {*has* [*been* (*eaten by the cat*)]} but employ the simple and simplistic arrangement in Figure 10.6.

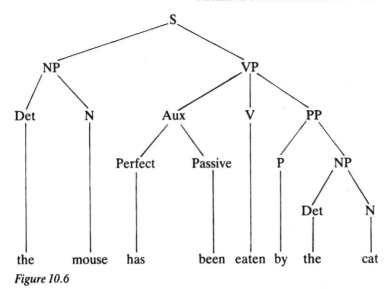

Figure 10.6

At the beginning of the chapter we talked of the different constructions in a language forming a network. We can now give an indication of what the network would look like. Consider **20**:

20 Was the cobra killed by the mongoose?

20 is related to (at least) two other sentences, **21** and **22**:

21 The cobra was killed by the mongoose
22 The mongoose killed the cobra

Our data contain two types of declarative sentences, active and passive, related by a transformation. The data contain declarative and *yes–no* interrogative sentences, likewise related by a transformation, subject–aux inversion. This transformation applies to both active and passive sentences. Now, we could devise a transformation that would directly link **22** and **20**, but there is no need to do so. The transformations that we already have are quite sufficient. The structure of **22** is shown in Figure 10.7.

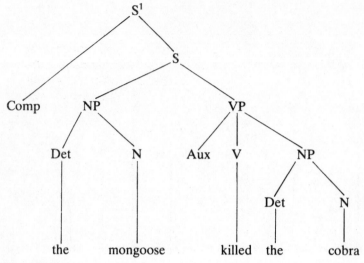

Figure 10.7

This structure is linked to the structure of **21** by the passive transformation, which gives the structure in Figure 10.8.

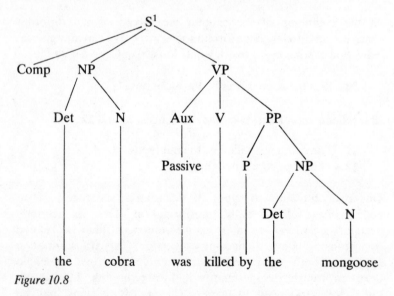

Figure 10.8

Finally, the link from **21** to **20** is given by subject–aux inversion, which gives the structure in Figure 10.9.

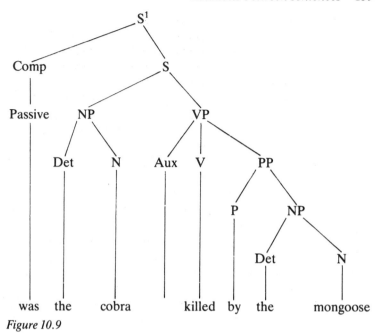

Figure 10.9

That is, it is not the case that each construction is directly linked with every other construction. Rather, one construction is taken as basic – the active declarative one – a route is mapped out from that basic construction to the others, and there may be a number of steps leading from one given construction to another. Figure 10.10 shows a piece of the network.

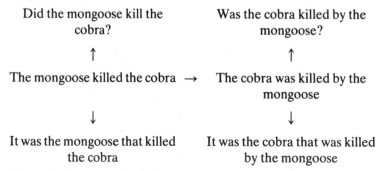

Figure 10.10

We stated above that another transformation linking **22** and **20** directly was not necessary. A stronger way of putting it is to say that the description should be kept as simple as possible and that another rule, not strictly necessary, is the way to unwanted clutter. This argument seems slight when we are dealing with a very small number of constructions, but we have to keep in mind that a detailed account of English will cover many constructions, and the description would be greatly inflated if we had a separate and direct link from each construction to every other construction.

In conclusion, we should warn the reader that the above sketch of transformations is intended to give only a rough idea of what is involved in writing a transformational grammar. In particular, the statement of the transformations is rough and ready, though quite adequate for this introduction. In the primary literature on transformational grammar, the transformations are stated far more rigorously, and the business of mapping routes from one construction to another turns out to be very complex.

Technical terms

adverb fronting
derivation
passive participle
subject–aux inversion

transformational grammar
transformational rule
WH interrogative
yes–no interrogative

Notes

1   GET is one auxiliary verb which is not generally accepted among the arbiters of good written English. In spite of its proscription, it is *the* passive auxiliary of informal spoken English and is now rapidly making its way into the written language. It differs in meaning from BE. The latter is static and can combine with participles to describe states and actions; *The table is well polished* describes a state, whereas *The table is well polished every morning* describes an action. The latter example is said to be dynamic, as opposed to static.
2   The class of participles includes forms such as *written*, *closed* and *dismissed*. These forms are related in meaning to the lexemes WRITE, CLOSE and DISMISS, and are obviously related to the other forms of these lexemes. The term 'participle' indicates that these forms participate in two classes of words; they are related to verbs but have properties of adjectives. For instance, they occur in NPs: *the closed shutters*, *the dismissed worker*, *the written word*. When they occur in active sentences, they are traditionally called past participles active; when they occur in passive sentences, the traditional label is past participles passive.

Exercises

(1) On page 132 it was stated that sentences such as *I like that pullover which Moira gave me* can be thought of as deriving from one sentence, *I like that pullover*, with another sentence embedded in it, *Moira gave me that pullover*.

   (a) Below are pairs of sentences. For each pair, embed the second sentence in the first to produce a sentence containing a relative clause.

      (i) The person seemed very worried
          The person phoned
     (ii) The picture is an early Picasso
          Helen liked the picture
    (iii) The book is in the library
          I found these facts in the book
    (iv) The student had made some mistakes
          I borrowed the student's notes

   (b) English has one relative clause construction introduced by *wh* words such as *who* and another construction introduced by *that*. Are both constructions possible for sentence pair (iii) above? Are there any differences between them, say, in possible word order?

   (c) Some relative clauses in English may have neither a *wh* word nor *that*. Look at the relative clauses you produced for sentence pairs (i)–(iv) above. In which examples can the *wh* word or *that* be omitted?

(2) Consider the following sentences.

      (i) A large dog lay on the rug
     (ii) On the rug lay a large dog
    (iii) The cat jumped through the window
    (iv) Through the window jumped the cat

   (a) Do you think any of the above sentences are systematically related? (See page 127.)
   (b) If your answer is yes, which construction would you take as your starting-point?
   (c) Describe the steps from your starting-point to the other construction.

(3)   Consider the following sentences and answer the same
      questions as for (2). (Hint: draw tree diagrams showing the
      constituent structure of the examples.)

     (i)   Fiona gave the message to Fred
   (ii)   Fiona gave Fred the message
  (iii)   Fiona bought a tie for Fred
  (iv)   Fiona bought Fred a tie

11 The sentence

Lyons defines the sentence as the maximum unit of grammatical analysis: 'A grammatical unit between the constituent parts of which distributional limitations and dependencies can be established, but which can itself be put into no distribution class' (1968, p. 173), and we adopt this definition. In other words, formal statements can be made about the distribution of sentence constituents, but not about sentences as wholes. Thus, we can talk about the distribution of NP (in environments like __ VP; V __; and Prep __) but no comparable distributional statements can be made with respect to the sentence itself, except, perhaps, that a text consists of a series of sentences S & S & S . . .![1]

Lyons's definition implies that the sentence has a certain sort of unity; it is grammatically complete; it can stand on its own, independent of context; and it has a degree of semantic independence. This is largely true of the units so far identified as sentences and used as examples. What, however, of the relationship between such units and, say, the orthographic sentences out of which this chapter is composed? Lyons suggests that no distributional statements can be made about such units – a text, it is suggested, consists of a series of sentences S & S & S . . . Consider, for example, the three orthographic sentences that form the preceding paragraph. The second and third begin with *In other words* and *Thus*, expressions which tie the relevant sentences to their predecessors. *In other words* indicates that the sentence is a rephrasing of the point made in the sentence before; *Thus* introduces an example of the point just made. We call such expressions 'binding expressions' since they bind sentences together into text. Without the binding expressions the three sentences could be rearranged in some other order – 3–2–1; 1–3–2; 2–1–3; and so on – with no substantial difference to the message conveyed, and with few other consequential amendments to the text (other binding expressions, or none, would be needed). Furthermore, if we disregard the binders, each sentence can stand on its own as a grammatically complete unit, and forms, in some sense, a complete message.

Orthographic sentences in texts are not always capable of such ready permutation. Consider, for instance, the following (read it as a text – (the numbers are for reference):

1   When John and Mary got back home, they found the front door had been left open. 2 John accused Mary. 3 She denied it. 4 John asked her to shut it. 5 She wouldn't.

The first sentence is grammatically and semantically capable of standing as an isolate, but none of the others is. If the second sentence were found as an isolate, one might reasonably inquire: 'What did John accuse Mary of?' In an isolate sentence ACCUSE requires a sentence frame NP – NP PP, where the subject NP is the 'accuser', the object NP is the 'accused', and the PP contains the 'accusation'. In connected text, however, ACCUSE permits the ellipsis or omission of the 'accusation', providing the 'accusation' is recoverable from the context, as in the example. Similarly, if 3 were found as an isolate, we might inquire: 'Who denied what?' The proforms *she* and *it* are understood in context as, respectively, 'Mary' and 'that she left the door open'. 4 further illustrates the use of proforms. 5 is another example of ellipsis – here understood as 'Mary wouldn't shut the door'.

The sentences 2–5 cannot stand alone. They are to a greater or lesser degree either grammatically and semantically incomplete or both: grammatically incomplete in so far as constituents have been elided; and semantically incomplete in as much as the sentences can only be understood with reference to their context. In both cases, these 'sentence fragments' are only fully understood by reference to some 'understood' fuller form, where the items that have been elided, reduced to proforms, and so on, are restored:

6a   John accused Mary of leaving the door open
6b   Many denied that she had left the door open
6c   John asked Mary to shut the door
6d   Mary wouldn't shut the door

The amount of grammatical and contextual interpretation necessary can be appreciated if we consider, for example, 5. Only in this particular context is it understood as 6d. In another context it might be understood as 'Mary wouldn't feed the cat'; 'Jane wouldn't give up smoking'; and so on.

Strings like 2–5 are entirely appropriate and natural in a text. By contrast, the series of sentences 1 and 6a–d do not form a text under any normal interpretation of text. On the other hand, each of 1 and 6a–d can stand alone as a well-formed grammatical sentence, and each is semantically self-contained. These sentences can be reordered to form a different text, perhaps:

> 7 John accused Mary of leaving the door open when they got back home and found it like that. 8 She denied it, but wouldn't shut it when John asked her to.

This time the 'accusation' is restored to ACCUSE; it is hardly possible in this context to elide this constituent since there is now no context from which it would be recoverable. *Wouldn't* has, this time, lost its subject, but gained its main verb, *shut*, the object of which now turns up as a proform; and *asked* has lost its complement which must now be recovered from the context.

Different arrangements of the 'understood' sentences have different consequences in terms of elision, pronominalization, and so on, and these processes produce sentence fragments, incapable of standing alone as sentences and relying for their interpretation on context and on the ability of the reader to reconstruct the 'understood' sentences to which they relate. Such processes can create sentence fragments that relate to almost any part of a sentence. Consider, as well as the examples in 2–5, 7 and 8, the relevant strings from the examples below, which are to be understood as exchanges between two speakers:

9a Nobody wants to go to the pictures
9b Except John

10a Anybody remember to feed the cat?
10b Yes, Kate did

11a What has John done now?
11b Broken another plate

12a Gill adores pastrami
12b Not adores, just likes

All of these might be appropriate exchanges, and the **b** fragments comprehensible and appropriate in context; all of them rely for their interpretation on the hearer's reconstructing the understood forms to which they relate.

The question arises, what is the status of sentence fragments? If our grammar generates these directly as expansions of the initial S symbol, that leads to an incoherent grammar, and destroys the very foundations of the grammar. We can postulate two sets of rules: first, grammatical rules which generate full sentences like **1** and **6a–d**; and second, a set of 'text formation rules' which produce, *inter alia*, sentence fragments. The rules allow for the ellipsis of contextually recoverable constituents, for intersentential proform formation, for the insertion of binding expressions, and so on. Text formation rules depend on linguistic and non-linguistic context. The rules for the formation of sentences, by contrast, are in principle independent of such constraints.

This is an attractive proposal, but it is far from clear whether it can be accomplished in any straightforward fashion. Let us look at the problems. We may begin by drawing a distinction between simple and complex sentences. Suppose simple sentences are those sentences that contain a single main verb, sentences with the sort of structure examined in earlier chapters:

13a   The dog frightened the cat
13b   The man put the lamp on the table

Complex sentences are those sentences that can be analysed as consisting of a number of simple sentences. We have already considered (Chapter 9.1) a sentence like:

14   John believes that Bill has married Mary

as having a constituent sentence (*Bill has married Mary*) embedded in a matrix sentence (*John believes NP*) with a structure as shown in Figure 11.1. Constituent sentences of this type are traditionally called subordinate sentences.

Many subordinate sentences bear overt markers of subordination:

15a   *When Mary came into the room*, John stood up
15b   *After entering the room*, John took off his coat
15c   John wanted *Bill to go*
15d   I don't like *your smoking so much*

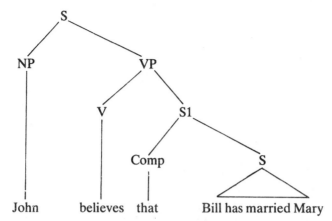

Figure 11.1

In **15** the strings deriving from embedded subordinate sentences are italicized. There are not only overt markers of subordination in complementizers (*that*) and subordinating conjunctions (*when*, and so on), but also grammatical constructions only open to subordinate strings: the 'infinitive construction' (*Bill to go*) and the 'gerund construction' (*your smoking so much*). (The derivation of these constructions is not considered further in this volume.)

The distribution of these subordinate constructions can be accounted for in terms of the distribution of the sentence constituent into which they are embedded. Thus NPs with sentences embedded in them operate much like other NPs; similarly temporal subordinate sentences (for example, **15a** and **15b**) form a class with adverbials of time and are distributed like them.

Subordinate sentences may be important for the strict subcategorization of various lexemes – we have already noted that nouns like RUMOUR and verbs like BELIEVE are subclassified precisely in terms of the fact that they can occur with complement sentences.

Finally, complex subordinate sentences cannot typically be resolved into a string of separate sentences without doing some violence to the dependency relations between the various constituents involved in a single sentence. This is obviously the case with complex sentences like:

16 John wanted Bill to go

which do not resolve into anything like:

17   *John wanted. Bill was to go

or even:

18   John wanted something. Bill was to go

since this breaks the relation of dependence; in these forms it is not necessarily the case that 'what John wanted' was for 'Bill to go'.

The same argument can be applied, though with perhaps less force, to examples like:

19a   Mary left the room because John started talking politics
19b   Mary left the room. John started talking politics
19c   John started talking politics. Mary left the room

In **19a** the causal relation is explicit. In **19c** the relationship may be causal, but it may equally well not be. In **19b**, even if the relationship is considered causal, and it need not be, the causality is 'reversed'.

The discussion leads to a number of conclusions. Our grammar needs to account for the formation of such sentences as those in **15** – it is not satisfactory to derive them by the use of text formation rules of any sort. The grammar must contain rules that account for strings that often resemble sentence fragments: a point we will return to.

First, however, consider another type of complex sentence, illustrated by:

20a   Mary came into the room and John stood up
20b   Jane doesn't buy books, but Mary buys a book whenever she passes a bookshop

Such sentences are 'co-ordinate complex sentences', and forms like *and* and *but* are 'co-ordinating conjunctions'. The structure of co-ordinate sentences can be shown schematically as in Figure 11.2.

Comparison with Figure 11.1 shows that in subordinate constructions the subordinate sentence is embedded in the matrix sentence, but in co-ordinate constructions the co-ordinate sentences are sisters; one sentence is not subordinate to the other. In principle, then, each of the conjunct sentences should be grammatically independent. Disregarding the conjunctions, this

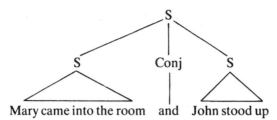

Figure 11.2

is true of the sentence in **20**, which can be resolved into two separate sentences:

21 Mary came into the room. John stood up

Now this is not the case for all co-ordinate sentences. Consider, for example, the following:

22a John wanted Harry to come and Bill to go
22b John uses a fountain pen when writing to his mother and when writing letters to the press
22c John asked Mary to shut the door but she wouldn't

In each of these the second conjunct is a string identical to the sort of string seen earlier in the chapter as sentence fragments. We now find ourselves on the horns of a dilemma. One uncomfortable horn prods us into allowing that sentences like **22** should be generated by our grammar, so the grammar will have rules for producing sentence fragments. The other equally uncomfortable horn goads us into proposing that co-ordinate sentences are formed by text formation rules and not by rules of the grammar at all! The former position entails an initial rule for the grammar of the sort:

23 $S \rightarrow S^*$

(where S^* is to be understood as allowing expansions S, S & S, S & S & S, and so on). This rule enables sentences to be generated of infinite length, identical to texts, except that where texts are typically subdivided into orthographic units the units are simply conjoined by conjunction. Children often produce texts of this sort (*We went to the seaside last Sunday and we played on the sands and*

Daddy bought us an ice cream and . . .). This approach also allows
us to treat binding expressions (of the sort discussed at the
beginning of this chapter) as a form of conjunction, which in many
cases they are! But the approach does have problems. We cannot
make distributional statements about constituent sentences
produced by such a rule since the rule produces no distinct
environments we can use. We also need to postulate some set of
rules to accommodate sentential sequence, and these rules must
take account of matters that go beyond the simple sentence as we
have so far considered it. Rules relating to various matters of word
order are taken up again in Part Three.

The arguments in the preceding paragraph lead to the conclusion
that conjoined sentences are not to be considered part of the
grammar at all, but are derived by text formation rules. This
conclusion is not wholly comfortable, but the logic of the argument
seems to force us into this position. It at least has the advantage that
it permits us to adopt the definition of the sentence with which we
began the chapter; the sentence is an abstract unit, established in
order to account for distributional regularities of its constituents.
The question of whether there are further distributional regularities
between sentences in some larger unit, say the paragraph, is
discussed in Part Three.

Technical terms

co-ordinate sentence   sentence fragment
co-ordinating conjunction   subordinate sentence
sentence   text formation rules

Note

1   This is a well-established descriptive viewpoint with a long history. Consider the
following quotation from *Hermes*, by James Harris (1751): 'The Extensions of
Speech are quite indefinite, as may be seen if we compare the Eneid to an
Epigram of *Martial*. But the *longest Extension* with which Grammar has to do is
the Extension here considered, that is to say a SENTENCE. The greater
Extensions (such as Syllogisms, Paragraphs, Sections and complete Works)
belong not to Grammar but to Arts of a higher order; not to mention that all of
them are but Sentences repeated.'

Exercises

The Introduction suggested that many of the data actually used by linguists to establish grammar are 'regularized'. In informal conversation we do not typically speak in units that can easily be recognized as grammatical sentences. Here is an extract from a transcription of part of a radio phone-in discussion on police pay. The speaker is a serving policeman. The items in brackets indicate interpolations from the chairman of the programme. The symbol + indicates a pause. The symbols *eh* and *um hum* indicate 'filled pauses'.

First of all + I would say that + I don't think any (1)
policeman wants a + wants a medal for + for eh the
profession which he's in + (No) every person + eh
decides + how his eh life is going to + be run (um hum)
We we'd work seven days shifts we'd be going to have (5)
our two days off (Yes) + and + I don't think + eh + the
people realize about shift allowance in England we will
receive no shift allowance for this (um hum) um I feel
that the press eh eh in a lot of cases give us a bad publicity
(Yes) + eh the article in fact that you have written + you (10)
+ read this morning about the + the Strathclyde eh
(Yes) the press reported that + the + this would + mean
a loss of wages about the overtime + about thirty-five
pounds a week (Yes) well in our local force here in the
county area + eh we're not actually allowed to be paid (15)
for overtime we're told that if we want to do overtime
then we must + take time off for it.

(1)   Make a transcription of the text for publication in a periodical.
      You should make sure that your transcription follows the
      usual orthographic conventions about punctuation, and so on,
      and that you write what, in the orthography, are considered to
      be grammatical sentences.
(2)   Make a note of what sort of things you have left out of your
      'cleaned-up' version (pauses, filled and unfilled; repetitions;
      false starts; and so on) and of the sort of things you have found
      it necessary to add. See if you can formulate these as a set
      of instructions to a secretary who was asked to do a similar
      task.

(3)   What is the relationship between the sort of units that are usually held to be sentences and any sort of unit you can discern in the text?

Part two

Morphology

12 Words and morphemes

12.1 Identifying words

All cultures which have a written language recognize the word as a unit. Children as they learn to read quickly come to recognize the established practice of the orthography, and for adults the word seems to represent a 'natural' unit. To be sure, there are marginal difficulties. In some cases it is not clear whether we should write one word or two (*all right* or *alright*?); in the case of 'compound words' like *windmill, water-mill* and *flour mill* there is some indeterminacy as to whether these should be written as a single orthographic unit, as a hyphenated unit or as two discrete units – an indeterminacy reflected in dictionaries. On the whole, however, literate societies do not find word divisions a great difficulty. In illiterate societies too speakers seem capable of segmenting their utterances into 'word-sized' units and when such languages are eventually 'reduced to writing' there is general agreement about the size of the unit established as a word. These facts seem to indicate the unit has some linguistic reality. It is not, however, easy to lay down criteria by which words are to be identified.

Three sorts of criteria are commonly called on – semantic, phonological and grammatical. A semantic criterion would be that a word is 'a unit of meaning'. This belief is widely held and represents a common intuition but cannot be made to apply in any straightforward way. For example, *reheat* is a word, yet it appears to have at least two relatively independent units of meaning. The first is the meaning attached to the prefix *re-*, perhaps something like 'again', and found in other words like *rewrite*; the second is the meaning associated with the stem *heat*, and also found as a component of words like *heater*. So if *reheat* is a unit of meaning, is not the string *heat again* also a unit of meaning, though it is usually considered to be a sequence of two words? The word *heat* itself seems to have a meaning we can represent as 'make hot', but *make hot* again is a string of two words. Clearly the semantic criterion by itself cannot be made to stand up. On the other hand, the notion that words have a kind of intuitive semantic unity is not totally to be discarded, particularly for compound words. A *blackboard*, as used in the classroom, may be a piece of 'board' which is 'black' (though with modern technology this is less and less the case), but the meaning of *blackboard* as a unit word is more than a simple conjunction of the meanings of the two stems from which it is composed, and is different from *black board*, in the sense 'a piece of board which is black'. We shall not call upon a semantic criterion for defining words, but it is not possible, and probably not desirable, to eliminate semantic considerations altogether.

Phonological criteria are more satisfactory. A common criterion is that of 'potential pause'; there is a potentiality for pause between word boundaries, but not within a word. This criterion indicates those points within an utterance where it is possible to insert a 'filled pause' – of the form usually represented orthographically as *er* or *um*. In general this works. The reader should test it by reading, say, this paragraph in this fashion. In most cases it is difficult to conceive of an *um* or *er* being interpolated into what are orthographically represented as words. This is particularly true with the 'inflected' forms of words (see section 12.2 below); thus *walk-um-s* (for *walks*) or *fill-um-ed* (for *filled*) is unlikely. However, with 'derived' words (see section 12.2) one might well find, say, *un-er-grammatical*, particularly if a speaker were hesitating between *ungrammatical* and *unacceptable*. There is no suggestion, of course, that speakers do in fact pause between words in normal speech. On the contrary, particularly in rapid speech, words are 'run together'. This is sometimes recognized in the orthography, regularly in forms like *can't* and *isn't*, and also in forms like *dunno* (*don't know*) and *wanna* (*want to*), and is a feature of humorous books dealing with particular accents of English (*jew asbestos to believe* . . .: *do you expect us to believe* . . .). Cases of this sort are usually recognized as instances of two or more words being 'fused' together by quite regular processes in rapid colloquial speech (see the discussion in Brown, 1990). The notion of potential pause tries to capture the generalization that if speakers are to pause within their utterances, they are most likely to pause between what we recognize as words. However, another difficulty is raised; it suggests that the recognition of places at which a pause is possible rests on a prior knowledge of word boundaries. This is a valuable clue to the recognition of word boundaries, but is not in itself criterial.

In some languages other phonological features correlate with word units. Thus in some languages the placement of accent is related to word structure. In Spanish, words ending with a consonant are typically accented on the final syllable (*avión* 'aeroplane'; *generál* 'general'; and so on), and words ending with a vowel are typically accented on the penultimate syllable (*muchá/cho* 'boy'; *blánco* 'white'; and so on). Other languages have different patterns of accent placement (Czech words are normally accented on the initial syllable; Turkish words on the final syllable; and so on). Some languages have rules of 'vowel harmony', usually associated with word units; in such languages the vowels are divided into two or more 'sets' and in any word all the vowels are chosen from one set; Akan and Turkish are instances. In these cases, however, the criteria for deciding the extent of the unit over which the rules (of accent placement, of vowel harmony, or whatever) hold is not a simple phonological decision – grammatical criteria also come into consideration (the affixation of suffixes to a word, for example). Such criteria, then, like potential pause, are useful indications, but do not by themselves suffice to identify words.

The most satisfactory criteria are syntactic criteria, among them the 'internal cohesion' and 'external distribution' of a word, and its ability to stand alone as a 'minimal free form'. Together these criteria show that a word has a unity that justifies its treatment as a unit. Consider, for example, the structure of a word like *uninterruptibility*. It is probably agreed that we can segment this word as *un-interrupt-ibil-ity*. The basis of this segmentation is the recognition that each of these segments can recur in other words, words given a related meaning by the common segment (note that meaning slips in here – it is hard to exclude!); thus we find UN-*intelligent*; *corrupt*-IBIL-ITY; *stupid*-ITY; and so on; and the form *interrupt* can itself stand as a word.

As far as the 'internal cohesion' of the word is concerned, it is not possible to interpolate any other segments between the segments we have isolated, nor is it possible to rearrange the order of the segments we have isolated. In other words, the item is bound together into a unit. This is not generally the case with strings of words – where it is almost always possible to add new items or rearrange the items within the sentence and still maintain a grammatical string. We can see this if we compare *black hat* (*black top hat, hat which is black*, and so on) with *blackcap* (in the sense 'type of bird'); and we can compare *blackcap* with *black cap* (*black corduroy cap, cap which is black*, and so on).

Similarly, in its external distribution a word operates like a unit. Either the whole word must be moved round the sentence or none of it can be moved round the sentence – you cannot move part of a word about. Thus, as the example *black hat* shows, each word is capable of a certain amount of independent movement, but in the case of *blackcap* either the whole word is moved or nothing is moved. These two criteria are reflected in the ability of a word to stand on its own as an isolate – the definition of a word as a 'minimal free form', which derives from Bloomfield (1935). *Uninterruptibility*, our example, is an appropriate one-word response to some such request as *Name a syntactic criterion for the identification of a word*. It is impossible to think of a comparable question which yields *ibil* as a response (except perhaps *Can you give an example of a segment of a word that cannot stand as an isolate?*). This leads to a distinction between 'free' and 'bound' forms (explored further on page 174). These criteria are in general satisfactory for an identification of words in English. Like all linguistic criteria, they apply to a greater or lesser extent with individual items. For the most part, forms that we wish to classify as verbs, nouns, adjectives and adverbs meet the criteria outlined. Some cases are less determinate, particularly compound words like *water-mill*. Other form classes do not so readily fulfil all these criteria. This is particularly the case with articles like *the* or *a*, as Bloomfield (1935) himself recognized; these are not usually found as isolates, and they are not usually detachable from the nouns with which they are in construction in an NP. On the other hand, they are not, in English, bound to their nouns in the way that a prefix like *un-* is bound; we can, for instance, interpolate other items (THE *great grey green greasy Limpopo* RIVER : *the river*). For this reason they are usually considered separate words. Having isolated those units that do fulfil all the criteria noted, other segments, which may fulfil only some of the criteria, must also be treated as words.

The foregoing discussion suggests that there is a certain indeterminacy about the definition of a word, and this is indeed the case. On the other hand, it does seem to be a unit that is unavoidable, and on to which a number of criteria converge. It will also not have escaped notice, and should be no surprise, that the criteria discussed, especially the syntactic criteria, turn out to be the same in kind as those used to identify phrases, and so on, and discussed in Chapters 1 and 2.

12.2 'Inflectional' and 'derivational' morphology

The study of the internal structure of words is 'morphology'. Many English words obviously have internal structure. The individual words in **1a** can uncontentiously be segmented as in **1b**:

1a The fearsome cats attacked the foolish dog
1b The fear-some cat-s attack-ed the fool-ish dog

The principal criterion for the analysis is the formal difference between sets of words. In the case of *cats*, we can start with the set *cat* and *cats*, which differ in that the former lacks and the second contains the segment -*s*, and then enlarge the set to include other pairs of nouns – *girl*: *girl-s*; *boy*: *boy-s*; *dog*: *dog-s*; and so on – which share this formal distinction. A formal analysis of this sort can also be related to a semantic distinction; *cat* (and analogously *girl, boy, dog*, and so on) is found in sentences appropriately applied to situations describing a single object and *cats* in sentences appropriately applied to situations describing more than one object of the same kind. In the case of *cat*: *cats*, since *cat* is common to both words, we assume that this form is associated with the semantic notion 'feline'; and since *cats* contains the additional segment -*s*, we assume that this can be associated with 'more than oneness'. The semantic criterion reinforces our formal analysis. The reader is left to pursue the analogous argument with *attacked*.

The analysis of *fearsome* as *fear-some* and of *foolish* as *fool-ish* is equally clear and can be pursued in the same terms. Formally *foolish* is segmentable as *fool-ish* on the analogy of forms, like *fool* and *fool-hardy*, on the one hand, and *boy-ish* and *girl-ish*, on the other. Semantically *fool* is applicable to individuals who are held to be simple minded and -*ish* can be associated with 'having the quality of being a . . .'. The reader is invited to subject *fear-some* to a comparable analysis.

In informal terms the principle is to isolate segments that have a 'common form' and a 'common meaning', though as we shall discover this is more a useful working heuristic than a proper definition.

The two pairs of words discussed in the preceding two paragraphs also illustrate an important division in morphological study. In the case of *cats* and *attacked* the analysis of the words corresponds to a grammatical analysis. *Cat* is a noun stem, -*s* is a plural marker (and plural is a term in the grammatical category of number), and the whole word is a noun (the 'plural form of CAT'). Analogously, *attack* is a verb stem, *-ed* is a past tense marker (and past is a term in the grammatical category of tense), and the whole word is a verb (the 'past tense form of ATTACK'). They are representative instances of 'inflectional morphology': that part of morphology which deals with the way in which lexical stems are brought together with grammatical markers like those for 'plural' or 'past tense'.

The analysis of *fearsome* and *foolish*, on the other hand, does not represent a grammatical analysis but describes the way lexical stems themselves are formed. In the case of *fool-ish* the addition of the 'adjective formative' *-ish* to the lexical stem *fool* forms the new lexical stem *foolish*. Similarly, in *fear-some* the adjective formative *-some* added to the noun *fear* produces the adjective *fearsome*. They are representative instances of 'derivational' or 'lexical morphology': that part of morphology which deals with the way lexical stems are formed.

Both kinds of morphology can be regarded as 'bridge' disciplines. In the case of inflectional morphology the bridge is between syntax and phonology. It relates to syntax in so far as it is concerned with the distribution of grammatical elements: for instance, the way it associates the 'noun stem' *cat* with the 'plural marker' *-s*. And it relates to phonology in that it involves the study of the phonological shapes of words; for instance, in *cats* (/kats/) the plural marker is phonologically realized as /-s/ since it is affixed to /kat/, whereas it would be /-z/ if it were affixed to /dɒg/ to form /dɒgz/ (the difference is explained in Chapter 13, section 13.2). In the case of derivational morphology the bridge is between the lexicon and phonology. It relates to the lexicon in so far as derivational morphology is concerned with the analysis of existing words and the creation of new ones, and to phonology in that it is concerned with the phonological processes involved.

For the rest of this chapter, and in the next two, we shall be concerned with 'inflectional morphology', returning to consider 'derivational morphology' in Chapter 15.

12.3   Models of inflectional morphology

In the previous section we introduced some of the terminology we will use in discussing inflectional morphology. Before we do so, however, a brief comment on the notion, introduced in the previous section, that morphology is a 'bridge' between syntax and phonology. In common with other 'bridge' disciplines, there are different views on the extent to which it can be considered as an independent discipline at all. We will consider two rather different views associated with the descriptions 'item and arrangement' and 'word and paradigm'.

The 'item and arrangement' model of morphology divides word formation between syntax and phonology. Syntax, as we have seen, involves the identification, labelling and bracketing of constituents from the largest (the sentence, which we studied in Part One) to the smallest (which we will call the 'morpheme' and which we begin to consider in this section). Under this view, *attacked* and *cats* in the sentence:

2a   The cats attacked the dog
2b   The cat-s attack-ed the dog

are given the syntactic analyses {ATTACK + past} and {CAT + pl}. The 'morphemes' {ATTACK}, {CAT}, {past} and {pl} are *items* (constituents) in a particular syntactic *arrangement*. We have seen that phrases are structures intermediate between words and sentences and if words have a similar kind of structure then there seems to be no difference between the 'arrangement' of the 'items' (here words) *the* and *cats* in the NP *the cats* and the arrangement of the items (here morphemes) {CAT} and {pl} in the noun *cats*. The kind of rules at issue are the same and the analysis continues down through the word, as it were, to the smallest constituent, the morpheme. Words, like phrases, may be important analytic units, but they are not the smallest. That honour is reserved to the morpheme. At this point phonology takes over with the rules which relate morphemes to phonological shapes.

A different view, the 'word and paradigm' model of morphology, sees the word as the smallest unit with which a *syntactic* description is concerned. The formation rules for words are seen as different in kind to the formation rules required for phrase or sentence structure. In this case, word formation necessarily involves an independent descriptive component. Elements like [past] are equally important under this view, but they can be seen as 'features' of a complex word unit rather than as constituents in their own right. To some extent the feature notation we used in Part One, where $\text{ATTACK}_{[past]}$ represents the whole word *attacked*, implicitly adopts such a view.

Many of the basic issues are the same in both approaches. Both approaches, for example, need to identify elements like 'ATTACK', 'past', 'CAT' and 'plural' even though they ascribe a different status to them, and both approaches are worth serious study. For reasons of space we will restrict our discussion to the 'item and arrangement' viewpoint, directing the interested reader to a discussion of similar problems in a word and paradigm approach in 'Further reading', page 373.

12.4   Some terminology

In section 12.1 we showed that the word is an important analytic unit. We should now observe that the word 'word' is used in a number of different senses, as Lyons (1968, pp. 196 ff.) points out, and that it is helpful to distinguish between them. We shall identify three.

The first is its use to refer to actually occuring physical forms. In this sense the sentence:

3   Mary loved John once, but she doesn't love him any more

contains eleven words. We shall use the term *word form* for this usage. There are eleven word forms in 3. From time to time it is convenient to make the further distinction between a phonological and an orthographic word form. Orthographic word forms, when used for exemplification within the text, are italicized; phonological word forms are represented in 'phonemic slashes', for example, *word forms* /wɜd fɔmz/.

The second usage can be illustrated by saying that in 3 *loved* and *love* are different forms of the word LOVE. This use of the term 'word' applies when we say we are going to look up the meaning of a particular word in the dictionary. We do not expect to find an entry for each of the different inflectional forms of LOVE, such as *loved, loves* and *loving*. We use the term *lexeme* to distinguish this usage. To distinguish lexemes from word forms we always use small capital letters to refer to lexemes, a usage established in previous chapters.

The status of these two terms is rather different. Word forms can, in some sense, be regarded as substantial units, as actually occurring forms; the words written on this page are word forms. The lexeme, on the other hand, is an abstraction. Word forms like *love, loves, loved* and *loving* can all be related to the lexeme LOVE, but none of them actually is the lexeme LOVE. If we associate dictionary entries with lexemes, we see that lexicographers have a problem; they must choose a word form to represent the lexeme in question. The particular choice of word form is a matter of convention in different languages. In English dictionaries verbal lexemes are typically represented by the 'infinitive' form; that is, LOVE is represented by *love*. The same is true in French and Spanish, so we find *aimer* in a French dictionary and *amar* in a Spanish dictionary. In Latin or Greek dictionaries, however, verbal lexemes are typically represented by the 'first person singular present indicative' form of the verb; thus we find *amo* rather than *amare* (the 'infinitive' form) in a Latin dictionary, and φῐλέω in a Greek dictionary.[1]

The difference between these two senses of word is clearly at issue if the question is asked, how many different words are there in this chapter? If we mean word in the sense of word form, then we count each instance of word forms like *is, are, be, was* and *were* as 'different words', and each instance of word forms like *word* as 'the same word'. If, on the other hand, we mean word in the sense of lexeme, then all the forms *is, are*, and so on, are different forms of the same word (= lexeme) BE, and we need to distinguish between WORD(1) (= word form) and WORD(2) (= lexeme). It is by no means always clear in word counts which of the two senses is at issue, but they need to be distinguished.

We will sometimes find it helpful to identify a third use of the term 'word' which can be illustrated by comparing the word forms *wrote* and *written* in *I wrote* and *I have written* with the word form *laughed* in *I laughed* and *I have laughed*. *Wrote* and *written* are different word forms, but the two instances of *laughed* are the same word form. However, if we describe *wrote* as the 'past tense form of WRITE' and *written* as the 'past participle form of WRITE', we will, analogously, want to describe *laughed* in *I laughed* as the 'past tense form of LAUGH' and *laughed* in *I have laughed* as the 'past participle form of LAUGH'. Syntactic descriptions such as 'the past tense form of . . .' describe *morphosyntactic words*. Typically a morphosyntactic word consists of a lexeme together with a grammatical description, as in 'past tense form of LAUGH', and there is often a correspondence between a morphosyntactic word and the word form by which it is realized, as in the examples given.[2]

We have identified three different senses of *word* – as word form, as lexeme and as grammatical word. In different circumstances we say that *laughed* and *laughed* in the examples given are the same word (= word form), are different forms of the same word (= lexeme), or are different words (= morphosyntactic word)! Unless the context makes it clear which sense is at issue, we need to make a terminological distinction between these three senses of word.

We have observed that many English words have internal structure. We now turn from different views of the word to the segments that make up the word. We have seen that in:

4   The cats attacked the dog

cats and *attacked* can be analysed as *cat-s* and *attack-ed* and that the constituent parts can be given grammatical descriptions. Thus the segment *attack* in *attack-ed* can be identified with the verbal lexeme ATTACK and the segment *-ed* with the grammatical description 'past tense'. The principle that permits this is that we identify the same segment in other forms of ATTACK (*attack, attack-s, attack-ing*) and other past tense forms contain the segment *-ed* (*kill-ed, walk-ed* . . .). Analogously the segment *cat* can be identified with the lexeme CAT and *-s* with the grammatical description 'plural'. In the 'item and arrangement' framework that we are adopting we can represent this analysis by constituent structure trees as in Figure 12.1.

Line (4) in the figure shows the segmentation of the words. We will refer to the word segments as 'morphs'; *attack* is a morph, and so is *-ed*. Line (3) shows an analysis in terms of 'morphemes',

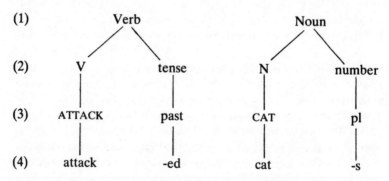

(the figures (1), (2), etc. are for reference only)

Figure 12.1

the minimal units of grammatical description; ATTACK is a morpheme, and so is 'past'. In line (2) the 'V' node identifies its daughter, ATTACK, as a member of the class of verbal lexemes, and the 'tense' node identifies its daughter, past, as a term in the category of tense. In line (1) the node 'Verb' identifies *attacked* as a verb constituent.

We noted in the preceding section that lexemes are 'abstract' units and that word forms are 'substantial' units. This statement needs to be widened to say that morphemes are abstract units (lexemes are one kind of morpheme) and morphs are substantial units (morphs are segments of word forms). The relationship between morpheme and morph is one of 'realization'; in the example the morpheme {ATTACK} is realized by the morph *attack*; and the morpheme {past} is realized by the morph *-ed*. This relationship is summed up in Figure 12.2.

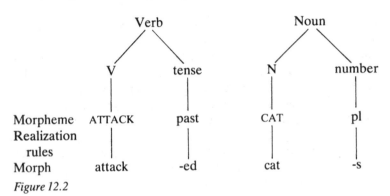

Figure 12.2

Many English words can be analysed in a comparable fashion. Now consider the words *ate* and *mice* in the sentence:

5   The cats ate the mice

If *attacked* in **1a** can, as a morphosyntactic word, be described as 'the past tense form of ATTACK', then it seems that analogously *ate* in 5 is 'the past tense form of EAT'. From a strictly syntactic point of view it is obviously desirable to be able to describe them in a parallel way: as {ATTACK + past} and {EAT + past}. However, whereas *attacked* may without disagreement be segmented as *attack-ed*, there is no obviously parallel segmentation available for *ate*. There seems no satisfactory way to identify a part of *ate* as realizing the lexeme {EAT} and another part as realizing {past}. Rather, *ate* as a unity realizes the morpheme string {EAT + past}. We could represent the analysis by a constituent structure diagram like those of Figure 12.3.

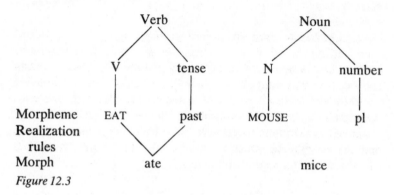

Figure 12.3

Down to the morphemic level the descriptions of *attacked* and *ate* are parallel; both consist of a verbal lexeme and a member of the category of tense. They differ in the way these morpheme strings are realized; in {ATTACK + past} the morpheme {ATTACK} is realized by the morph *attack* and the morpheme {past} by the morph *-ed*; in {EAT + past} the morpheme string as a whole is realized by the single morph *ate*.

It should be clear that there are advantages in identifying two different sorts of units: the abstract morpheme which we need for syntactic descriptions, and the substantial morph which we need for the actual structure of word forms. The abstract morpheme is part of the syntactic description, and from the viewpoint of the syntactic description the relation between morpheme and morph is of no consequence. The substantial morph, on the other hand, is a word form or part of a word form. When a word form can be segmented into smaller units, which cannot in their turn be segmented, these smaller units are morphs. Thus word forms may consist either of single morphs (as with the unsegmentable *ate*) or of a string of morphs (as *attack-ed*). In these terms a morpheme is not part of a word form at all; it is an abstract element whose distribution is determined by the syntactic description; the relationship between a word form, or the morph(s) that compose(s) it, and a morpheme or string of morphemes, is one of realization; a morph realizes a morpheme or a string of morphemes.

To distinguish morph from morpheme in discussion we enclose morphemes in curly brackets, {past}, {ATTACK + past}, and represent morphs, like the word forms of which they may be part, in italics, *-ed, attack-ed*.

12.5 Lexical and grammatical morphemes

We have described the morpheme as an abstract unit whose distribution is accounted for in the syntax. Strings such as {ATTACK + past} and {MOUSE + pl} are strings of morphemes. There are two distinct types of morpheme: items like {ATTACK} and {MOUSE}; and items like {past} and {pl}. The former type we call lexical morphemes, or lexemes, and the latter grammatical morphemes. There is an important distinction between them.

Lexical morphemes, lexemes, are listed in the lexicon, and are inserted into syntactic derivations by a lexical insertion rule, in the manner described on page 43 (though these rules need some amendment now that we have embarked on a morphological description). Lexical morphemes, we have seen, are inserted in tree diagrams under terminal nodes labelled Noun, Verb, Adjective, and so on. Terminal nodes of this sort are called lexical category nodes, since lexemes are inserted beneath these nodes, and, as we have seen, lexemes can be categorized into classes of Noun, Verb, and so on. Classes like Noun and Verb we call lexical categories; in the lexicon each lexeme needs to be characterized in terms of the lexical category to which it belongs. Lexical categories are, in principle, open; it does not seem possible to list exhaustively the membership of any major lexical category, since it is always possible to introduce new items. Thus, in English, the category of Noun can be extended by the addition of new members as cultural needs dictate; a new artefact, for example, is often given a name, and this name, syntactically, is a noun. Nor is it the business of a syntactic description of a language to determine the total distribution of a particular lexeme; other considerations are important – for instance, the semantic restrictions of the sort discussed as selection restrictions in Chapter 5.3. Thus, while the syntax determines the distribution of the category Noun, the total distribution of a particular noun is only in part determined by the syntax.

Grammatical morphemes, items like {past}, {non-past}, {sing} and {pl}, are somewhat different. These morphemes too can be grouped into categories, such as tense or number, which we call grammatical categories. The important distinction between lexical and grammatical categories is twofold. The first distinction is that whereas the membership of a lexical category is in general open, the membership of a grammatical category is closed; it is possible to list exhaustively the membership of grammatical categories. Thus, in English, the category number has two terms – we shall refer to members of grammatical categories as 'terms' in the particular category at issue – singular and plural. These two terms are established by the fact that there is, in English, just this opposition possible in this category and no other. It is not a necessary characteristic of any language that there should be just two terms in the category number; some languages have a third term, dual, characteristically applied to objects that occur typically in pairs. Thus in classical Greek we find:

6   *singular*   *dual*   *plural*

   ὁ πούς   τώ πόδε   οἱ πόδες

   'the foot'   'the (two) feet'   'the feet'

Note the formal contrast between the noun forms, echoed by the concordial forms of the article (ὁ – τώ – οἱ). Such a formal contrast is not available in English, so we say that English has only two terms in its number system. The number of terms in a grammatical category is determined by formal characteristics of the language in question and cannot be assumed in advance.

The second distinction between grammatical morphemes and lexemes is that the distribution of purely grammatical categories is, in principle, describable purely within the syntax. This distinction can best be illustrated by the following fragment of a grammar:

7   *Constituent structure rules:*

S	→	NP	VP
VP	→	V	NP
V	→	Verb	Tense
Tense	→	{past,	present}
NP	→	Art	N

N	→	Noun	Number
Number	→	{sing,	pl}

Lexical rules:

Noun	→	{BOY, DOG, CAT, HOUSE . . .}
Verb	→	{FRIGHTEN, AMUSE . . .}

In this grammar the distribution of morphemes like {past} or {sing} is totally determined by the constituent structure rules. On the other hand, whereas the distribution of the class Noun or Verb is determined by the constituent structure rules, the distribution of an individual noun – HOUSE, say – is determined in part by the distribution of the class Noun, but also by semantic considerations which are external to the syntax proper.

Having drawn this distinction, we can observe that in many languages certain grammatical categories are typically associated with certain lexical categories. In English the category of tense is typically associated with verbs. So the morphs associated with the morpheme {past}, orthographically realized as -*ed*, are found in verb words (*kill-ed*, *walk-ed*, and so on), not in noun words. Conversely, the grammatical category of definiteness is realized in English by articles, which, although they are not affixed to nouns, only occur in association with nouns (*the man, a walk*, and so on).

A further distinction commonly used in grammatical discussions is between grammatical and lexical words. Grammatical words are those words that realize only grammatical morphemes; lexical words are those items whose stems realize lexemes. This is why it is possible to recognize in nonsense poetry the fact that the poem is, in some sense, in English:

8 'Twas brillig and the slithy toves
    Did gyre and gimble in the wabe

The grammatical words are all clearly English – *and, the, did* – it is the lexical words that have 'nonsense' stems – *tove, gyre, gimble, wabe*. Take *slithy*, for instance; it is in the syntactic position for an adjective (Art Adj N), and it has the morph -*y*, a common marker of a derivational process deriving adjectives from nouns (cf. *slime*: *slimy*; *grime*: *grimy*; and so on). There are lexical classes truly open to new membership. On the other hand, it would probably be impossible to interpret 'nonsense' where the lexical stems were related to 'regular' English lexemes, but where the 'grammatical' words were nonsense.

12.6   The morpheme as an abstract unit

Distinguishing between the substantial morph and the abstract morpheme has a number of advantages. It frees syntactic description from an unnecessarily close identification with word forms and allows us to postulate units, morphemes, that are useful for a syntactic description. Conversely, it allows us to study the structure of words without necessarily seeking a syntactic correlation for every morph we may wish to postulate. In this section and in Chapter 14 we will see abundant justification for this separation from the point of view of syntax, and in Chapter 16 we will explore some of the advantages for word formation.

We have seen that, syntactically speaking, word forms like:

9a   walk-ed; attack-ed
9b   ate; wrote; went

can all be represented by morpheme strings like {WALK + past} and {GO + past}, irrespective of the fact that in the examples in **9a** there is a direct correspondence between morphemes and morphs whereas in **9b** the words are not readily segmentable. Now consider the word forms:

10a   large   larg-er
10b   bad   worse
10c   foolish   more foolish

The forms in the left-hand column have traditionally been called the 'simple' forms of the adjectives concerned (LARGE, BAD, FOOLISH), and the forms in the right-hand column the 'compared' forms. Simple adjectives have a different distribution from compared adjectives; the forms are not, for example, freely interchangeable:

11a   My house is large, but yours is larger than mine
11b   My essay may be bad, but yours is worse than mine

but not:

12a *My house is larger, but yours is large than mine

12b *My essay may be worse, but yours is bad than mine

From a syntactic point of view there are advantages in attributing the same structure – say, {comp(ared) + Adj} – to all the compared forms. From the point of view of word formation, however, all the forms are different; *larg-er* consists of two morphs, *worse* is a single unsegmentable word form, and *more foolish* is two separate word forms. Furthermore, in the case of *more foolish* the morph realizing {comp} precedes the adjective stem, whereas with *larg-er* it follows. For syntactic description we need one type of statement, but for word formation we need another type.

The last observation distinguishes between the ordering of morphemes in a syntactic description and the ordering of morphs in word formation. In the case of morphs order is clearly crucial. They must be ordered in the sequence in which they actually occur; in a form like *walk-ed* the morphs can only occur in that order and never in the impossible *ed-walk*. The morpheme, however, is an abstract unit, so why should we not order morphemes in whatever way makes a grammatical statement most revealing and economical? In the grammar we may order the morphemes that are realized by *walked* as {past + WALK} if there seems good reason to do so; and as we shall see in Chapter 14.3, there is good reason. The realization rules that relate morphemes to morphs ensure that the morphs occur in the correct order.

We will look at the morphology of English verb forms in Chapter 14, but to illustrate the principle let us consider a different and more straightforward example involving verb forms in the following Akan sentences.[3] The second word in each sentence is the verb word. The verb stem is *fura* (FURA 'wrap round, put on, wear'). The descriptions to the left of each sentence are the names used to refer to the various verb forms, and we can regard these as identifying the relevant morphemes; so in **13a** *fura* realizes the morphemes {hab + FURA}:

13a	hab	Kofi fura ntoma	'Kofi wears a cloth'
13b	prog	Kofi re-fura ntoma	'Kofi is putting on a cloth'
13c	fut	Kofi be-fura ntoma	'Kofi will put on a cloth'

| 13d | pret | Kofi fura-a ntoma | 'Kofi put on a cloth' |
| 13e | perf | Kofi a-fura ntoma | 'Kofi has put on a cloth' |

hab(itual); prog(ressive); fut(ure); pret(erite); perf(ect)

The verbal affixes form a five-term category {hab, prog, fut, pret, perf}, which we call the category of Aspect. The affixes are mutually exclusive and no verb can have more than one, so *a-re-fura*, *be-fura-a*, and so on, are impossible. From a syntactic point of view it is clearly most illuminating to postulate rules like:

| 14 | Verb | → | Asp V |
| | Asp | → | {hab, prog, fut, pret, perf} |

which associate each verb stem with an aspect marker and place it before the verb. Realization rules will then ensure that the habitual verb form has no affix, the preterite has a suffix, and all the other forms have a prefix. It is not possible to devise rewrite rules that maintain the generalization that all five terms belong to the same category of Aspect and also to derive the morphemes in the correct surface order (the reader is invited to try).

We conclude that the compositional structure of words is to some degree independent of the syntactic description of a sentence and that it is necessary to distinguish between the morpheme – an abstract unit whose distribution is accounted for by the syntax – and the morph – a substantial unit whose distribution is not wholly accounted for by the syntax.

Technical terms

bound form
derivational morphology
free form
grammatical category
grammatical morpheme
homograph
inflectional morphology
item and arrangement
lexeme
lexical category

lexical morpheme
morph
morpheme
morphosyntactic word
orthographic words
phonological words
potential pause
realization
word form

Notes

1   This terminology also allows us to talk sensibly about some traditional problems. So, for example, 'homography' arises when two different words (= lexemes) are orthographically represented by the same word (= word form). Thus the same word form *mace* may realize either the lexeme MACE(1) with the sense 'spice' or the lexeme MACE(2) with the sense 'staff of office' – a fact usually recognized in dictionaries by according each lexeme a different entry.

2   In section 12.3 we distinguished between 'word and paradigm' and 'item and arrangement' models of morphology. In the former the grammatical word will generally be the head lexeme and its associated features (e.g. *laughed*: LAUGH$_{[past]}$ or LAUGH$_{[past\ part]}$); in the latter the grammatical word will be a string of morphemes (e.g. *laughed*: {LAUGH + past} or {LAUGH + past part}.

3   The sentences are represented in the orthographic form. Tone markings have been omitted, although these are also relevant to a complete description of the verbal system. This does not affect the point at issue.

13   Morphemes and morphs

In the previous chapter we established a distinction between morphemes, abstract units used in the grammar, and morphs, concrete units that are 'parts of words'. We described the relation between the abstract morpheme and the concrete morph as one of realization. In this chapter we look at different kinds of morphs and begin to explore realization.

13.1   Morphs

When a word form can be analysed into smaller forms, which cannot themselves be analysed into yet smaller forms, the smaller forms are morphs. A morph is thus a word form (if it cannot be analysed) or part of a word form. In this section we introduce some terminology for talking about morphs.

Word forms that can be analysed into a string of two or more morphs are morphologically complex. Word forms that consist of a single morph are morphologically simple; *walk-ed* is morphologically complex; *went* or *ran* is morphologically simple.

A morph that can stand alone as a word is a free morph; *boy, tea, time, half, back, happy* and *long* are free morphs. A morph incapable of standing alone as a word is a bound morph: *-ish, un-, -ed* and *-ness* in *boy-ish, un-happy, walk-ed* and *good-ness* are bound morphs. We show bound morphs preceded or followed by a hyphen: *-ish, -un,* and so on.

By definition a morphologically simple word must consist of a single free morph. A morphologically complex word may consist of a free and a bound morph (*boy-ish, un-happy, good-ness*, and so on), two free morphs (*tea-time, half-back*, and so on), or any appropriate combination of free and bound morphs.

In discussing morphologically complex words it is convenient to have some terminology for various different types of constituent. That part of a word form to which derivational or inflectional affixes can be added is a *stem*. A stem may be morphologically simple or morphologically complex; a morphologically simple stem is often called a *root*. An *affix* is an inflectional or derivational morph added to a stem. Affixes which precede their stem are *prefixes*; affixes which follow their stem are *suffixes*; and affixes inserted within their stem are *infixes*.

So, for example, in the forms *duck, duck-ling* and *duckling-s*: *duck* consists of just a simple root; *duck-ling* consists of the stem *duck*, which is also a root, and the derivational suffix *-ling*; and *duckling-s* consists of the stem *duckling*, which is not a root because it is morphologically complex, and the inflectional suffix *-s*.[1]

Prefixes and suffixes can easily be illustrated in English. *im-, un-* and *pre-* are prefixes in the words IM-*possible*, UN-*likely* and PRE-*fix*; *-ed, -ment* and *-ly* are suffixes in *walk*-ED, *conceal*-MENT and *ungentleman*-LY. Infixes do not regularly occur in English, though one might consider *im*-BLOODY-*possible* as a peculiar example of infixation. Infixation does, however, occur in children's 'secret' languages. A quite widely spoken secret language, sometimes called 'aigy-paigy', is formed by infixing the syllable *aig* (pronounced /eig/ as in the proper name Craig) before every vowel nucleus of 'regular' English: *Thaigis aigis haigow yaigou taigalk saigecraigetlaigy*: *th-is -is h-ow y-ou t-alk s-ecr-etl-y*. In this language *aig* is an infix in a word like *th-is*, yielding *th-aig-is*. Many Semitic languages can be analysed as containing infixes; in modern Arabic, a root like *k-t-b* 'write' appears in words like *katab* 'he wrote', *kita:b* 'book' and, with prefixes, *ma-ka:tib* 'places for writing, studies', *ma-ktab* 'places for writing, study' and *je-ktab* 'he is writing'; similarly, the root *g-l-s* appears in *galas* 'he sat', *ga:lis* 'sitting person', *ma-ga:lis* 'councils' and *ma-glas* 'council' (Bloomfield, 1935, pp. 243–4).

13.2 Morphs and allomorphs

In the previous chapter we described the relation between the abstract morpheme and the substantial morph as one of realization. For the sake of simplicity, in all the examples we looked at a particular morpheme was always realized by the same morph. So, for example, in looking at English plural forms we deliberately chose examples in the traditional orthographic representation where {plural} is uniformly realized by *-s*, as in *cat-s* and *dog-s*. It is, however, by no means the case that a morpheme is always realized by a single morph. When a morpheme is realized by a series of different morphs, the alternative realizations are called allomorphs. In this section we will look at cases of allomorphy and consider what factors condition the choice of one allomorph rather than another.

Consider the phonological forms for English plurals:

1   *The plural forms of English nouns:*

buses	/bʌs-ɪz/	hats	/hat-s/	hags	/hag-z/
cheeses	/tʃiz-ɪz/	sacks	/sak-s/	bags	/bag-z/
bushes	/bʊʃ-ɪz/	maps	/map-s/	knobs	/nɒb-z/
garages	/garɑʒ-ɪz/	proofs	/pruf-s/	eaves	/iv-z/
patches	/patʃ-ɪz/	moths	/mɒθ-s/	lathes	/leɪð-z/
judges	/dʒʌdʒ-ɪz/			bees	/bi-z/
				paws	/pɔ-z/

Three distinct morphs realize {plural} in English: /-ɪz/, /-z/ and /-s/. In the example, the distribution of these allomorphs is determined by the phonological characteristics of the stem final segment, thus:

2   *Allomorphs of English {plural}:*

/-ɪz/   occurs after stems ending in /s, z, ʃ, ʒ, tʃ, dʒ/ that is, after stems ending in a voiced or voiceless sibilant
/-z/   occurs after stems ending in a voiced segment other than a sibilant
/-s/   occurs after stems ending in a voiceless segment other than a sibilant

When the distribution of allomorphs can be described in phonological terms, the allomorphs are said to be phonologically conditioned.

In the example quoted there is some phonological similarity between the appropriate allomorph and the stem to which it is affixed; /s/ and /z/ are voiceless and voiced alveolar fricatives, affixed to stems ending in voiceless and voiced segments.

There is no need for phonological conditioning to involve phonological similarity. Thus in the following data from Tsotsil (taken from Nida, 1949, p. 23) we find dissimilation – that is, the affixes are phonologically dissimilar in a regular fashion from the stem vowels:

3 *Tsotsil:*

-k'uʃ	'wedge'	-k'uʃi	'to put a wedge in'
-ʃik'	'prop used beneath an object'	-ʃik'u	'to put a prop under'
-ʃon	'prop used against an object'	-ʃoni	'to put a prop against'
-vov	'crazy'	-vovi	'to go crazy'
-t'uʃ	'wet'	-tuʃi	'to become wet'

The suffix is the front vowel /-i/ when the stem vowel is a back vowel /u/ or /o/; and the back vowel /-u/ when the stem is the front vowel /i/.

There can be phonological conditioning even when there is no apparent phonological similarity between a stem and its phonologically conditioned affixes (Tojolabal data from Nida, 1949, p. 18):

4 *Tojolabal:*

-man	'to buy'	hman	'I buy'
-il	'to see'	kil	'I see'
-k'an	'to want'	ak'an	'you (sing) want'
-al	'to say'	awal	'you (sing) say'
-lap	'to dress'	slap	'he dresses'
-u	'to drink'	yu	'he drinks'

Given this limited amount of data the affixes appear to be as follows:

5 *Tojolabal person affixes:*

'first person'	/h-/	preceding consonants
	/k-/	preceding vowels
'second person'	/a-/	preceding consonants
	/aw-/	preceding vowels
'third person'	/s-/	preceding consonants
	/y-/	preceding vowels

If this analysis accurately represents the situation in the language as a whole, we see that in the case of the first and third person pronouns there appears no obvious phonological similarity between the pre-consonantal and pre-vocalic allomorphs; the distribution, however, is clearly phonologically conditioned.

The selection of allomorphs is not always phonologically conditioned. There may be other conditioning factors. Consider the following data, from English:

6 *More English plural forms:*

house	/haus/	houses	/hauz-ɪz/
calf	/kɑf/	calves	/kɑv-z/
elf	/ɛlf/	elves	/ɛlv-z/
sheaf	/ʃif/	sheaves	/ʃiv-z/
wife	/waif/	wives	/waiv-z/
bath	/bɑθ/	baths	/bɑð-z/
path	/pɑθ/	paths	/pɑð-z/

The distribution of the plural affixes (in the right-hand column) is entirely regular, and follows the rules for English plurals given in **2**. In this case it is the stem that shows allomorphic variation: /haus/: /hauz-/, and so on. There appears to be no phonological reason for this alternation, since comparable forms are entirely regular:

7 *English plurals again:*

piece	/pis/	pieces	/pis-ɪz/	*not*	*/piz-ɪz/
reef	/rif/	reefs	/rif-s/	*not*	*/riv-z/

as, indeed, are the 'possessive' forms:

8 *Some possessive forms in English:*

		plural		*sing possessive*	
wife	/waif/	wives	/waiv-z/	wife's	/waif-s/
youth	/juθ/	youths	/juð-z/	youth's	/juθ-s/

You are invited to discover the other allomorphs for the singular possessive. You will find that they are identical to those for plural (*-s*, *-z* and *-ɪz*), and have the same phonologically conditioned distribution.

We are thus forced to say that with items like (HOUSE) the allomorph /hauz-/ is chosen in the environment {plural}. When the selection of the appropriate allomorph is determined by circumstances which cannot be described phonologically, then these allomorphs are said to be grammatically conditioned. Grammatically conditioned affixes in English include the plural affixes *-im* and *-en* in *kibbutz*: *kibbutz-im, seraph*: *seraph-im* and *ox*: *ox-en*. These irregular forms include loans (*kibbutzim*) and linguistic 'fossils' (*oxen*).

Occasionally morphs may be in free variation; in such cases it does not matter which of two (or perhaps more) allomorphs is chosen. Thus the forms *burned* and *burnt* seem to be free variants in the past tense (*I burned*: *I burnt . . .*) and the past participle (*I have burned*: *I have burnt*). If this is the case, then /-d/ and /-t/ are in free variation as realizations of past tense and past participle in construction with {BURN}.

The grammar may sometimes have a morphemic distinction when there is no overt marker of this particular distinction in actual word forms. In such cases a 'zero' morph or allomorph is sometimes postulated. This is usually represented by $\emptyset$. Zero allomorphs are often postulated when the structure of a series of related forms is such that there is a 'significant absence' of a formal marker at some point in the series. In English plural is usually marked with *-s*, as in *dog*: *dogs*, and so on, but with some nouns there is no morphological variation between the singular and plural; thus we find *sheep*: *sheep, salmon*: *salmon, grouse*: *grouse*, and so on:

9a   I shot two dogs yesterday
9b   I shot two grouse yesterday
9c   *I shot two grouses yesterday

We can postulate that the plural form of GROUSE is *grouse-$\emptyset$*.

Zero morphs are often postulated when the general structure suggests that the absence of any morphological marker is itself of significance. For example, in Totonac the subject pronouns are as follows:

10   *Totonac subject pronouns* (see Nida, 1949, p. 46):

k-	first person singular	-wi	first person plural
-ti	second	-tit	second
$\emptyset$ -	third	-qú	third

The third person singular is never indicated overtly and it is the 'significant absence' of an affix that indicates the third singular. Remember the Sherlock Holmes story where the great detective perceived the significance of the fact that the dog did *not* bark.

In this section we have been looking at the way a morpheme may be realized. In some cases, the relationship is invariant and a morpheme is realized everywhere by the same single morph – DOG, for instance, is always realized as /dɒg/. In other cases a morpheme may be realized by one of a set of allomorphs; the selection of the particular allomorph may be conditioned by phonological factors (for example, **2**), or by grammatical factors (for example, **6**), or the allomorphs may be in free variation. We have also seen that a morpheme may have no realization at all, a 'zero' morph, and that zero may be either an allophone (for example, **9**) or an invariant realization (for example, **10**).

13.3   Realization

The relationship between morpheme and morph is 'realization' and in this section we will look at one way of dealing with realization with an 'item and arrangement' grammar. For illustrative purposes we will consider how to account for the English plural and possessive forms illustrated in Figure 13.1. The regular allomorphs for {pl(ural)} and {poss(essive)} are identical and they are phonologically conditioned as illustrated in **2** above. It is not possible to have both a plural and a possessive marker.

	CAT	DOG	BUS	SHEEP	WIFE
N	kat	dɒg	bʌs	ʃip	waif
N + poss	kats	dɒgz	bʌsɪz	ʃips	waifs
N + pl	kats	dɒgz	bʌsɪz	ʃip	waivz
N + pl + poss	kats	dɒgz	bʌsɪz	ʃips	waivz

Figure 13.1

To deal with these kinds of data we will need a little grammar of the kind we developed in Part One. We need a constituent structure rule like **1** in Figure 13.2 to develop the structure of a noun into the terminal symbols of the grammar, the lexical category symbol N and the grammatical category of number, here represented by the optional {pl}. We also need a lexical rule to insert a lexical item to the lexical category symbol. For our illustrative purpose we will assume that lexical insertion can be achieved by the simple phrase structure rule **2** in Figure 13.2. To these rules we need to add a set of 'morphological realization rules', rules (3)–(10) of Figure 13.2,

to realize the various lexical and grammatical morphemes introduced by the grammar.

Constituent structure rule:

(1)   Noun   →   N (+ pl)   (+ poss)

Lexical rule:

(2)   N   →   {CAT, DOG, BUS, SHEEP, WIFE}

Morphological realization rules:

(3)	CAT	→	/kat/	
(4)	DOG	→	/dɒg/	
(5)	BUS	→	/bʌs/	
(6)	SHEEP	→	/ʃip/	
(7a)	WIFE	→	/waiv/	in the environment__pl
(7b)			/waif/	elsewhere
(8)	pl	→	∅	in the environment/ʃip/__
(9a)	poss	→	∅	in the environment pl__
(9b)			/ɪz/	in the environment 'sibilant C' __
(9c)			/s/	in the environment 'voiceless C' __
(9d)			/z/	elsewhere
(10a)	pl	→	/ɪz/	in the environment 'sibilant C' __
(10b)			/s/	in the environment 'voiceless C' __
(10c)			/z/	elsewhere

Rules (3)–(7) introduce bases
Rule (7a) introduces a bound form
Rule (7b) introduces a free form
Rules (8)–(10) introduce suffixes
Rules (3)–(6) introduce invariant morphs
Rule (7) introduces grammatically conditioned allomorphs
Rule (9a) introduces a grammatically conditioned zero
Rules (9b)–(d) and (10) introduce phonologically conditioned
  allomorphs

Figure 13.2

Figure 13.3 illustrates some derivations using these rules.

Rule				Rule			
(1)	N	+ pl	+ poss	(1)	N	+ pl	+ poss
(2)	DOG	+ pl	+ poss	(2)	WIFE	+ pl	+ poss
(4)	/dɒg/	+ pl	+ poss	(7a)	/waiv/	+ pl	+ poss
(9a)	/dɒg/	+ pl		(9a)	/waiv/	+ pl	
(10c)	/dɒg/	−z/		(10c)	/waiv	−z/	
(1)	N	+ pl	+ poss	(1)	N	+ poss	
(2)	SHEEP	+ pl	+ poss	(2)	WIFE	+ poss	
(6)	/ʃip/	+ pl	+ poss	(7b)	/waif/	+ poss	
(8)	/ʃip/		+ poss	(10b)	/waif	−s/	
(9c)	/ʃip		−z/				

Figure 13.3

We observed above that a noun cannot be marked for both possessive and plural. These rules handle this by deleting {poss} when it co-occurs with {pl}, rule (9a), which achieves the correct result but only if the rules are applied in the order stated. Figure 13.4 shows what happens if these rules are applied in another order.

Rule				Rule			
(1)	NS	+ pl	+ poss	(1)	NS	+ pl	+ poss
(2)	BUS	+ pl	+ poss	(2)	SHEEP	+ pl	+ poss
(5)	/bʌs/	+ pl	+ poss	(6)	/ʃip/	+ pl	+ poss
(10a)	/bʌs	-ɪz/	+ poss	(9c)	/ʃip	−s	+ poss
(9b)	/bʌs	-ɪz	-ɪz/	(10a)	/ʃip	−s	−ɪz/

Figure 13.4

Technical terms

agglutinative rules	free variation
allomorph	grammatical category
base	grammatical conditioning
bound morph	grammatical morpheme
category	grammatical word
concord	infix
derivational affix	inflectional morphology
derivational morphology	lexical category
free morph	lexical morpheme

lexical word	prefix
morph	realization rule
morpheme	root
morphological realization rule	rule ordering
morphologically complex	stem
morphologically simple	suffix
null-realization rules	tense
number	term (in a grammatical category)
phonological conditioning	zero

Note

1 Sometimes a further terminological distinction is drawn between stems to which inflectional elements can be added, which are called stems, and stems to which derivational elements are added, which are called bases. Thus *duck* in *duckling* is a base, since *-ling* is a derivational affix; and *duckling* in *duckling-s* is a stem, since *-s* is an inflectional affix.

Exercises

(1) *Noun classes in Luganda (a language from Uganda)*
     In Luganda, as in other Bantu languages, nouns can be analysed as having the structure prefix + stem (for example, *omu-kazi*). The alternation between singular and plural is shown by different prefixes (for example, *omu-kazi* 'woman', *aba-kazi* 'women'). Nouns can be assigned to 'gender classes' depending on the form of the singular and plural prefixes. Four different noun classes are illustrated in the data. They have been assigned arbitrary numbers for ease of reference.

	singular	*gloss*	*plural*	*stem*
(i)	omu-kazi	woman	aba-kazi	-kazi
	omusajja	man	abasajja	-sajja
	umuntu	person	abantu	
	omwana	child	abaana	
	omwezi	sweeper	abeezi	
	omwozi	washerman	aboozi	
(ii)	eŋkoko	chicken	eŋkoko	-koko
	eŋgo	oil	eŋgo	

	ente	cow	ente
	endiga	sheep	endiga
	embogo	buffalo	embogo
	emmese	rat	emmese
(iii)	omugga	river	emigga
	omuggo	stick	emiggo
	omwaka	year	emyaka
	omwezi	moon	emyezi
(iv)	ekisolo	animal	ebisolo
	ekintu	thing	ebintu
	ekyalo	village	ebyalo
	ekyenyi	forehead	ebyenyi

Segment the words into morphs. Write the stem form in the right-hand column above. Fill in the matrix below with the prefix forms. When a prefix is realized by two or more allomorphs, there is a space for each allomorph. State the appropriate environment that conditions the allomorphs. Make your statements as general as possible. In the worked example, __ C means 'in the environment preceding a consonant' and __ V means 'in the environment preceding a vowel'.

class	singular		plural	
		in the environment		*in the environment*
1	omu-	__ C		
	omw-	__ V		
	/	/		
2				
3				
4				

(2) *The verb word in Luganda*

In Luganda the verb word is usually marked with a prefix which represents the subject, and with a morph which shows the 'tense' of the verb; it may also, in certain circumstances, be marked with a morph which represents the object. Each of the verb words below could stand as an independent sentence, with the meaning glossed. In this exercise you are asked to analyse the verb words below:

(i)	ndigenda	I shall go
(ii)	yagenda	He went
(iii)	nkyagenda	I am going
(iv)	twagenda	We went
(v)	aligenda	He will go
(vi)	wagenda	You (sing) went
(vii)	baligenda	They will go
(viii)	mukyagenda	You (pl) are going
(ix)	mwagenda	You (pl) went
(x)	tukyagenda	We are going
(xi)	baagenda	They went
(xii)	nnagenda	I went
(xiii)	akyaŋkuba	She is beating me
(xiv)	baamukuba	They beat him
(xv)	bakyakulaba	They are looking at you (sing)
(xvi)	yatukuba	She beat us
(xvii)	ndibagoba	I shall chase them
(xviii)	akyandaba	He is looking at me
(xix)	tukyabalaba	We are looking at them
(xx)	olitugoba	You (sing) will chase us
(xxi)	twabalaba	We saw you (pl)
(xxii)	tulibalaba	We shall see you (pl)
(xxiii)	nnabakuba	I beat them
(xxiv)	mulindaba	You (pl) will see me

(a) Give the morphs associated with the following translation meanings; where a given morpheme is realized by two allomorphs, state the environment (that is, what conditions the choice of one allomorph rather than another).

subject pronouns		
		in the environment
I		
you (sing)		
he/she		
we		
you (pl)		
they		

object pronouns		
		in the environment
me		
you (sing)		
him/her		
us		
you (pl)		
them		

tense/aspect affixes		
		in the environment
future		
past		
progressive		

Verb stems		
		in the environment
'*go*'		
'*beat*'		
'*chase*'		
'*see/look at*'		

(b)   What is the order of affixes within the word?

(c)   Supply the probable forms for the following meanings:
I shall beat them   You (pl) saw me

(3)   *Syntactic analysis*

Here is an extensive morphological and syntactic exercise.
The data come from a Xhosa (a Bantu language of Southern
Africa) folk tale.

The data are presented in three lines. In the first line is the
language text; the second line is a fairly literal 'word-by-word'
gloss into English; the third line contains a more idiomatic
English translation. You should beware of taking the glosses
literally, since the grammatical structure of the language
differs from English and a full word-by-word translation is not
possible without a lot of further explanation.

Following the text are a number of questions designed to
help you towards an analysis. You will not be able to make an
exhaustive grammatical description of Xhosa on the basis of
the amount of data you have here. The texts do, however,

have enough data to give some idea of the structure of the language as a whole.

Amasela (*Thieves*)

Ngenye imini, udyakalashe nomvolufu babona inqwelo yeentlanzi   (1)
One   day   Jackal   and Wolf   they saw a wagon of fishes
One day Jackal and Wolf saw a wagon of fish

Kwa oko udyakalashe wathi 'Mvolufu, ndilambile. Ndifuna intlanzi.'   (2)
Then   Jackal   he said Wolf   I hungry   I want   a fish
Then Jackal said, 'Wolf, I am hungry, I want a fish.'

Mvolufu wathi 'Uya kuzifumana njani iintlanzi?' Udyakalashe   (3)
Wolf   he said You will find them how   the fishes Jackal
Wolf said, 'How are you going to find the fish?' Jackal

wathi 'Uya kubona.' Udyakalashe yena wabaleka waya   kulala   (4)
he said You will see   Jackal   he   he ran   he went to lie down
replied, 'You will see.' Jackal, he ran and lay down in the road

endleleni   phambi kwenqwelo. Umqhubi wasibona esi silo   (5)
in the road in front of the wagon Driver   he saw this   creature
in front of the wagon. The driver saw this creature

wacinga   ukuba sifile. Wasiphakamisa ke   wathi 'Ndiya kumhlinza   (6)
he thought that   it dead He picked it up   then he said I will flay him
and thought it was dead. Then he picked it up and said, 'I will flay

lo   dyakalashe ekhaya. Ndiya kwenza umnweba ngesikhumba.   (7)
this Jackal   at home I will make   a caross   with the skin
this Jackal at home and make a caross with the skin

ndiwuthengise,   ndifumane imali.' Kwa oko   (8)
I sell it   I find   money Then
and sell it to make money.'

wamphosa enqwelweni waya   kuhlala   esihlalweni sakhe   (9)
he threw him on the wagon he went to sit down on the seat   of him
Then he threw him on the wagon, went and sat down on his seat

waqhuba inqwelo. Wavuka udyakalashe, wathatha iintlanzi   (10)
he drove the wagon He got up Jackal   he took   the fishes
and drove on. Jackal got up and took the fish

waziphosa   phantsi emva kwenqwelo, watsiba   ke   enqwelweni,   (11)
he threw them down   behind the wagon he jumped then from the wagon
he threw them down behind the wagon. Then he jumped off it

wahlala phantsi, watya. Umvolufu wayibona le   nto. Wabaleka   (12)
he sat   down   he ate Wolf   he saw it this thing He ran
and sat down and ate. Wolf saw this happening and ran

kudyakalashe, wafika   wathi 'Dyakalashe, nam ndilambile.'   13)
to Jackal   he arrived he said Jackal, I   also I hungry
to Jackal. On arrival he said, 'Jackal, I am hungry too.'

Waphendula udyakalashe wathi 'Mvolufu, ukuba ulambile, yiya   (14)
he answered Jackal   he said Wolf   that you hungry you go
Jackal answered, 'Wolf, if you are hungry, go

kulala   phaya endleleni. Umqhubi uya kucinga ukuba ufile.   (15)
to lie down there in the road The driver he will think that   you dead
and lie down there in the road. The driver he will think that you are dead.

Uya kukuphakamisa, akuphose   enqwelweni aye kuhlala esihlalweni (16)
He will pick you up   he throw you on the wagon he go to sit on the seat
He will pick you up, throw you on the wagon and go and sit on his seat
sakhe aqhube inqwelo. Wena ke uya kuvuka, uthathe iintlanzi,   (17)
of him he drive the wagon You then you will get up you take the fishes
and drive the wagon. Then you get up and take the fish
uziphose   phantsi utsibe   ke enqwelweni, uhlale phantsi,   (18)
you throw them down   you jump then from the wagon you sit down
and throw them down. Then you jump down from the wagon, sit down
utye.' Umvolufu walithatha eli cebo, wabaleka waya   kulala   (19)
you eat Wolf   he took it this advice he ran   he went to lie down
and eat.' Wolf took this advice, and ran and went and lay down
endleleni. Kodwa umqhubi waqonda   ezi zilo   (20)
in the road But   the driver he understood these creatures
in the road. But the driver now knew that these creatures
zamqhatha.   Wambetha kakhulu umvolufu emzimbeni.   (21)
they were cheating him He beat him hard   Wolf   on the body
were cheating him. So he beat Wolf hard on his body.
Umvolufu wakhala,   wavuka, wabaleka. Udyakalashe sisilo   (22)
Wolf   he cried out he got up he ran way Jackal   it a creature
Wolf cried out, got up and ran away. Jackal is a creature,
nomvolufu sisilo   naye. Zizilo   zonke. Kodwa udyakalashe (23)
and Wolf   it a creature too They creatures both   But   Jackal
and so is Wolf. They are both creatures. But Jackal
uhlakaniphile, umvolufu sisidenge.   (24)
he clever   Wolf   he stupid.
is clever and Wolf is stupid.

(a) Make a list of all the verb stems in the data, and gloss
     each item (for example, *bona* 'see'). List the stems in the
     form in which they occur, or in which you think they
     would occur, in the simple past tense form. Do not try to
     account for forms which are translated in the free English
     translation by 'I am __', 'They are __', 'I want __', and so
     on; that is, forms with the 'present' tense (for example,
     ndilambile, line 2; *ndifuna*, line 2; and the forms in lines
     22–4).

(b) Diagram the structure of past tense verb forms in terms
     of the morphs that obligatorily and optionally occur. Make
     a list of subject and object morphs, and gloss them in some
     way so that the relevant concordial relationships are clear.

(c) Diagram the structure of those verb forms that are
     apparently (judging from the glosses provided) used to
     refer to future events, and so on. Note that there are two
     types of form (for example, in sentence beginning line
     16). Describe their distribution.

(d)   There appear to be three different types of locative expression (they translate such phrases as 'on the road' and 'in front of the wagon'). Diagram their structure. (Note the following nouns: *umzimba* 'body'; *isihlalo* 'seat'; *indlela* 'road'.)

(e)   Make an analysis of the sentence *Uya kukuphakamisa . . . aghube inqwelo* (lines 16–17) into morphs. Separate the morphs in each word by hyphens (for example, *u-dyakalashe*) and identify each morph (for example, personal name class prefix – Jackal). Ignore the word *sakhe*.

14 The morphology of the English verb

14.1 Singular and plural: a problem in analysis

We have distinguished between the morpheme (a distributional unit of the syntax) and the morph (a distributional unit connected with word formation). The relationship between the two we have called realization. We have seen that the relationship between morpheme and morph is not always one-to-one, and have established a model of description which involves two basic components: (1) constituent structure and lexical rules and (2) morphological realization rules. This chapter looks at problems in the analysis of English verbs in these terms.

The facts of agreement between verbs and their subjects involve the issue of how we treat number in both nouns and verbs, so we will start the discussion by considering the forms of the nouns and verbs in simple sentences like:

1a The boy yawns
1b The boys yawn

and their past tense counterparts

2a The boy yawned
2b The boys yawned

We must consider the various forms in sentences, rather than in isolation, since the questions that interest us have implications that go beyond word formation. Consider first the apparently straightforward description of the singular and plural forms of English nouns. The 'regular' paradigm for English nouns is illustrated in such pairs as:

3   *singular*   *plural*
     boy   boys
     girl   girls

The paradigm is 'regular' because it applies to the vast majority of English nouns, and to all new borrowings (for example *sputnik*: *sputniks*). For simplicity we shall take our examples from the written rather than the spoken form of the language and do not consider questions of allomorphy; so we will represent the regular plural morph simply as -*s*.

Given that these are the singular and plural forms of the relevant lexemes, a possible analysis is to take {sing(ular)} and { pl(ural)} as terms in the category of {number}, and analyse *boy* as {BOY + sing}, and *boys* as {BOY + pl}. We can represent this analysis in the little grammar in Figure 14.1, which generates the trees in Figure 14.2.

Constituent structure rules:

NP	→	Art Noun	
Noun	→	N Num	Num(ber)
Num	→	{sing, pl}	sing(ular); pl(ural)

Lexical rule:

N	→	{BOY, GIRL . . .}

Figure 14.1

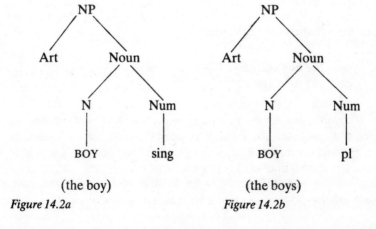

(the boy)   (the boys)

Figure 14.2a   *Figure 14.2b*

If we now think about the rules for realizing the various morphemes, there is a problem. Each of the morphemes in Figure 14.2b can be related to a single morph – Art: *the*; BOY: *boy*; pl: *-s*. But what about Figure 14.2a? We appear to have one too many morphemes – Art: *the*; BOY: *boy*; but sing:?

Before we examine this problem further, consider some of the 'irregular' noun forms in English:

4
singular	plural
man	men
mouse	mice
goose	geese

As we have noted before, there appears to be no acceptable segmentation into morphs of the plural forms. An analysis into morphemes is, however, not only possible but clearly desirable. We want to say that *man* realizes the morpheme string {MAN + sing} and *men* the morpheme string {MAN + pl}, in exactly the same way as *boy* realizes the morpheme string{BOY + sing} and *boys* the morpheme string {BOY + pl}. This implies that we should expand the lexical rule in Figure 14.1 to:

5 N → {BOY, GIRL, MAN, MOUSE, GOOSE, . . .}

Let us now turn to morphological realization rules. Consider first the plural forms. As far as the rules for forms like *boys* are concerned, no great problem arises. We can have quite straightforward rules of the form:

6 BOY → *boy*
    pl → *-s*

We will call rules of this sort 'agglutinative' rules; such rules have a single morpheme on the left-hand side of the rule matched to a single morph on the right-hand side. As far as rules for forms like *men* are concerned, we can, since we have decided that these forms are unsegmentable, have rules of the form:

7 MAN + pl → *men*

We call rules like this 'fusional'; fusional rules have more than one morpheme on the left-hand side of the rule matched to a single morph on the right-hand side. A rule like this seems to capture well the fact that *men* is unsegmentable, and that it realizes two morphemes.

Let us now turn to the singular forms where, as we noted above, we seem to have one morpheme too many. There are a number of possible solutions. One is a fusional realization rule here too:

8 BOY + sing → *boy*

Alternatively, we might say that BOY corresponds to *boy* and that there is no singular morph, that is, an analysis involving the use of a 'zero' morph, as discussed in the preceding chapter. However, postulating zero morphs brings problems (and if we follow this solution we will need a lot of zero morphs to account for the relevant facts of English, even in this small area). Instead, we propose the following rule:

9 N + sing → N

This rule can be understood to mean: for any string {N + sing}, delete the morpheme {sing}. In other words, simply delete {sing}. We call rules like this 'null realization rules'.

A different kind of solution is more radical. Since only plural forms have a marker, we could consider {pl} to be optional. In this analysis singular forms will simply be unmarked for number. This implies the constituent structure rules:

10 NP → Art N
      N → N (+ pl)

These rules yield the tree diagrams of Figure 14.3.

Consider each solution in turn. The last solution, using the rules in **10**, is superficially attractive, since it seems to suggest that we need only postulate a morpheme when we find a corresponding morph. But we have already seen that this is unsatisfactory for all forms, for example, the irregular plurals. A more fundamental problem is that rules like those of **10** fail to give any systematic account of the category of number. This is a drawback at a theoretical level since we expect our grammar to give a systematic account of such categories and even at a practical level a systematic

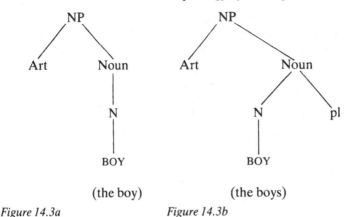

Figure 14.3a   Figure 14.3b

account of the category of number makes easier the description of the facts of such grammatical characteristics as number agreement between subjects and verb, to which we turn shortly.

The solution of **8** is perfectly possible, but it too misses a proper generalization: that singular nouns appear in the base form alone. This leaves solution **9**; it has the advantage of being able to postulate a morpheme {sing} and allows us to state the correct generalization that singular nouns are never marked by any morph; they occur in their simple stem form. We can summarize our rules as in Figure 14.4.

Constituent structure rules:

NP	→	Art Noun
Noun	→	N Num	Num(ber)
Num	→	{sing, pl}	sing(ular); pl(ural)

Lexical rule:

N → {BOY, GIRL, MAN, MOUSE . . .}

Morphological realization rules:

MAN + pl	→	*men*
MOUSE + pl	→	*mice*
N + sing	→	N
MAN	→	*man*
MOUSE	→	*mouse*
BOY	→	*boy*
GIRL	→	*girl*
pl	→	*-s*

Figure 14.4

In the morphological realization rules, the first two are fusional rules, the third is a null realization rule and the rest of the rules are agglutinative. As we saw in the last chapter, rules of this kind must be ordered, or at least partially ordered, or incorrect derivations arise (for example the first rule must precede the fourth and the last or we shall produce forms like *mans*; children, of course, sometimes do).

14.2   Subject–verb concord

Now consider the verb forms in our example sentences:

> **11a**   The boy yawns (= **1a**)
> **11b**   The boys yawn

> **12a**   The boy yawned (= **2a**)
> **12b**   The boys yawned

The forms shown are the 'regular' forms of the verb, since they are the commonest, and are used with new borrowings or coinings. As far as a morphological analysis is concerned, there are three distinct word forms, which can be analysed as *yawn*, *yawn-s* and *yawn-ed*. The formal identification of these morphs can be reinforced by semantic criteria. The forms in **12a** and **12b** are appropriately applied to a situation which happened at some time previous to the time of utterance, whereas those in **11a** and **11b** are more appropriately applied to a situation describing either a general truth or habit (it is the habit of boys to yawn, and so on), or possibly to a situation actually happening at the moment of utterance – rather in the fashion of a commentary. The distinction is usually characterized as past (**12a** and **12b**) and non-past (**11a** and **11b**). An analysis into morphemes needs to postulate the same distinction, which we can, following tradition, identify as the category of tense.

Now consider the pair of forms *yawns* and *yawn* in **11a** and **11b**. We have already identified the distinction between *boy* and *boys* as involving the grammatical category of numbers; we now note that the distinction between *yawn* and *yawns* correlates with this. We find sentences like **11a** and **11b**, but we will not find:

> **13a**   *the boy yawn
> **13b**   *the boys yawns

and this relationship is, of course, shared by other different sentences similar to **11a** and **11b**:

14a   the cat yawns; the cats yawn
14b   the boy walks; the boys walk

The selection of the appropriate verb form depends on the number of the subject NP; if the subject is singular, then the verb too has to be singular, and this is marked by the -*s* suffix; if the subject is plural, then the verb too has to be plural, though this is not marked overtly. This suggests we should characterize the distinction in the verb forms too as one of number.

Note at this point that the criteria for setting up these morphemes of number in the verb involve syntactic considerations (that is, the need to account for concord or agreement) that go beyond a strict analysis into morphs. We are now able to postulate that the morphemes realized by the forms *yawns* and *yawn* are:

15a *yawns*:   {YAWN + non-past + sing}
15b *yawn*:   {YAWN + non-past + pl}

This morphemic analysis can be represented in constituent structure trees of the form shown in Figure 14.5.

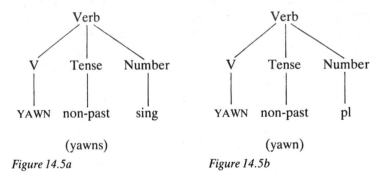

(yawns)   (yawn)

Figure 14.5a   *Figure 14.5b*

Once again we have more morphemes than morphs, and as before a number of solutions suggest themselves. We could have fusional rules:

16a   YAWN + non-past + sing → *yawns*
16b   YAWN + non-past + pl → *yawn*

but they are open to the same objection as the comparable rule for the singular forms of nouns discussed in **8**, they miss an obvious generalization. More realistically we could have a rule for the lexeme YAWN:

    17 YAWN → *yawn*

and then consider realization rules for the grammatical morphemes. Here a fusional rule may seem appropriate for the singular form:

    18 non-past + sing → -*s*

But what of the plural form? Neither {non-past} nor {pl} have a realization. We can have a rule:

    19 V + non-past + pl → V

analogous to rule **9**; that is, a 'null realization' rule. Yet another solution is to say that {non-past} has no realization in either the singular or plural forms, that singular is realized by -*s*, and plural has no realization. This suggests rules like:

20a	V + non past	→	V
20b	sing	→	-*s*
20c	V + pl	→	V
20d	YAWN	→	*yawn*

We provisionally adopt this last solution. Before leaving these rules, observe that the rules in **17–19** and those in **20** make somewhat different generalizations about the forms in question. The first set of rules, **17–19**, asserts that -*s* is a marker of both tense and number, that is, that it is a singular tense marker. The second set of rules, **20**, asserts that there is no marker of tense and that -*s* is merely a singular marker.

Now consider *yawned* in **12a** and **12b**. These forms have already been characterized as being {past} in comparison with the forms in **11a** and **11b** which are {non-past}. We need to consider whether *yawned* in **12a** is {sing} and yawned in **12b** is {pl}, paralleling the singular/plural description of *yawn* and *yawns*. We may take either of two opposite positions. We can assert that verb forms always concord, or agree, with their subject nouns in number, but that in past tense forms there is no overt marker of this agreement; *yawned* in **12a** realizes {YAWN + past + sing}. Alternatively, we can say that verbs only concord with the subject NPs in the non-past, as suggested by **20**, and there is no concord at all in the past. So *yawned* in both **12a** and **12b** simply realizes {YAWN + past}, and the question of number agreement is irrelevant, since verbs in the past do not concord.

A problem for either of these analyses is just how to capture the relevant generalization in terms of rules. There are two problems: one related to the realization of the tense morphemes and the other related to the number morphemes. Let us consider them in turn.

Tense is a category that, in English, is associated with the verb. We have suggested that this category has two terms: {past} and {non-past}. We have further hypothesized that {past} can be associated with the morph *-ed* and {non-past} has a null realization. It may be argued then that we can dispense with a morpheme {non-past} altogether. But this raises the same sort of objections as we raised to a comparable situation with singular nouns, discussed with respect to **10**; it misses an important generalization about English verb groups. Furthermore, we find the morphemes {past} and {non-past} useful for other purposes, for example co-occurrence restrictions with adverbs of time, which can be accounted for, at least in part, in terms of co-occurrence restrictions with tense morphemes; the tense morphemes have a syntactic function irrespective of the fact that one of them need not be realized by any overt morph. We therefore retain tense morphemes in the verb.

Number morphemes pose a different problem. We can argue, for English, that number is primarily a category associated with the noun, only secondarily a category associated with the verb; the subject noun controls the number morpheme on the verb. For example, the verb cannot be in the singular form if the subject noun is plural (**the boys yawns*). In traditional terms this relationship is called concord and the noun considered to be the 'controller' of the concord. But does the subject noun always require the verb to show concord? As we have seen, this question can be answered in two ways. We can say that the verb always agrees in number with the subject (that is, always has a number morpheme) but that this agreement is not always marked with an overt morph of number agreement. This solution can be diagrammed, informally, as:

21a $\{N + sing\} - \{V + non\text{-}past + sing\}$ (*yawns*)
     $\{N + sing\} - \{V + past + sing\}$ (*yawned*)
21b $\{N + pl\} - \{V + non\text{-}past + pl\}$ (*yawn*)
     $\{N + pl\} - \{V + past + pl\}$ (*yawned*)

At the other extreme, we can say that the verb only concords with the subject in number when the subject is singular and the verb is non-past. This solution we can diagram as:

22a $\{N + sing\} - \{V + non\text{-}past + sing\}$ (*yawns*)
     $\{N + sing\} - \{V + past\}$ (*yawned*)
22b $\{N + pl\} - \{V + non\text{-}past\}$ (*yawn*)
     $\{N + pl\} - \{V + past\}$ (*yawned*)

As far as morphology is concerned, the solution shown in **22** is simpler in that we have fewer morphemes to account for that have no overt realization; the solution shown in **21** leaves us with a number of morphemes with no overt realization. Solution **22** also enables us to say that a form like *yawned* is simply the past tense form of YAWN (there being no number agreement in the past), where the solution **21** entails our having to say that *yawned* is either the past tense singular form of YAWN or the past tense plural form of YAWN. A further advantage of **22** is that it enables us to make clear in the grammar that number is primarily a category of the noun, and that it is a verbal category only secondarily, and by concord.

How, then, can we express this generalization in terms of rules? Constituent structure rules for these phenomena suffer two drawbacks. First, they are extremely clumsy to write (the reader is invited to try), but more importantly they do not express the generalization so clearly. More appropriate is to formulate a transformational rule that has the effect of copying the morpheme of number from the NP subject on to the verb. This means that in the constituent structure we only need to develop number as a category of the noun (which is what we want); the transformational rule then copies it on to the verb (also what we want). The rules in Figure 14.6 do this.

For example, the constituent structure and lexical rules can develop a tree shown in Figure 14.7. The concord rule operates on this structure since the structure meets the structural analysis specified in SA (a singular N is followed by a non-past verb). The

Constituent structure rules:

S	→	NP VP
VP	→	Verb
NP	→	Art Noun
Noun	→	N Num
Num	→	{sing, pl}
Verb	→	V Tense
Tense	→	{past, non-past}

Lexical rules:

N	→	{BOY, GIRLS . . .}
V	→	{YAWN . . .}

Subject–verb concord:

SA: $_{NP}(Art + N + sing) - _{Verb}(V + _{Tense}(non\text{-}past))$

SC: $_{NP}(Art + N + sing) - _{Verb}(V + _{Tense}(non\text{-}past + sing))$

Figure 14.6

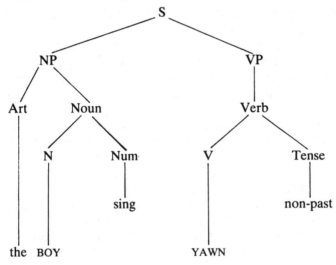

Figure 14.7

structural change (SC) specifies that we must add a morpheme {sing} to the tense node; the reason for this particular analysis will become clear later in the chapter. The resultant structure is shown in Figure 14.8. Realization rules operating on Figure 14.8 yield *The boy yawns*.

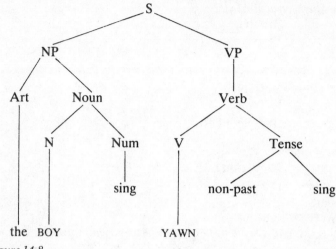

Figure 14.8

Consider the advantages of the analysis proposed. To begin with, we have identified the categories of number and tense as being primarily categories of, respectively, the noun and the verb; this is shown by the constituent structure rules. We have identified the category of number as only secondarily a category of the verb (shown by the fact that it is derived by the concord rule) and then only a category under certain conditions (that is, when the verb is non-past and singular).

Before closing the discussion, note that, just as we find irregular noun plurals in English (for example *goose*: *geese*), so too we find irregular past tense forms of verbs – *run*: *ran*, *think*: *thought*, and so on. It is clear that the relevant past tense forms can be analysed as realizing morpheme sequences such as {RUN + past} and {THINK + past}. Morphological realization rules for such forms are shown in Figure 14.12 below. They are similar to those introduced for the noun forms discussed at the beginning of the section.

Before completing this section, we will illustrate concord rules with a further example. Consider the following NPs:

23a   the boy
23b   the boys

24a   a boy
24b   some boys

The opposition *the* : *a* has been traditionally described as one of definiteness, the category of definiteness having the terms definite and indefinite. This is done on the grounds that in uttering a sentence like:

25 I want the boy to come and see me this evening

the speaker typically has some particular individual in mind, whereas in uttering a sentence like:

26 I want a boy to come and see me this evening

no particular boy is in the mind of the speaker and any boy will serve. This characterization suffices for our present purposes, and we postulate morphemes {def(inite)} and {indef(inite)} to account for the distinction. What, then, of the plural forms **23b** and **24b**? Consider first the forms **23a** and **23b**. The article morph is the same in both cases: *the*. We encounter the problem discussed with respect to agreement in the verb. If we analyse *the* in **23a** as 'the singular form of the definite article' and *the* in **23b** as 'the plural form of the definite article' then the forms correspond, respectively, to morpheme strings {def + sing} and {def + pl}. Alternatively, we can say that *the* is simply the definite article, realizing the morpheme {def} and no question of number arises. The latter seems a more satisfactory solution since it leads us to postulate fewer morphemes that have no overt realization.

In the forms of **24a** and **24b**, it is possible to argue that the forms *a* and *some* are, respectively, 'the singular form of the indefinite article' and 'the plural form of the indefinite article'. Evidence for such an analysis is shown if we compare **26** with:

27 I want some boys to come and see me this evening

In **26** the speaker has no particular boy in mind and any boy will serve, but the speaker clearly has only a single boy in mind; in **27** the speaker has a number of boys in mind, though no particular number and no particular boys. The opposition appears to be between a single unspecified individual and an unspecified number of unspecified individuals. This leads us to postulate that *a* and *some* realize, respectively, the morpheme strings {indef + sing} and {indef + pl}.

If we accept this analysis we need to consider how it can be incorporated in our grammar and once again a concord rule seems an appropriate mechanism. The rules in Figure 14.9 will serve. The concord rule is to be understood exactly as the previous rule, except that here we have an additional notational convention; an item in one pair of square brackets is matched with the corresponding item in the other pair of square brackets. For example, the constituent structure rules generate the trees in Figures 14.10a and 14.10b.

Constituent structure rules:

NP $\rightarrow$ Art Noun
Noun $\rightarrow$ N Num
Num $\rightarrow$ {sing, pl}
Art $\rightarrow$ {def, indef}

Article–noun concord:

SA: $NP(_{Art}(\text{indef}) - N - \begin{bmatrix} \text{sing} \\ \text{pl} \end{bmatrix})$

SC: $NP(_{Art}(\text{indef} + \text{sing}) - N - \begin{bmatrix} \text{sing} \\ \text{pl} \end{bmatrix})$

Figure 14.9

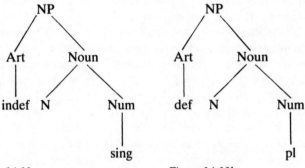

Figure 14.10a   *Figure 14.10b*

The concord rule operates on the structure in Figure 14.10a to yield the derived tree shown in Figure 14.11. Note that the concord rule cannot operate on the structure of Figure 14.10b because it does not meet the structural analysis. This description corresponds to our observation that the definite article does not concord with the noun in number.

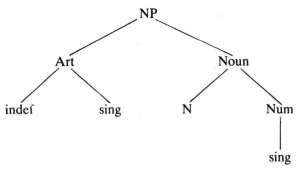

Figure 14.11

The rules we have proposed are summarized in Figure 14.12, to which have been added appropriate realization rules.

Constituent structure rules:

S	→	NP VP
VP	→	Verb
NP	→	Art Noun
Noun	→	N Num
Num	→	{sing, pl}
Art	→	{def, indef}
Verb	→	V Tense
Tense	→	{past, non-past}

Lexical rules:

N	→	{BOY, GIRL . . .}
V	→	{YAWN . . .}

Subject–verb concord:

SA: $_{NP}(Art + N + sing) - _{Verb}(V + _{Tense}(non\text{-}past))$

SC: $_{NP}(Art + N + sing) - _{Verb}(V + _{Tense}(non\text{-}past + sing))$

Article–noun concord:

SA: $_{NP}(_{Art}(indef) - N - \begin{bmatrix} sing \\ pl \end{bmatrix})$

SC: $_{NP}(_{Art}(indef + sing) - N - \begin{bmatrix} sing \\ pl \end{bmatrix})$

Morphological realization rules:

(1)	MAN + pl	$\rightarrow$	*men*
(2)	GOOSE + pl	$\rightarrow$	*geese*
(3)	N + sing	$\rightarrow$	N
(4)	BOY	$\rightarrow$	*boy*
(5)	GIRL	$\rightarrow$	*girl*
(6)	MAN	$\rightarrow$	*man*
(7)	GOOSE	$\rightarrow$	*goose*
(8)	pl	$\rightarrow$	*-s*
(9)	RUN + past	$\rightarrow$	*ran*
(10)	V + non-past	$\rightarrow$	V
(11)	RUN	$\rightarrow$	*run*
(12)	YAWN	$\rightarrow$	*yawn*
(13)	WALK	$\rightarrow$	*walk*
(14)	sing	$\rightarrow$	*-s*
(15)	past	$\rightarrow$	*-ed*
(16)	def	$\rightarrow$	*the*
(17)	indef + sing	$\rightarrow$	a
(18)	indef + pl	$\rightarrow$	*some*

Figure 14.12

This grammar produces trees like Figures 14.13 and 14.14, the output after the operation of the concord rules and the morphological realization rules. There are observations on the operation of the concord rules below each diagram.

Before closing this section it is useful to point out some implications of our grammar. There is nothing 'given' about our model; it is the result of analytic decisions taken about various aspects of the structure of sentences and their constituents. Different decisions would have resulted in a different grammar. Note also that the formalization of the grammar makes totally overt those analytic decisions we have made, for instance, our observations on the scope of concord relations, and to which category the categories of number and tense 'primarily' apply.

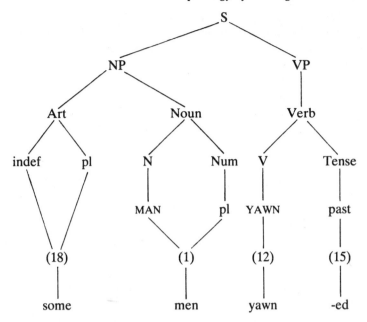

1 The numbers in brackets identify morphological realization rules from Figure 14.12.
2 Subject–verb concord has not operated since verbs only concord in number, according to our rule, when they are non-past, and when the subject is singular; neither condition is satisfied in our tree.
3 Article noun concord has operated since the article is indefinite and the noun is plural. The output is shown in the tree.

Figure 14.13

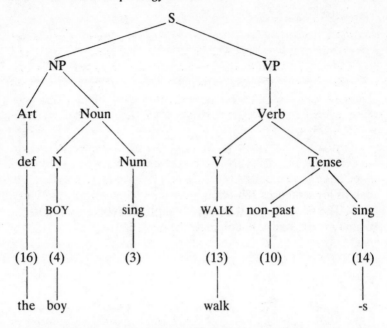

1 The numbers in brackets identify morphological realization rules from Figure 14.12. Note that {sing} in the NP (rule **3**) and {non-past} in the V (rule **10**) have null realization.
2 Subject–verb concord has operated since the subject NP is singular and the verb non-past.
3 Article–noun concord has not operated since this rule only applies to indefinite articles, and the article here is definite.

Figure 14.14

14.3   Tense and aspect in the English verb

We now turn to consider the morphology of English verb forms in more detail. Consider the sentences:

28a   The dog *bit* the cat
28b   The dog *has bitten* the cat
28c   The dog *is biting* the cat
28d   The dog *has been biting* the cat
28e   The dog *will bite* the cat
28f   The dog *may have bitten* the cat

All the sentences have the same subject NP (*the dog*) and the same object NP (*the cat*). They differ in the internal structure of what we will call the 'verb group', italicized in the examples. Each verb group consists minimally of a form of the verb BITE, which we call the main or lexical verb. It is always the last constituent. The main verb may be preceded by one or more other verbs – in our examples we have forms of the verbs BE, HAVE, WILL and MAY. We call these auxiliary verbs.

We will consider first those sentences like **28b–28f** which contain auxiliary verbs, and return later to consider sentences like **28a**, which has only a main verb. An appropriate constituent structure analysis for sentences **28b–28f** is illustrated schematically in Figure 14.15. The node Aux will be developed to dominate one or more auxiliary verbs, and V to dominate the main verb.

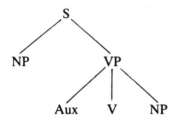

Figure 14.15

The principal function of the main verb is to introduce appropriate lexical content – all the sentences have to do with 'biting'. The principal function of the auxiliaries, on the other hand, is to relate the sentence to 'temporal', 'modal', 'aspectual' and 'voice' distinctions.

Temporal distinctions locate an event in time:

29a The dog *is* biting the cat (*now*)
29b The dog *was* biting the cat (*yesterday afternoon*)
29c The dog *will* bite the cat (*tomorrow, I expect*)

The grammatical category of 'tense' is described in more detail with respect to example **43** below and the way the category of tense relates to temporal distinctions of the kind illustrated in the examples is discussed in Chapter 16.

Modal distinctions are realized by a class of 'modal auxiliary verbs' including MAY, CAN, WILL, SHALL and MUST and relate, *inter alia*, to the speaker's judgement as to the possibility (likelihood,

probability, etc.) that the event described in the sentence is true
(see Palmer 1986 for a thorough discussion of modality):

30a   The dog *may* have bitten the cat
                (it is possible that it did)
30b   The dog *must* have bitten the cat
                (it is probable that it did)

If there is a modal auxiliary it must be the first auxiliary in the verb
group (compare **31a** and **31b**) and no verb group can contain more
than one modal auxiliary (**31c**):

31a   The dog may have bitten the cat
31b   *The dog has may bitten the cat
31c   *The dog may will have bitten the cat

Furthermore, whatever verb follows a modal auxiliary must be in its
'base' form:

32a   The dog will *bite* the cat
32b   The dog may *be* biting the cat
32c   The dog can't *have* bitten the cat

Aspectual distinctions describe the way an event is distributed
over time. The aspectual distinctions overtly realized in the English
verb group are 'perfective' and 'progressive'. Perfective aspect is
realized by the 'perfective auxiliary verb' HAVE and indicates that
an action has been completed

33a   The dog *has* bitt*en* the cat (non-past perfective)
33b   The dog *had* bitt*en* the cat (past perfective)

As the examples indicate it may combine with tense. When the
perfect auxiliary HAVE is chosen then the following verb, main or
auxiliary, must be in the 'past participle' form. Exactly what shape
the past participle takes depends on the particular verb involved,
but it is frequently a form which ends in the suffix *-ed* or *-en*:

34a   The dog *has* frighten*ed* the cat
34b   The dog may *have* bitt*en* the cat
34c   The dog *has* be*en* biting the cat

though not always:

35a The man *has hit* the dog
35b John *has swum* the Channel

To remind us of the formation rules for the perfective auxiliary we represent it as {HAVE + pp}; HAVE because the auxiliary involved is a form of HAVE and pp to indicate that the following verb is in the past participle form.

Progressive aspect is realized by the 'progressive auxiliary verb' BE and indicates that an action is or was in progress:

36a The cat *is* bit*ing* the dog (non-past progressive)
36b The cat *was* bit*ing* the dog (past progressive)

When the progressive auxiliary is chosen then the following verb must be a 'present participle'. This is always an *-ing* form:

37a The dog has *be*en bit*ing* the cat
37b The dog may *be* bit*ing* the cat

As before, to remind us of the formation rules for the progressive auxiliary, we will represent it as {BE + *-ing*}; BE because this is the progressive auxiliary and *-ing* to indicate that the following form is an *-ing* form.

Voice indicates whether the sentence is in the active or passive form (cf. Chapter 10.2). As we have seen, passive sentences involve the additional 'passive auxiliary verb' BE.

38a The dogs have bitten the cat
38b The cat has *be*en bitt*en* by the dogs

39a The dog is biting the cat
39b The cat is *being* bitt*en* by the dog

When the passive BE is chosen the following verb is in the 'past participle' form. On the same principles as before, we will describe this as involving {BE + pp}. Note that example **39a** involves the progressive auxiliary, {BE + ing} and the corresponding passive sentence, **39b**, thus involves both the progressive (BE + *ing*: *is* be*ing*) and the passive (BE + pp: *be*ing bitt*en*). Progressive and passive both involve forms of BE; they are distinguished by the form of the following verb.

The above account shows a number of peculiar features about the structure of the verb group in English; in particular, the choice of a particular auxiliary has consequences for the verb that immediately follows it. This fact makes it extremely cumbersome to describe the English verb group using constituent structure rules. We therefore resort to a more 'abstract' type of representation for the auxiliaries: {HAVE + pp}, {BE + *-ing*} and {BE + pp}, noting that pp and *-ing* represent the formation rules for the *following* item, whatever that happens to be. We can now say that the verb group consists of, minimally, a main verb, and the main verb may, optionally, be preceded by one or more auxiliaries. These must be in the order shown schematically in Figure 14.16. In the example sentence the first auxiliary is MAY. A modal must be followed by a base form, hence the base form *have* of the perfective auxiliary HAVE. This is followed by the past participle form of BE, *been*. This BE is the progressive BE and is therefore followed by the *-ing* form, *being*. This time BE is the passive BE, and so is followed by the past participle form of the main verb, *bitten*.

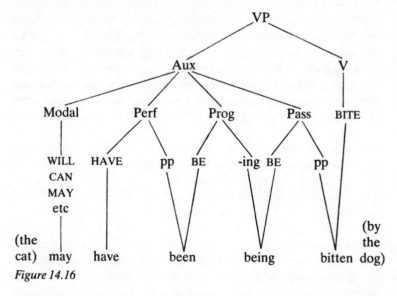

Figure 14.16

In the example all the auxiliaries have been chosen. Obviously, it is not obligatory to have them all: none, all, or any may be chosen, providing only that those that are chosen maintain the order shown in Figure 14.16. Note that verb groups cannot be formed with the auxiliaries in arbitrary orders:

40a *Modal Prog Perf
40b *The dog will be having bitten the cat

41a *Modal Pass Prog
41b *The cat will be been biting by the dog

42a *Prog Modal
42b *The dog is canning bite the cat

We must now look at verb groups with no auxiliary:

43a The dog bites the cat (every day)
43b The dog bit the cat (yesterday)

The distinction shown between the forms *bites* and *bit* is generally described as one of 'tense', the form in **43b** being the 'past tense' form, and that in **43a** the 'non-past' form. The typical function of the 'past' form is to refer to events located in 'past' time, that is, time previous to the moment of utterance of the sentence involved. The other form, as we have noted, is usually contrasted as the 'non-past' form. The form often used in this sense is the present progressive (*the dog is biting the cat* (*at this moment*)), and this verb group involves the progressive auxiliary. Typical uses of the non-past form are to refer to habits (as in **43a**), general truths (*dogs bite cats*), and so on.

In the orthographic form of the language the past form of most main verbs is generally formed by the addition of the suffix *-ed* to the stem (*kill-ed, frighten-ed, want-ed*, and so on), but this is not the case for all verbs, as, for example, *bit* in **48a**, rather than **bited* (and similarly *run: ran, think: thought*, and so on). For now we follow the traditional account and simply refer to all such forms as 'the past form of KILL', 'the past form of BITE', and so on. The past : non-past alternation shown in **43a** and **43b** is also characteristic of verb groups that contain auxiliaries:

44a The dog has bitten the cat
44b The dog had bitten the cat

45a   The dog is biting the cat
45b   The dog was biting the cat

46a   The dog can bite the cat
46b   The dog could bite the cat

47a   The dog bites the cat
47b   The cat is bitten by the dog

48a   The dog bit the cat
48b   The cat was bitten by the dog

In all cases the first verb in the verb group shows the alternation in tense, however many items there are in the group. Only this first position in the verb group is open to this alternation, since the form of verbs other than the first is determined by what precedes them. This is most clearly shown in the last two pairs of examples. In **47a** and **48a** the first verb in the verb group is the main verb itself, and this consequently shows the tense alternation. In the corresponding passive sentences **47b** and **48b** the passive auxiliary is introduced before the main verb: the passive auxiliary is now the first verb in the verb group, and consequently shows the tense alternation. The main verb itself must be in the past participle form, since this form, as we have seen, is the form that follows the passive auxiliary.

How are we to treat these facts? Hitherto our description has by and large followed the surface order, but as we saw in Chapter 12, section 12.6 we do not need to do this. We will instead adopt a description which treats tense as a sort of auxiliary and, furthermore, as the first auxiliary in the verb group. What is at issue can be seen by considering the verb groups in **47** and **48** as represented in Figures 14.17 and 14.18. Figure 14.17a and Figure 14.18a are identical except for the introduction of the passive auxiliary – and similarly Figures 14.17b and 14.18b.

To accommodate this new approach we must modify the schematic constituent structure representation for the verb group shown in Figure 14.16, to that shown in Figure 14.19. We can summarize the description captured in Figure 14.19 as follows. Of the auxiliaries, only Tense is obligatory (since all verb groups in simple sentences are tensed) and this category has two terms {past} and {non-past}. The other auxiliaries are optional, but if they occur they must occur in the order shown. The category Modal can be

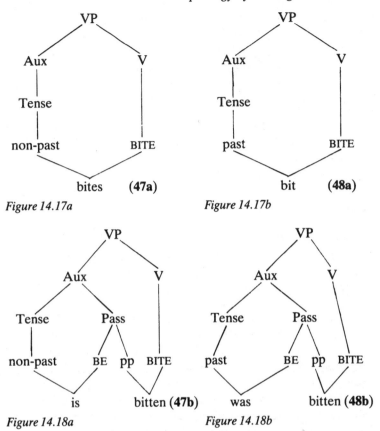

Figure 14.17a   Figure 14.17b

Figure 14.18a   Figure 14.18b

realized by any one of the modal auxiliaries (a form of CAN, WILL, MAY, and so on). The category Perf is realized by a form of HAVE, which form depending on what other auxiliary immediately precedes it, and is followed by a verb in the past participle form, this we represented by the notation {HAVE + pp}. The category Prog is realized by a form of BE, which form depending on what precedes, and it is followed by a verb in the *-ing* form; we have shown this as {BE + *-ing*}. The category Pass is also realized by a form of BE, but this time followed by the past participle form: {BE + pp}. The realization of Perf, Prog and Pass is 'discontinuous': they are realized by two non-contiguous morphs. An example, for the verb group *has been walking*, is shown diagrammatically in Figure 14.20. In Figure 14.20 *has* is formed by the fusion of non-past + HAVE. *been* and *walking* are formed agglutinatively by the suffixation of *en*

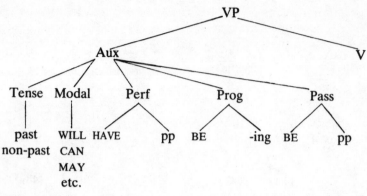

Figure 14.19

and *-ing* to the stems *be* and *walk*. Perf is realized discontinuously by (*has . . . -en*), and Prog by (*be . . . -ing*).

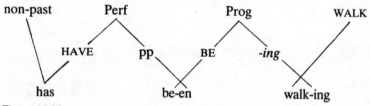

Figure 14.20

Constituent structure rules:

S	→	NP VP
NP	→	Art Noun
Noun	→	N + Num
Num	→	{sing, pl}
Art	→	{def, indef}
VP	→	Aux Verb
Aux	→	Tense (Modal) (Perf) (Prog)
Tense	→	{past, non-past}
Modal	→	{CAN, WILL, MAY . . .}
Perf	→	HAVE pp
Prog	→	BE *-ing*

Lexical rule:

V	→	WALK

Figure 14.21

The most economical grammar to deal with these facts supposes that a constituent structure rule introduces those elements that are later to be discontinuous as a single constituent; the discontinuity is handled by a later reordering rule. Let us see how this might be managed for the examples we already have. We propose the rules in Figure 14.21. These rules product strings like:

49a   past   WALK

49b   past   Perf   WALK
       past   HAVE   +   pp   WALK

49c   past   Perf   Prog   WALK
       past   HAVE   +   pp BE + *-ing*   WALK

49d   non-past   Modal   Prog   WALK
       non-past   WILL   BE   +   *-ing* WALK

To account for the discontinuities we propose a rule:

50   *Affix hopping:*

Any affix which is found to the left of a verb is to be moved to the right of that verb. An affix may hop a verb only once; past, non-past, pp and *-ing* are affixes; any modal HAVE, BE and any item categorized as V and introduced by a lexical rule are verbs.

Applying this rule to the strings in **49** we get the results shown in **51**

51a   past   WALK
     →   WALK + past
          (*walked*)

51b   past   HAVE + pp   WALK
     →   HAVE + past   WALK + pp
            had   *walked*

51c   past   HAVE + pp   BE + *-ing*   WALK
     →   HAVE + past   BE + pp   WALK + *-ing*
            had   *been*   *walking*

51d non-past   WILL   BE + *-ing*   WALK
→   WILL + non-past   BE   WALK + *-ing*
             will   *be*   *walking*

We now need morphological realization rules. For the data we have been considering we can propose those in Figure 14.22 (formulated as 'orthographic rules'). Our examples now become:

52a   *walked* (the past of WALK)
52b   *had walked* (the past perfective of WALK)
52c   *had been walking* (the past perfective progressive of WALK)
52d   *will be walking* (the non-past modal WILL progressive of WALK)

The reader is invited to try other combinations as permitted in the rules.

Morphological realization rules:

HAVE + past	→	*had*
HAVE + non-past	→	*have*
BE + past	→	*was*
BE + non-past	→	*is*
BE + pp	→	*been*
HAVE	→	*have*
BE	→	*be*
CAN + past	→	*could* (and similarly for
CAN + non-past	→	*can* WILL and MAY)
pp	→	*-ed*
past	→	*-ed*
WALK	→	*walk*

Figure 14.22

We now try to accommodate within this type of description the facts of number agreement between subject and verb. We discussed some aspects of this problem earlier in the chapter, but two amendments are needed to bring our account into line with our new model. The first is needed to deal with number agreement as it affects all the verbal auxiliaries (our previous account dealt only with verb groups with a single verb, past or non-past – forms like *walk, walks, walked*). The second has to do with the order of morphemes: our previous account supposed that tense was introduced following the verb, and we have now decided to place it as the first auxiliary; the changes that this new analysis requires are relatively trivial.

The facts of English number agreement are complex and can, as we have seen, be analysed in a number of different ways. In line with our previous discussion, we will suppose that verbs only agree in number when there is an overt marker of number on one of the auxiliaries or on the main verb. With this assumption, the facts can be summarized as follows:

(1)   Number agreement is only shown on the first item in the verb group, whatever that is:

53a   The man walks/ the men walk
53b   The man is walking/ the men are walking
53c   The man has walked/ the men have walked

Note that the first item in the verb group is also the item that shows tense. Tense and number go together, even in interrogatives:

54a   Does the man walk/do the men walk?
54b   Is the man walking/are the men walking?
54c   Has the man walked/have the men walked?

Tense and number are said to be cumulated, that is, realized together, on the first verb in the verb group.

(2)   Modal verbs never show number agreement:

55a   The man can go/the men can go
55b   The man could go/the men could go

(3)   With non-past verb forms, when the subject is singular, HAVE, BE and the main verb show number agreement:

56a   The man has gone
56b   The man is going
56c   The man goes

(4)   With non-past verb forms, when the subject is plural, only BE shows number agreement (but not HAVE or the main verb, which are in their stem forms):

57a   The men have gone
57b   The men are going
57c   The men go

(5)   With past verb forms, only BE shows number agreement in both singular and plural:

58a   The man was going/the men were going
58b   The man had gone/the men had gone
58c   The man went/the men went

We can summarize these facts in terms of the three rules in Figure 14.23.

Verb number agreement (obligatory):
(a)   SA: $X - N - sing - _{Tense}(non\text{-}past) - V - Y$
        SC: $X - N - sing - _{Tense}(non\text{-}past + sing) - V - Y$
        (on condition V is not a modal)

(b)   SA: $X - N - pl - _{Tense}(non\text{-}past) - BE - Y$
        SC: $X - N - pl - _{Tense}(non\text{-}past + pl) - BE - Y$

(c)   SA: $X - N - \begin{bmatrix} sing \\ pl \end{bmatrix} - _{Tense}(past) - BE - Y$
        SC: $X - N - \begin{bmatrix} sing \\ pl \end{bmatrix} - _{Tense}(past + \begin{bmatrix} sing \\ pl \end{bmatrix}) - BE - Y$

Figure 14.23

The summary in (1)–(5) above is expressed in these rules as follows:

(1) is shown by the fact that the number morpheme is adjoined as a sister to tense (and dominated by tense), showing that the two are cumulated. The generalization is expressed like this so that in formulating the question rule we can say that tense hops over the subject NP, and tense brings number along with it (see **54**).

(2) is shown by the fact that modals are specifically excluded from the scope of any of the rules proposed.

(3)–(5) are directly represented in the rules (a)–(c) in Figure 14.23 respectively.

The number agreement rule, expressed this way, simplifies our morphological realization rules, though it clearly leads to a complex statement of the number agreement rule. It is possible to state the number agreement rule in a different way. We can, for instance, assert that all verbs agree in number with their subjects; but this complicates the morphological realization rules since we then must say, for example of modals, that whereas they agree in number with their subjects (as stated by the rule), number agreement is never realized in any way. It seems preferable to formulate the rules as we have done in Figure 14.23 so number agreement is only held to occur when there is an overt marker of this agreement.

Technical terms

affix hopping	null realization
agreement	number
aspect	paradigm
auxiliary	perfective aspect
concord	progressive aspect
cumulation	

Exercises

1 *Number agreement*

In English present-tense verbs agree with the subject noun in number: *the boys are leaving* vs *the boy is leaving*. A plural noun requires a plural verb. Agreement in English presents certain subtleties, as the form of the noun can be misleading with respect to its number. A distinction is drawn between syntactic number agreement and semantic number agreement, and the following examples illustrate the problem. For each example, decide whether it is acceptable. For each unacceptable example, try to determine why it is unacceptable. Note: Number agreement works differently in different varieties of English. The examples below are to be judged relative to standard written (British) English.

1   The news from Auchtermuchty were not encouraging
2   The scissors is in the top lefthand drawer
3   Your trousers has just been put into the washing machine
4   Linguistics is easy
5   These statistics were not easy to interpret
6   Statistics are taught in some schools
7   Statistics are a useful tool
8   The committee are discussing the problem
9   The team is celebrating victory
10 Liverpool is unhappy about the referee [during commentary]

Draw up a list of other nouns that create the same problems of agreement.

2   *Concord in Luganda*
This exercise builds on exercises in Chapter 13. In the data below, all the strings are morphologically analysed. All the six strings in any one group have the same structure, indicated at the head of the group. Within each group of six the first three examples are 'singular' and the second three are 'plural'. The first example in each group of three contains a noun from class 1 as established in previous exercises, the second from class 2 and the third from class 3. As before, the noun word can be analysed as consisting of prefix + stem, the form of the prefix depending on the class of the stem. Adj(ectives), Dem(onstratives), Num(erals), and so on, can also be analysed as consisting of prefix + stem. The verb also, where appropriate, has a prefix concording with the subject noun.

NP(N + Adj + Dem1 (+ Num))

omu-kazi omu-lungi o-no	this pretty woman
en-te en-nungi e-no	this nice cow
omu-ggo omu-lungi gu-no	this nice stick

aba-kazi aba-lungi ba-no aba-satu   these three pretty women
en-te en-nungi zi-no es-satu   these three nice cows
emi-ggo emi-rungi gi-no e-satu   these three nice sticks

NP(N + Adj + Dem2) + Vb

omu-sajja omu-kadde oy-o a-li-fa   that old man will die
en-jovu en-kadde ey-o e-ri-fa   that old elephant will die
omu-ti omu-kadde ogw-o gu-li-fa   that old tree will die

aba-sajja aba-kadde ab-o ba-li-fa   those old men will die
en-jovu en-kadde ez-o zi-ri-fa   those old elephants wil! die
emi-ti emi-kadde ogy-o gi-li-fa   those old trees will die

NP(N + Adj + Dem3 (+ Num))

omu-sajja omu-tono o-li   yonder small man
en-te en-tono e-ri   yonder small cow
omu-ggo omu-tono gu-li   yonder small stick

aba-sajja aba-tono ba-li aba-taano   yonder five small men
en-te en-tono zi-ri et-taano   yonder five small cows
emi-ggo emi-tono gi-ri e-taano   yonder five small sticks

(a)   Identify the various prefixes and stems and fill in the matrix below.

class	noun	adjective	numeral	demonstrative		
				'this'	*'that'*	*'yonder'*
1 sing	omu-	omu-	—	o-	oy-	o-
pl						
2 sing			—			
pl						
3 sing			—			
pl						

(b)   Describe the pattern of 'concord' or 'agreement' shown in the examples. You can do this either in words or in terms of a rule or formula of some kind.

15   Lexical morphology

We have drawn a distinction between lexical (or derivational) morphology and inflectional morphology. The formation of new words, in the sense of new lexemes, is the field of lexical or derivational morphology. So by lexical derivation we can form the new lexemes *writ-er* and *re-write* from *write*, and from *sail* the new lexeme *sail-or*. By contrast, the grammatical forms *write-s, wrote* and *sail-s, sail-ed* are a matter of inflectional morphology. In these terms the words *writing* in the sense of 'handwriting' in *Your writing is illegible* and *sailing* in *Sailing is my favourite hobby* are both derivational formations; they are nouns. On the other hand, when part of a verb group *writing* in *He is writing a letter to his girlfriend* and *sailing* in *He is sailing round the world* are inflectional formations, both are present participles. Inflectional morphology is a matter for the grammar. We shall argue that derivational morphology is a matter for the lexicon.

We have seen that many grammatical words like *sail-ed* can be analysed into segments, which we have called morphs. We have also seen that in this case the analysis corresponds to a grammatical analysis in terms of morphemes; thus in *sail-ed* the grammatical morpheme {past}, realized as *-ed*, is affixed to the lexical morpheme SAIL, realized as *sail*.

It is obvious that many lexemes can also be analysed into segments: *writ-er, re-write* and *sail-or*. We will identify these segments too as morphs. In these examples, however, the analysis does not correspond to a grammatical analysis; this suggests that we should not treat *-er* and *re-* as morphemes, in the sense in which we have defined morpheme, as the minimal unit of the grammar. Instead we will refer to them as lexical formatives; thus in *sailor* the lexical formative *-or* is affixed to a lexical stem, *sail*.

Lexical stems may themselves be unanalysable, as in *sail*, or may themselves be complex, as for example the stem in *un-realistic*. The derivational process by which this is formed proceeds as follows. To the adjective stem *real*, which is a root, and morphologically simple, we suffix the noun formative *-ist* to form the noun *realist*. To this stem, which is complex, we suffix the adjective formative *-ic* to form the adjective *realistic*. Finally, we prefix the adjective formative *un-* to form the adjective *unrealistic*.

This suggests that the word has the internal constituent structure represented in Figure 15.1.

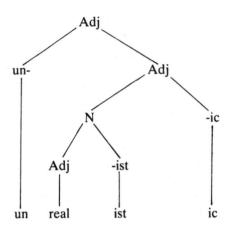

Figure 15.1

The fact that words can be analysed as having an internal constituent structure of the sort shown in Figure 15.1 suggests some general 'word formation rules'. **1–3** show a selection. Note that the rules in **1** illustrate 'noun formatives', those in **2** 'adjective formative', and so forth:

1a	Adj + *ist*	→ N	real-ist
1b	V + *-al*	→ N	refus-al
1c	V + *-ion*	→ N	confus-ion
1d	N + *-hood*	→ N	man-hood
1e	Adj + *-th*	→ N	leng-th
2a	N + *-ic*	→ Adj	angel-ic
2b	*un-* + Adj	→ Adj	un-real
2c	N + *-ish*	→ Adj	girl-ish
2d	V + *-able*	→ Adj	read-able
2e	N + *-y*	→ Adj	trend-y

3a	Adj + -*en*	→	V	rip-en
3b	N + -*ify*	→	V	beaut-ify

Rules of this sort need to be supplemented by further rules indicating whether the suffix does or does not induce phonological and orthographic change in the stems to which it is affixed. We will mention two kinds of phonological change, stress shifting and segmental change. -*ic*, **2a**, requires the syllable preceding the suffix to be stressed: ANgel: anGELic, ALcohol: alcoHOLic, and so on (stress is shown in small capitals); -*able*, **2d**, has no effect on stress: reLY: reLIable; MANage: MANageable, and so on. Segmental changes often follow on stress shifts (*angel*, /eindʒəl/ : *angelic* /andʒɛlik/) but need not do so: *alcohol* /alkəhol/ : *alcoholic* /alkəholik/. Orthographic changes can be illustrated by **1b** where the stem form loses its final -*e* before the affix: *refuse: refusal*.

Rules like this capture valuable generalizations about the structure of lexical items but have a different status from 'rewrite rules' and have therefore not been formulated as such. A rewrite rule like:

4   N → Adj + -*ist*

captures the wrong generalization; we do not want to say that a noun has the constituents Adj + -*ist* (which is not generally true) but rather that in appropriate cases a noun may be formed from an adjective stem by the suffixation of -*ist*: the generalization captured in rule **1a**.

We consider word formation rules like those in **1–3** as belonging to the lexicon rather than rules that belong to the grammar as we have previously considered grammar. There are a number of reasons for this.

In the first place, formation rules like **1–3** are of limited rather than general productivity. By productivity we mean the general applicability of a rule. Inflectional rules are of general productivity. So the rule that affixes the {past} morpheme to a verb stem is one that applies to all verb stems. The rules are productive in so far as they apply to a range of stems: **1b**: *arrival, rebuttal, perusal, acquittal* . . .; **1c**: *deduction, action, procession, edition* . . . On the other hand, they are of limited productivity, because it is not the case that any V can undergo these rules, but also they apply to lexical stems in a somewhat arbitrary fashion. **1b** applies to many verb stems (*arrive, rebut*, and so on), but clearly not to all (*expect*:

*expectal, act: *actal). Stems like *deduct* and *act* must instead derive nouns by rule **1c** (*deduct: deduction, act: action*). In general, if a verb stem undergoes one formation process (like *refuse*), then an alternative process is not open to it (**refusion*) and in the few cases where both forms are available (*remit: remittal, remission*) each of the derived forms has a different sense.

Rules are productive to different degrees. The suffixation of *-y* (*length-y, fox-y*) is still an active productive process in contemporary spoken forms like *trendy*, or *a very linguisticy sort of solution*. So too is the suffixation of *-ish*, established in words like *girlish* and *bookish*, but also to be found in spoken forms like *five o'clockish* and *a very smokerish reaction* ('the typical reaction of a smoker'), which you will not attest in a dictionary. Conversational forms like *smokerish* or *linguisticy* suggest that a rule like **2e** is an active part of a speaker's word formation rules. By contrast, **1e**, the derivational process that relates *long: length, strong: strength, wide: width*, and so on, seems to be no longer productive.[1]

Word formation rules, then, are of limited rather than general productivity; some are still productive, others fossilized; and they have a somewhat arbitrary application to particular stems. In all of these respects they contrast with the centrally grammatical rules, such as the rule forming noun plurals, which are generally productive and of wide application.

We have already noted a second reason (page 171); from the point of view of the grammar, the process by which a lexeme is formed is not relevant. For the adjectives STUPID and FOOLISH in the environment *a __ boy*, it is not relevant that STUPID is a root and FOOLISH a derived form. No grammatical rules need to have access to the information that FOOLISH is derived from a noun root. Thus in Figure 15.1 grammatical rules operate only on the topmost Adj node; the subordinate N and Adj nodes are not subject to grammatical rules. The rule ascribing number to a noun cannot apply to the string *realist* when it is part of the adjective *realistic* (there is no form **realists-ic*), nor can *realistic* be compared like an adjective when part of the form *unrealistic* (**un-more-realistic*). Indeed, it only confuses the grammar to include such information, because if we do we need to put special restrictions on our rules; for example, we would need to state that the rule ascribing number to a noun does not apply when a particular noun stem is itself dominated, as in Figure 15.1, by an Adj node.

This is confirmed by two supporting observations. One is that grammatical affixes are usually 'peripheral', and derivational affixes are usually 'internal'. Schematically, we find strings like GA + DA + STEM + DA + GA (where GA = grammatical affix and DA = derivational affix) but not strings like *DA + GA + STEM + GA + DA, where the grammatical affixes are internal and the derivational affixes peripheral. In English, for instance, we find *morphemeicized* (STEM + DA + DA + DA + GA) but not, say, **morph-eme-s-ic-iz-ed* (STEM + DA + GA + DA + DA + GA) where the number affix (*-s*) is sandwiched between two derivational affixes. This generalization appears true of many, perhaps all, languages.

The second observation is that derivational processes are often cyclical – a simple lexeme can undergo a derivational formation to produce a derived lexeme, which can then go through another derivational formation which can go through another derivational process, and so on. Thus *morph* (N) → *morpheme* (N); *morpheme* (N) → *morphemic* (Adj); *morphemic* (Adj) → *morphemicise* (V). Grammatical processes do not cycle like this, and, as we have seen, we cannot apply a grammatical process to a lexeme and use that as the base for another lexical formation. The grammatical rules are part of the grammar, and it is not relevant to the grammar whether a given lexeme is a root or a derived form.

Thirdly, lexical rules can involve recategorization. **2a** and **2c–e** are 'class changing'; they take a stem of one category and produce a lexeme of another category; **2a**, for example, derives adjectives from nouns. Lexical rules are not always class changing; in **2b**, for example, the derived category is the same as the original category and it is 'class maintaining'. By contrast, the issue never arises with inflectional rules; they are always class maintaining.

A fourth reason has to do with the semantic properties of rules such as those in **1–3**. A derived lexeme generally has some semantic relation to the lexeme from which it is derived, usually through the root which both lexemes share. As far as the stem is concerned it is not always clear what generalizations can usefully be made about which aspects of meaning are retained in the derived form. Consider the stems *boy*: *boy-hood*, *knight*: *knight-hood* and *sister*: *sister-hood*. The same is true for the derivational affix; an affix often has some general meaning, but its meaning will have to be stated in extremely general terms. For example, nouns formed by the affixation of *-hood* are typically abstract (*man*: *manhood*) and the 'central' sense seems to be 'state, quality or rank'

(Partridge, 1958, p. 848), but Partridge also notes 'resultant secondary senses' – a 'concrete instance' in *falsehood* or, perhaps from 'rank', the sense of 'collectivity' in *brotherhood* and *sisterhood*. A similar example is *remit*: *remission, remittal*, noted earlier in the chapter. The two derived noun forms clearly share some aspect of the meaning of the corresponding verb, but the particular aspects of shared meaning differ in each pair. Such changes of meaning are more appropriately accounted for in the lexicon than in the grammar.

The examples considered so far have all involved the affixation of a lexical formative to a lexical stem, the lexical correlate perhaps of agglutination in inflectional morphology. It is worth observing that lexical formation can also involve the correlate of fusion, as in **5**:

5a N + 'sound change' → V *bath*: *bathe*
5b N + 'stress shift' → V CONvict: conVICT

or the correlate of 'zero', a process usually known in lexical morphology as 'conversion' and illustrated in **6**:

6 N → V They manned the ship
They shipped the men

Another common source of new lexemes is composition or compounding, illustrated by words like *bookmark* and *halfback*. In compounding, each part of the compound is itself a lexical stem, and typically a free morph, as with *book* and *mark* in *bookmark*. In compounding there is often a considerable problem about word division, and orthographic conventions offer little help; sometimes compounds are written as a single word (*waterfall*), sometimes hyphenated (*water-drop*), sometimes as two words (*water bottle*) – the examples are all taken from the *Shorter Oxford English Dictionary*. A recent history of English (Strang, 1970, p. 39) treats as 'morphological units' the following: *middle distance, market research, cost effectiveness* and *standing ovation*. The criteria used have been discussed (pages 157–8); typically no further item can be inserted between the two elements; they cannot be transformationally separated, one element cannot be pronominalized or be taken as the antecedent for pronominalization, and so on. However, there is little clarity as to what counts as a compound word and what is a modifier–head construction where the modifier is a noun. Thus it is curious that in the *Shorter Oxford English Dictionary*, of the forms *field mouse* and *harvest mouse* only the latter has an entry (under *harvest*). Compounding is an extremely productive source of new lexical items in English, even though its boundaries are unclear.

As a final consideration, we may ask how far it is sensible to carry the process of derivational analysis within words. Clearly the basis for analysis is the fact that words share common phonological material and a common element of meaning. Thus *strawberry* is analysed as *straw-berry* on the analogy of *dew-berry, logan-berry, rasp-berry*, and so on. One can easily justify the *berry* morph, and in the case of *strawberry*, the *straw* morph, but *logan-* and *rasp-* are more difficult and it would perhaps be best to consider *loganberry* and *raspberry* as simple non-derived forms.

Another problem area involves 'phonaesthemes' (formatives with phonaesthetic properties) in onomatopoeic words. Some analysts have wished to make an analysis of such words. Thus Bloomfield (1935, p. 245) sees 'intense, symbolic connotations' associated with the 'prefixes' and 'affixes' in such words as:

7a *fl-*   'moving light': flash, flare, flame, flicker . . .
7b *gl-*   'unmoving light': glow, glare, gloom, glint . . .
7c *sl-*   'smoothly wet': slime, slush, slip, slide . . .
7d *-are*   'big noise or movement': blare, glare, flare . . .
7e *-ash*   'violent movement': bash, crash, slash . . .

An analysis of this sort can, with some ingenuity, be made quite extensive.

A similar and more problematical area involves the etymology of words. Thus in the following set of words:

8   re-ceive   re-cur   *re-duct   re-duce
        de-ceive   *de-cur   de-duct   de-duce
        con-ceive   con-cur   con-duct   con-duce
        *in-ceive   in-cur   in-duct   in-duce

some analysts recognize 'etymemes' (formatives with etymological relevance). As with phonaesthemes, the problem with this sort of analysis is how far to go. The analyst with a background in the historical study of a language might well wish to go further than an analyst without such a background. For ordinary speakers of the language there is no perception of the etymology of many words;

orchard derives from Old English *ort-geard*, the first element probably deriving from Latin *hortus* 'garden'; *caterpillar* is said to derive from Old French *chate* 'cat' + *piller, pilour* 'pillager'. Probably only an etymological dictionary would wish to analyse examples such as these and they certainly do not seem to be within an individual's productive lexicon. Items like *receive* are more problematical, partly because *re-* is still productive (*re-electrification*) and partly because of the possible analogies with *deceive*, and so on, as in **9**. On the other hand, the 'stem' *-ceive* is no longer usable in any productive way; its status is rather like *logan-* and *rasp-* mentioned above. It is probably best to treat items like *receive* (whose internal structure relates to etymological considerations which are no longer productive) and items like *flash* (whose internal structure relates to phonaesthetic considerations) as simple, underived lexemes.

Our conclusion, then, is this. It is useful to distinguish between inflectional and derivational morphology. Inflectional morphology deals with the distribution of categories introduced by the grammar, and is general and productive. Derivational morphology deals with the production of new lexemes, is less productive and often arbitrary in application; as such it belongs with the lexicon rather than the grammar. It can also be extended to make generalizations about the internal structure of some lexemes that otherwise one would wish to treat as units (see the discussion of phonaesthesia and etymology).

Technical terms

back formation
class changing
class maintaining
composition
compound word
conversation
derivational morphology
etymeme

lexical formative
lexical morphology
lexical stem
onomatopoeia
phonaestheme
productivity
recategorization

Note

1   In some cases words appear to have been derived by a productive process, when this is not in fact the case. Thus we have *aggression*, but not usually **aggress*, *butler* and *vicar* but no **buttle* or **vic* (though in fact all of the starred forms can be found – the latter two in novels by P. G. Wodehouse). Such forms are 'back formations'; *think*: *thinker* suggests **vic*: *vicar*.

Exercises

(1)   The relationship between *kind* and *unkind* (and other similar pairs of words like *helpful*: *unhelpful*) can be described by a lexical rule *un-* + Adj → Adj; that is, prefixing the lexical formative *un-* to an Adj(ective) stem yields another Adj. This is a 'class-maintaining' rule in that the base form and the derived form both belong to the same class, in this case Adj. Similarly, the relationship between *teach*: *teacher* and *rule*: *ruler* can be described by the rule V + *-er* → N; that is, suffixing the lexical formative *-er* to a V(erb) stem yields a N(oun). This is a class-changing rule.

Consider these words:

beautify	beauty	central
centrality	centralize	class
classification	classify	equal
equality	equalize	glorification
glorify	glory	legal
legality	legalization	legalize
popular	popularity	popularize
pure	purify	purity
simple	simplification	sterile
sterility	sterilization	

Analyse the words and:

(a)   List the stems that are further unanalysable and assign them to a word class.

(b)   Devise lexical rules to account for the derivational relationships between the various words.

(c)   One of the examples at the head of the exercise is V + *-er* → N. If *rule* is the verb stem, simple affixation would yield **ruleer*; this could be avoided by adding an orthographic rule. What orthographic rules are needed to derive the correct forms of the words in the exercise?

(d) If you compare the stress patterns of the derived and the underived forms you will find that sometimes the same syllable of the stem is stressed in both forms (for example, GOVern: GOVernment) and sometimes the stress 'shifts' (for example, divORce: divorcEE). For each of your rules say whether it is a 'stress shifter' (and what happens to the stress) or not.

(e) Can you assign any general 'meaning' to the various lexical formatives you identify (for example, *un-* in the example at the top of the exercise is 'negative')?

(2) (a) List ten examples of *class-changing lexical rules* (other than any illustrated above). For each rule:

(b) Illustrate it with a few examples.

(c) Assign a general 'meaning' to the various lexical formatives you identify.

16   Form classes and grammatical categories

16.1   Form classes: nouns, adjectives and verbs

Previous chapters discussed the principles by which form classes are established. The discussion assumed that the application of the principles was relatively straightforward and would yield a determinate set of classes. In this chapter we reopen the question.

Earlier chapters identified two different types of morpheme: lexical morphemes or lexemes, and grammatical morphemes. Lexical morphemes were grouped together into classes, called lexical categories, to which we assigned names like Noun, Verb and Adjective. We saw that in principle such classes are 'open', in that new items can be added to them. So, for example, *sputnik* has been added to the lexical category of Noun in English. Grammatical morphemes too were grouped together into classes, called grammatical categories, to which we gave names like Tense and Number. Each of these categories has a finite number of terms; they are 'closed' in that new items cannot arbitrarily be added to them. So, for example, the English category of Number has the two terms singular and plural; it is difficult to see how a new term, say 'dual', could be added since it would have extensive repercussions for the whole grammar of the language.

In discussion hitherto we have supposed that the distribution of a grammatical category, like number, and of the terms of the category, like singular and plural, is totally definable within the grammar. This is shown by the fact that our constituent structure rules develop structures which include such items as singular and plural. By contrast, whereas the grammar can define the distribution of some lexical category as a whole, it is unable to define the distribution of individual members of the category. So, for example, we can use the grammar to define the distribution of the class Verb, but we cannot in the grammar define the total distribution of some particular verb – this would require, amongst other things, a statement about the selection restrictions for the verb in question, and we have not included such information in the grammar.

A further distinction between lexical and grammatical categories is this: lexical categories are realized either as free forms (for example, *dog, walk*) or as the stems of complex forms (for example, *dog-s, walk-ing*). Grammatical categories, on the other hand, are very often realized as bound forms (for example, *-s, -ing, -ed*) though they may on occasion be realized as individual words (for example, the auxiliary verbs). These facts are reflected in oppositions commonly found in grammars between lexical (or 'full') words and grammatical (or 'form') words – lexical words are typically those that contain a lexical stem, and grammatical words are those that realize grammatical categories alone. The distinction is quite useful but not entirely clear-cut, and is not always easy to draw. The fact that grammatical categories are often realized as bound morphs leads, in many languages, to a typical association between a lexical category and a grammatical category or categories. So, for example, in English the category of Number is realized on the Noun and the category of Tense is realized on the Verb – an important point to which we return.

Considerations of this sort lie behind the establishment of a system of 'parts of speech' for a language. Discussions of parts of speech often distinguish between the 'major' (Noun, Verb, Adjective, Adverb) and the 'minor' (Article, Preposition, Conjunction, and so on). The major parts of speech are, or have stems which are, lexical categories. In descriptions of particular languages linguists have usually (but not invariably) been able to identify classes to which they assign the names of the major parts of speech. The minor parts of speech often realize grammatical categories, and descriptions of different languages vary as to the number of minor categories identified and the names given to them. For example, English is usually described as having a category Article, but in many languages, Latin for instance, no such category is identified.[1]

In traditional grammars, which do not recognize the morpheme as a relevant linguistic unit, parts of speech are classes of words (the traditional word corresponding to the orthographic unit). In some more recent treatments, parts of speech are regarded as classes of stems – a classification that works best with the major parts of speech, with a lexical stem, but which also works with other stems realizing only grammatical categories. The two approaches are obviously somewhat different, but not necessarily in conflict. Thus Hockett (1958, p. 221) defines a part of speech as: 'A form class of stems which show some similar behaviour in inflection, in syntax, or both. The part of speech system of a language is the classification of all its stems on the basis of similarities and differences of inflectional or syntactical behaviour.' Compare this definition with the definitions given for some of the parts of speech in classical Greek by Dionysius Thrax, a Greek grammarian of the first century BC – he is often regarded as the forerunner of the Western tradition of grammatical description (see Robins 1967, p. 33):

The noun is a part of speech inflected for case, signifying a person or thing.

The verb is a part of speech without case inflection, but inflected for tense, person and number, signifying an activity or process performed or undergone.

The preposition is a part of speech placed before other words in composition and in syntax.

Both Hockett and Thrax mention two types of criteria: inflectional and syntactic. As we have seen, inflection involves the internal structure of a word form, perhaps by affixation of a bound morph, and so on. In the case of the major parts of speech inflection typically involves the affixation, and so on, of bound morphs realizing grammatical categories to a lexical stem – as in Thrax's definition of the Noun and Verb in Greek. Syntactic criteria are distributional criteria, reflecting the external distribution of a form. It was these two criteria that we used to establish form classes on pages 25–7. Nowadays syntactic criteria are usually held to be primary; in those languages that do not inflect at all they are the only criteria available; in the case of languages in which some but not all parts of speech inflect, they are the only possible criteria for the non-inflecting parts of speech – as in Thrax's definition of the Preposition in Greek. When languages do inflect, however, inflections will obviously be an important criterion.

Thrax's definitions also include a semantic criterion lacking in Hockett's ('. . . signifying a person or thing', and so on). We have already observed that we cannot rely on notional definitions (see pages 50–3). A moment's thought uncovers many forms that are syntactically nouns but do not 'signify a person or thing' – ACTION,

ACTIVITY, MOVEMENT, and so on. Indeed, nouns like this 'signify an activity', supposedly the criterion for verbs. We do not take semantic criteria as criterial in establishing form classes. It is a different matter when we come to naming a class; since it is indeed the case, in for example English, that the formally defined class of Noun includes many items that do 'signify a person or thing', it seems sensible to retain the traditional name for this class rather than inventing a new arbitrary name. The question of naming (which may as well relate to some central semantic feature, and will yield an easily remembered name) is a different matter from the formal establishment of a class (which ignores such criteria).[2]

To exemplify inflectional and syntactic criteria, consider how we might identify the class Noun in English. English is not particularly rich in inflections and the only inflectional criterion we can apply is that members of this class co-occur with the plural morph -*s* (or inflect for number by fusion *man*: *men*, and so on). The inflectional criterion that they co-occur with the genitive morph -*s* is only marginally useful in English since this item might more profitably be considered to be an affix to the NP as a whole rather than to the noun specifically (*the woman next door's cat = the cat of the woman next door*).[3] Distributional criteria reflect the ability of the noun to operate as head of the NP, and hence to co-occur with articles, numerals, and so on, within the NP. Then, as NPs they have a distribution as subject, object, and so on, of the verb.

If we apply these criteria to a set of items we find a class, including MAN, BOY, DOG and CAT, that will meet them all. We call these the 'central members' of the class. Other forms meet some but not all of the criteria. Some are 'defective' with respect to the inflectional criteria; abstract nouns (SINCERITY, WARMTH, BEAUTY) and proper nouns (JOHN, FIDO) do not occur in the plural; a few nouns occur only in the plural (SCISSORS, TROUSERS, SUDS, and so on). Others are 'defective' with respect to some of the distributional criteria; proper nouns do not typically occur with articles, and so on. However defective their morphology may be, and however restricted their co-occurrence possibilities with the NP are, all the items we have mentioned occur as the head noun of an NP, and hence as subject, object, and so on, of the verb. These latter are perhaps the most important criteria – note that they are syntactic. There are, however, a few items that we would probably wish to identify as nouns that barely meet even this minimal criterion; they are items like HEADWAY and TABS (*They kept tabs on him*) that occur only, or mainly, in idioms.

The preceding paragraph illustrates the principle used to establish form classes – a given set of criteria identifies a particular class. It also shows up a problem – particular items meet these criteria to a greater or lesser extent. We can establish a class of 'central members' that meet all or most of the criteria. There remain various subclasses that meet the criteria to a greater or lesser extent or, on the margins, hardly at all! To some extent we can turn this fact to our advantage since it allows us to identify subclasses of the major category – in a previous chapter, for instance, we established the class of Proper Nouns in terms of the fact that they do not co-occur with the definite article. It does, however, have a drawback; the categories have no 'hard, definable edges'. Let us give a non-linguistic example to define the problem. Individuals may be assumed to have criteria by which they assign a particular plant to the category 'tree' or 'bush'. There seem to be central members of these classes; we speak of *pine* or *beech trees*, not *bushes*, and similarly of *rhododendron* or *lavender bushes* not *trees*. But what of *holly* or *hawthorn*? There is a comparable sort of indeterminacy between form classes.

We will consider this question by looking at the distinction between adjectives and nouns, and then at the distinction between adjectives and verbs in English.

We have already outlined criteria for the class Noun. Adjectives are usually defined in terms of four criteria, one inflectional and the other three syntactic. The syntactic criteria are: (1) that adjectives occur attributively as modifiers of the noun in NP (*a poor man*); (2) that they occur predicatively after the copula (*the man is poor*); and (3) that they can themselves be modified by intensifying expressions (*very poor, rather poor*). The inflectional criterion is (4): they occur in comparative and superlative forms (*poor: poorer, poorest*). On the evidence POOR is a central member in that it satisfies all four criteria. Less central members include adjectives: that do not occur attributively (**an afloat boat*, **an ablaze building*); that do not occur predicatively (**The difficulty is same*; **The reason is principal*); that cannot be modified by intensifying expressions (**rather afloat*, **very major*); and that do not compare (**more major*, **most major*). These restrictions need not in themselves worry us.

The criteria for adjectives and nouns obviously do not overlap.

Now we come to the problem. We identified POOR as centrally an adjective. Yet we find that it occurs in most of the environments taken to be criteria for nouns; it co-occurs with articles (*the poor, those poor*, and so on), and it can be subject or object of a verb (*The poor are always with us*; *He pities the poor*, and so on). There are, to be sure, restrictions – it does not, for instance, occur in the plural (*The poors). But the 'adjective' POOR seems to occur in more of the typical noun environments than a peripheral 'noun' like TABS! The converse is also true. CONCRETE, which appears to be a noun, occurs in some of the adjective environments: *a concrete floor, the floor is concrete*. It does not meet all the criteria, however – it does not compare (*more concrete, *most concrete) and can hardly occur with modifiers (*rather concrete). Here we find the 'noun' CONCRETE occurring in more of the typical adjective environments than a peripheral 'adjective' like AFLOAT. How are we to tackle this problem?

A number of possible solutions have been mooted. We discuss four, and exemplify them with POOR.

The first is to say that we have two distinct, though homophonous, items; POOR(1) is an adjective and POOR(2) is a noun. One drawback to this solution is that POOR(2) still retains some adjective-like properties – it can be intensified (*He only pities the very poor*; cf. **He only pities the very man*) and it can, just, be compared (*He only pities the poorest*; cf. **He only pities the most man*). Nouns cannot be intensified or compared.

A second solution is to say that POOR is 'basically' an adjective, but can be 'recategorized' as a noun in certain types of structure. A drawback of this solution is that we must then say that some adjectives can recategorize easily (for example, POOR, BEAUTIFUL, GOOD), that others do not recategorize at all (for example, MAJOR, ABLAZE) and that yet others recategorize in some circumstances (for example, BLACK, PINK). This seems to involve adding a statement in the lexicon for each adjective to indicate the ease with which it can be recategorized.

A third solution is to assert that POOR is an adjective, but that in certain structures additional material is 'understood'; with this solution *the poor* might derive by a transformational deletion rule from a structure like *those who are poor* or *those people who are poor*. This solution is attractive in that it sets out a semantic reading of the usage of POOR concerned, but it has problems if we extend the principle widely; *I want the black* might be related to *I want the black dress, I want the black ball* (in snooker), *I want the black man*, and so on; the 'understood' items depend on the context of utterance.

A final solution is to say that in *the poor are always with us* POOR functions as the head of an NP, and to relax our rules on the structure of NPs to allow adjectives in certain circumstances to take on this syntactic function. This solution involves distinguishing the syntactic function of an item (as head of an NP, and so on) from its syntactic class (as adjective, and so on). This final solution seems attractive in the case of items like CONCRETE, noted above, where, in a structure like *a concrete floor*, it functions as the modifier of a noun head. Many items we wish to class as nouns can occur as modifiers (*a picnic basket, a bus station, iron railings*, and so on); it does not seem sensible in these cases to identify either two items (PICNIC(1) an adjective, and PICNIC(2) a noun) or to say that PICNIC has been recategorized.[4] This solution is also attractive in the case of structures like *the down line* (a preposition modifier) and *the very man* (an adverbial modifier). The discussion seems to suggest that there is no unique satisfactory solution. Some instances are best handled in one way, others in another.

We now turn to consider the relationship between adjectives and verbs. We have already seen (Chapter 4) that the distinction drawn in English between adjectives and verbs is not drawn in the same way, if at all, in some languages; in these languages items that are syntactically verbs translate into English adjectives. What is the position in English? The inflectional criterion for a class Verb in English is that the category of tense and the 'aspectual' categories of progressive and perfect may be realized on verb stems. The situation is complicated by the fact that in English all these categories cannot be realized simultaneously on the verb stem, instead auxiliary verbs are introduced to carry them (see discussion in Chapter 18).[5] Syntactic criteria for verbs would include their distribution within the VP, their 'strict subcategorization' possibilities and so on. We should also note that verbs can be subcategorized in terms of inherent features (rather in the manner in which we subcategorized nouns by features like [±animate], and so on, on pages 69 ff.). The feature most usually discussed in this connection is [±state] (which we discuss in more detail on page 293). For now we note that some verbs do not readily co-occur with the progressive auxiliary: *He is knowing Chinese*; *He is seeming intelligent*; or in the imperative (as a command) *Know Chinese*, *Seem intelligent*. These, usually known as 'stative' verbs, can be characterized as [+ state]. Other verbs that do occur with the progressive and in the imperative are known as 'active' or 'action' verbs; they can be characterized as [− state]: *He is turning off the light*; *Turn off the light*; and so on.

At first glance the criteria for verbs seem to be distinct from those for adjectives. A few items can be used either as adjectives or verbs (*The grass is yellow*; *The grass is yellowing*), and there are a number of systematic derivational relationships between adjectives and verbs (RIPE: RIPEN, CLEAR: CLARIFY, and so on). On the other hand, the two classes do not overlap inflectionally. The category of tense, for example, can be marked on verb stems (*He walks*; *He walked*) but not on adjective stems (**He poors*; **He poored*). But then we come to auxiliary verbs. Suppose we say that the verb BE is introduced as a 'dummy verb' with adjectives to carry the tense distinction (this sort of analysis seemed appropriate to account for the occurrence of the 'dummy verb' DO in negative and inter- rogative constructions on pages 129–30), giving **He walksn't* but *He doesn't walk*; **Walks he?* but *Does he walk?* Perhaps, by analogy, BE is a 'dummy verb' for adjectives – **He poors* but *He is poor*; **He poored* but *He was poor*. If we adopt this analysis, we can treat adjectives in English as another subclass of verb, distinguished by the fact that they require the introduction of the dummy BE!

Such a proposal is not entirely fanciful (and indeed is adopted by some linguists). If we adopt it, how do the other distinguishing criteria for verbs work out? To begin with, adjectives, like verbs, have a distribution within VP – both are 'predicators'. We can use much the same kinds of strict subcategorization frames for adjectives as we can for verbs. Some verbs take sentential complements (*I believe that the world is flat*), others (RUN, PAINT) do not. Similarly some adjectives take sentential complements (*It is odd that the world is flat*), and others (RED, INTELLIGENT) do not. Some verbs are transitive and others are not. Adjectives can be considered in a similar light if we note that non-subject NPs in this case require prepositions: *I like reading*: *Reading is easy for me*; *I delight in syntactic analysis*: *Syntactic analysis is delightful to me*; *I can't understand the argument*: *The argument is incomprehensible to me*; and so on. A further similarity involves the characterization [±state]. Just as we have stative and action verbs, so we have stative and action adjectives; RED and POOR are [+ state] (**I am being poor*; **Be poor*); CAREFUL and CLEVER may be [− state] (*I am being careful*; *Be careful*). Some verbal forms occur attributively like adjectives – *singing bird, roaring fire*. We could derive NPs like these by the same rules as we use for attributive adjectives.

We note that verbs and adjectives are related; earlier we showed that adjectives and nouns were related. Does this mean that nouns and verbs are also related? Well, we could extend the classification [±state] somewhat. Nouns like PERSON and VIRGIN seem to be [+state] [*She is being a virgin*; *Be a virgin*) in contrast to HERO (*He's being a hero*; *Be a hero*). Similarly we note that some nouns take sentential complements, like RUMOUR and INSINUATION (*Have you heard the rumour that the world is flat?*), and some nouns do not, like CAT and BOY.

The position reached in the last paragraph does not seem very helpful. If we group all these items into one large class, called, say, 'contentives', then we would still need to distinguish between those contentives that typically introduce BE to carry tense (the former class of adjectives), those that permit tense to be shown on the lexical stem (the former class of verbs) and those that may occur with articles (the former class of nouns)! For English at least it seems more sensible to retain the original classes and recognize that the classification of stems is not wholly without problems.

In any given sentence it is usually clear whether a particular lexical stem is being 'used as' a noun or adjective or verb. We were after all able to set up three separate and non-overlapping criteria for these classes. The typical problem is whether we are able to assign a particular stem to one or other class independent of its use in a sentence, and this is not always straightforward. A speaker, by using a given lexical stem in more than one class, can make subtle distinctions of meaning; English may be unusually liberal in the latitude it allows to individual stems to occur in different classes. Other languages do not seem to allow quite such freedom!

16.2   Grammatical categories

We now turn to a different though related problem: the relationship between subclasses of a lexical category and the number and type of grammatical categories that we may wish to establish in a language. As a preliminary, we distinguish between 'overt' and 'covert' categories. Some categories are overt in that at least one term of the category is identified by a formal marker of some sort; in the English category of tense, the term past is overtly marked by the morph -*ed*. Similarly, the term plural in the category of number is overtly marked by the morph -*s* affixed to noun stems. Even though the singular term is not also overtly marked we say that the category is overt. Such categories have other syntactic implications. Thus, for example, there are co-occurrence restrictions between nouns and numerals that can, at least in part, be related to the singular : plural distinction. The numeral *one* cannot co-occur with plural nouns, and numerals other than *one* cannot co-occur with singular nouns. Some verbs require non-singular subjects or objects (so we can have *he gathered the men into a group* but not **he gathered the man into a group*), and so on. The category of number in English controls verb concord and, to a limited extent, concord within the NP. We saw on pages 63 ff. that co-occurrence restrictions and facts like concord were important in establishing the category of number. Other categories may be 'covert', in that no term in the category can be identified with a formal marker; on the other hand, co-occurrence restrictions or other grammatical phenomena enable us to establish the existence of the category. Thus the French category of gender is a covert category; nouns, which are assigned to gender classes, are not themselves usually marked for gender, but the gender is clear from co-occurrence with, for example, article forms. There is no overt marker of gender in a noun like *chaise* but it must co-occur with the article *la* rather than *le*; although the category of gender is inherent in the noun, the actual formal marking of gender occurs not on the noun but on the article which it is in construction with. Covert categories are no less important in a description than overt categories.

This particular distinction also brings us into direct confrontation with problems concerned with the relation between 'notional' and 'formal' categories. This can be illustrated by considering the category of number in English. At first sight it seems a fairly straightforward matter. The grammatical category of number is an overt category with two terms, singular and plural, shown by the alternation between pairs of forms like *cat: cats*. The grammatical category correlates, more or less, with a notional category which we may suppose also has two terms, 'oneness' and 'more-than-oneness' – we use *cat* to refer to a single 'cat', and *cats* to refer to more than one 'cat'. So far as it goes this is correct, and the names given to the grammatical category reflect these semantic facts. Note that the particular distinction drawn in English is not universal; we have already noted that some languages, classical Greek and Arabic for example, have a three-term number category, with an additional term, 'dual', used to refer to things that typically go in pairs (arms, legs). English has no grammatical category of dual. English can and does have the means to refer to pairs of items – for example, the lexical items *both* and *neither* – but the distinction is not 'grammaticalized', realized as a formal system in the grammar, but is rather 'lexicalized'.

16.2a   Number: singular, plural; count, mass; collectives

We return to the question of number in English. It can be argued that, prior to any singular : plural distinction, a mass : count distinction is needed, the number distinction of singular : plural only applying to count nouns. Consider the following. Count nouns in general are used to refer to discrete objects that can be counted – thus *two chairs, twenty cigarettes, a hundred pipers*, and so on. Mass nouns, on the other hand, are characteristically used to refer to items perceived not in terms of individual members, but in some mass terms: items like *water, sand, butter* and *ink*. The count : mass distinction is covert, in that nouns in English are not marked in any way to show their membership of either subclass. The distinction can, however, be established on the basis of the co-occurrence relationships of the two classes of noun (see discussion in pages 69–78). Mass nouns do not co-occur with numerals (*one sand, *two waters, and so on), nor in the plural (*butters, *inks, and so on); they do not co-occur with the indefinite article (*an ink, *a water), but do occur with the determiner *some* (pronounced /sm/) (*some butter, some ink*). Count nouns are the opposite; they occur with numerals (*one boy*), in the plural form (*boys*), with the indefinite article (*a boy*), but not, in the singular, with /sm/ (*sm boy). We also observe that, for the purposes of concord, both subject–verb concord and concord within the NP, mass nouns operate like singular count nouns (*This butter is . . .*; **These butter are . . .*). There are, of course, idiosyncrasies; a few mass nouns are plural in form and take plural concord (*clothes, guts, suds*); a few are not overtly plural but take plural concord (*gentry, cattle, clergy*); and so on. These idiosyncrasies apart, they offer no particular problems.

The count : mass distinction may be held to be a reflex of a notional distinction which we call a distinction between 'individuated' and 'non-individuated' referents.

The descriptive problem begins to arise when we find nouns that we might wish to regard as 'basically' mass nouns occurring with the syntax of count nouns:

1 I always have a coffee at this time of the morning
2 Two milks, please
3 I don't like either of these two wines

The converse also occurs:

4 The scrum was not producing enough ball for the backs
5 He is collecting worm for his fishing
6 This room smells of cat

As with our discussion of POOR (pages 239–40), we can adopt one of a number of solutions, each seeming attractive for some items and less attractive for others. We can suppose that two items are involved – COFFEE(1), the mass noun, and COFFEE(2), the count noun, and so on. Or we can suppose that COFFEE is basically a mass noun, and has been recategorized in 1. Alternatively, we can suppose that some relevant quantifying expression has been elided – *I always have [a cup of] coffee* .

The first solution seems attractive when the phenomenon is well established in usage, and this fact is often reflected in dictionaries. So, for example, LAMB is given in two senses in the dictionary, LAMB(1) the 'animal' and LAMB(2) the 'meat of the animal', reflected in sentences like:

7 I would like a lamb
8 I would like lamb

This solution is reinforced by the fact that in some cases the animal and its meat receive two different lexical realizations PIG: PORK; COW: BEEF; and so on. A similar solution is open to items like BEAVER(1), the 'animal' and BEAVER(2) the 'skin of the animal'; OAK(1) the 'tree' and OAK(2) the 'wood of the tree'. Such usages seem well established. There are, however, two points to be made. First, the type of understood categorization depends to a large extent on context – in a draper's shop 8 would typically refer to the 'skin' rather than the 'meat' of the animal (and the converse in a restaurant). Secondly, the extent to which the process is established in usage (if dictionaries are any guide) is variable. Thus we might not expect to find POTATO(1) the 'vegetable' (*Give me a potato*) and POTATO(2) (*Would you like some* (= *sm*) *potato?*), and similarly APPLE, BANANA, and so on.

The second solution seems attractive for examples like **4–6**. Usages like this do not seem to be established in the language – though **4** is becoming established in television commentary on rugby football, in Britain at least – and are clearly heavily context-dependent for their interpretation.

The third solution seems attractive in cases like **1–3**, though it is not without problems. In a case like *two milks* we need to account for the resiting of the plural marker (compare *two pints of milk*), but we can doubtless get round this. More difficult is that the precise quantifying expression relies once again on context; **2** relates to *two [pints of] milk* in a note to the milkman, but to *two [cups/glasses, and so on, of] milk* in a café.

The count : mass distinction appears to rest on a perceptual distinction, at least to some degree. Some things are characteristically perceived as non-individuated (like 'sand' and 'water'), but they may be individuated in quanta (*a bucket of water, a heap of sand*) and then expressed like count nouns (*two waters*). Conversely, some things are typically perceived as individuated (like 'ball' and 'cat'), but may, or some of their attributes may, be perceived as non-individuated, and then be expressed as mass nouns (see **4–6**).

A similar problem arises with the class of 'collective' nouns (COMMITTEE, GOVERNMENT, HERD, and so on). These occur with either singular or plural concord:

    9   The committee has agreed to the appointment
   10   The committee have agreed to take no further action

The usual account of such sentences is that the number choice depends on whether the collective is thought of as acting as a single body (*the committee has . . .*) or as a collection of individuals (*the committee have . . .*). With such nouns, even though they take plural concord on the verb, concord within the NP remains in the singular (*this committee have . . .*)! As in the count : mass distinction, the assignment of number appears to rest on a perceived or imputed semantic perception.

To account for this, we might suppose that in some community some 'typical' perception such as 'individuated : non-individuated' and 'oneness : more-than-oneness' is 'grammaticized' into a formal grammatical category – count : mass, singular : plural. The grammatical category is reflected in a range of syntactic behaviour; once established as a grammatical category, it is open to exploitation for semantic effect. (Not all communities grammaticize the same 'typical' percepts.)

An interesting way of looking at this problem is proposed by Jespersen (1929, p. 46). He suggests that we can regard language as involving three interrelated levels of description: a level of forms (the actually occurring morphological markings); a level of grammar (with formally established categories like count : mass and singular : plural); and a level of meaning (with notional categories like individuated : non-individuated and oneness : more-than-oneness. The grammatical level faces both ways: towards the level of form and towards the level of meaning as in Figure 16.1.

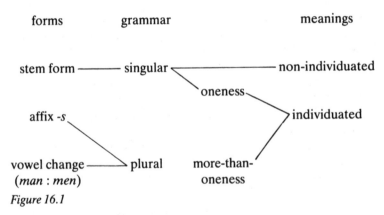

Figure 16.1

A perceptual characterization is reflected in a particular grammatical choice, which is realized as a particular form. This approach allows us both to maintain the principle of a grammar established on formal principles (the formal opposition of number, and so on) and to understand how this formal system is related to, and can on occasion be manipulated by, the semantics.

We can incorporate it into our previous description in the following manner. Recall that we suggested (page 69) that nouns should be characterized in the lexicon in terms of a set of syntactic features, [±count], and so on. We also saw that a characterization, say [±count], had consequences for co-occurrence with articles, and so on. Suppose now we say that whereas a particular lexical item may be characterized as 'typically' [+count] or [−count], this characterization may be altered by a semantic consideration. However, once they have been altered, the grammatical consequences are predicted by the grammar. We can also accommodate within such an account those irregularities we have noted during the discussion – SUDS, for example, can be characterized as [−count], [+ pl].

A further advantage is that this way allows us to accommodate both the situation described above for [±count] nouns in English, where a semantic characterization can influence a grammatical choice, and the sort of situation found with French gender, where the grammatical characterization is relatively uninfluenced by semantic considerations. In different languages different categories are influenced to different degrees by semantic considerations. In French, and other European languages, nouns cannot be switched from gender class to gender class for communicative effect (one might think, for instance, that French would allow *une homme* as a characterization of an effeminate man – but this sort of thing is not permissible). Many languages do permit it; so in Lugisu, a Bantu language from Uganda, we find *mu-twe* 'head' 'recategorized' as a diminutive *ka-twe* 'pin head', or as an augmentative *gu-twe* 'big head' by changing gender class – the effect is derogatory.

16.2b   Tense

Let us now turn to another grammatical category in English, that of tense. How should our description account for the relationship between notions of time and the formal opposition between 'past' and 'non-past' established and discussed on page 209? The category is an overt two-term category, called tense, because it often corresponds to notions of time, but the correspondence is far from direct. There is a frequent correspondence between past time and past tense (*I was in London last week*; *We went to America last summer*, and so on) but there are circumstances when a past tense form is used, with no implication of past time. If the main verb in reported speech is in the past tense, the verb in the reported speech may also be in the past tense, irrespective of the time reference. If my daughter says to me at breakfast one morning '*I am going to the pictures this evening*' (using a non-past tense verb form), I can report this to my wife at lunch-time with the words '*Jane said she was going to the pictures this evening'* (using a past tense verb form). Past tense is also often used for 'unreal conditionals' – as in *If my daughter were to go to the pictures . . ., If only I understood what it was all about . . ., I wish I knew . . .*, and so on. In yet other circumstances the distinction between the past and non-past tense does not reflect any time distinction at all, as in: *I wonder/wondered if you would like a cup of coffee*; *I think/thought you would be interested to know that . . .* The most striking cases of non-correspondence occur with the modal auxiliary verbs, where very frequently the use of a morphological past tense form bears no relation at all to past time: *I might go if you asked me*; *I could stop smoking if I tried*; *I wouldn't have the slightest idea*; and so on.[6]

Next consider sentences with a non-past verb form. They can sometimes be found with a 'present' time reference: *Dalglish shoots and it's a goal*; but, as we have already observed, this is not the usual way to refer to actions taking place at the time of utterance. More frequently the simple non-past verb form is used in a 'timeless' sense – *Honesty is the best policy*; *War solves no problems*; to refer to 'habits' – *I cycle to work every morning*; *I always get drunk at Hogmanay*; to refer to 'states' – *I belong to Glasgow*; *I speak Chinese*; and so on. Non-past verb forms may also be used to refer to future events – *I leave for Paris in the morning*; and indeed to past events (the so-called 'historic present') – *Earlier this morning I come into the kitchen and what do I find?*; and past states of affairs – *Shakespeare draws his characters from real life*. The correspondence between 'present time' and the non-past form of the verb is even less straightforward than the correspondence between 'past-time' and the past form of the verb.

What, then, do we make of characterizations like 'timeless', 'habit' and 'state', characterizations frequently met with in grammars? There are, to be sure, occasions when the correspondence between some such category and a term in the category of tense is reasonably direct; thus 'timeless' is typically realized by a non-past verb form (*God was good*; *Christmas was on 25 December*; *Cocks crowed at dawn* seem anomalous if they are to be understood as statements of 'general truth' which hold regardless of time!). Similarly 'past instantaneous actions' are usually realized by a simple past verb form (*I bought a coat this afternoon*; *I gave my wife a diamond ring for Christmas*). But usually the relation is less direct. 'Present habits' usually correlate with a non-past verb form, but past habits frequently occur, not with a simple past form, but with a form of USED TO (*I cycle to work every morning*; *I used to cycle to work every morning*). Similarly, as we have observed before, 'present instantaneous' actions are often realized by the progressive rather than the simple non-past verb form (*I am typing this sentence now*). The relationship between notions like 'habit' and some formal overt grammatical category is often indirect, but such notions can play an important part in controlling other features of the sentence. Thus, for example, 'timeless' statements usually require a noun of general reference as subject, and are restricted as to the type of adverbial modifiers they permit; *Cocks crow at dawn* can be held to be a timeless statement, but *My favourite red rooster crows at dawn most mornings* cannot. Similarly 'past habits' impose restrictions on adverbial expressions – one can hardly say **I used to cycle to work this morning*!

Notions like 'timeless' and 'habit' seem to have relevance for more than the single category of tense. Grammatical features that can be correlated with such notions extend throughout the sentence and may be relevant for grammatical selection at various places. A valuable discussion of some of these notions is Crystal (1966) to which the reader is referred (see also Leech, 1971).

The difficulty may be summarized thus. Categories like 'timeless', 'habit' and 'unreal condition' have syntactic implications in relation to such matters as co-occurrence restrictions relating to adverbs, and so on; on the other hand, there is no single overt category to which they can be tied in any straightforward way. There is a further problem with respect to the notional categories – it is not clear how many such categories we need to postulate, or what the distinctions are between them. For example, we have suggested a category of 'state' – but this is clearly not a unitary category at all; there are all sorts of states. We might recognize: inherent states (*I am a man*); resultant states (*My coffee is cold* (*now, but it was hot ten minutes ago*)); transitory states (*It is fine now* (*but will be raining again in ten minutes*)); and so on. It is far from clear that reliable distinctions can be drawn clearly between them.

This is at least true for English where such categories are not relatable to a formal distinction in the grammar. In terms of our former discussion, they are not 'grammaticalized'. The situation is different in some other languages. In Finnish the distinction between 'transitory' and 'inherent' states is reflected in a difference in the case form adopted by the noun. In Akan the distinction between 'states' and 'actions' is reflected in the existence of a special 'stative' verb form, open only to verbs that describe states; the distinction between 'inherent' and 'resultant' states is typically marked by different aspect markers on the verb.

As far as English is concerned, it does not seem profitable to set up categories like 'timeless' as grammatical categories, on a par with the grammatical category of tense – though attempts have been made. It would seem more appropriate to account for such distinctions in terms of a model of description like that hinted at on page 247, but we shall not pursue this further here.

Technical terms

closed category	lexical category
collective noun	lexical word
count noun	mass noun
covert category	open category
form word	overt category
full word	part of speech
grammatical category	recategorization
grammatical word	

Notes

1 Such observations raise a host of interesting questions that we do not have the space to explore. For example, to what extent is there a similarity between the classes named Verb in Akan, Gaelic and English which justifies their being called by the same name? Do all languages have a syntactic class to which we can appropriately apply the name Verb? Those interested in pursuing this question are directed to Lyons (1968, ch. 7) and the references there. An interesting review of word classes in a variety of languages is *Lingua*, vol. 17, 1967.

2 At one time it was fashionable to discard even the names Noun, Verb, and so on, since it was thought that these might smuggle in undesirable semantic considerations. Thus Fries (1952) conducts a rigorous distributional analysis of English and labels the classes he establishes with numbers and letters. It is no surprise to discover that these classes, although given arbitrary labels, turn out to be the familiar classes of Noun, Verb, and so on. It is worth consulting Fries to see how far such an analysis can be pursued.

3 Various derivational affixes are also limited to noun forms – like the *-ness* in *goodness, helplessness*, and so on. But since *-ness*, and others like it, is a lexical formative and not an inflectional affix, we do not consider such items further here.

4   This solution is not, however, open to the sort of grammar that we have been considering so far; we have no satisfactory way of identifying grammatical 'functions' like modifier. The grammar is set up to account for the distribution of categories. We return to this problem in Chapter 19.

5   The situation is different in other languages where the verb stem can carry both tense and aspect categories – see, for example, the brief exemplification of Akan on page 51. Such languages often do not have a category of auxiliary verb; Akan doesn't.

6   There are some cases where past tense and past time do correspond: *I can speak French quite well now*; *I could speak German when I was younger*; but this is not the regular pattern for modal verbs. There is an argument that some so-called past tense forms among modal verbs are better thought of as simply separate items. An example is *should* when used in the sense of 'duty', e.g. *You should always give up your seat on the bus to an old lady*. Replacing *should* by *shall* produces a sentence of doubtful acceptability! The interested reader is referred for further discussion to Leech (1971) and Palmer (1986).

Exercises

In the grammatical analysis of languages words are assigned to *word classes* on the formal basis of *syntactic behaviour*, supplemented and reinforced by differences of *morphological paradigms*, so that every word in a language is a member of a word class. Word class analysis has long been familiar in Europe under the title 'parts of speech', and since medieval times grammarians have operated with nine word classes or parts of speech: noun, verb, pronoun, adjective, adverb, preposition, conjunction, article (determiner – E.K.B./ J.E.M.) and interjection (Robins, 1964).

(1)   Adjectives in English are recognized by the following properties:

    (i)   In an NP, they precede the N and may be preceded by a determiner.

    (ii)   They occur after certain verbs: for example, BE, BECOME, GET, GROW, SEEM.

    (iii)   EITHER *-er* and *-est* are added to build comparative and superlative forms, OR the adjective is preceded by *more* or *most*.

    (iv)   They can be preceded, in an AP, by *very, quite*, and so on.

    (v)   *-ly* can be added to build an adverb.

The lexical items below are usually considered to be adjectives. Apply the criteria to them. What problems arise?

QUICK, PRINCIPAL, MAJOR, MAIN, AWAKE, WOODEN, FAST, DUMB, SHEER, LOATH, LATE, PERFECT, EXCELLENT

(2) Devise criteria for classifying English words as verbs. Apply the criteria to:

SLEEP, HAVE, KNOW, BELIEVE, OUGHT, MAY

(3) To what word classes (in the list given by Robins above) would you assign the words in the following, and why?

> 'Twas brillig, and the slithy toves
> Did gyre and gimble in the wabe;
> All mimsy were the borogroves,
> And the mome raths outgrabe.
>
> 'Beware the Jabberwock, my son!
> The jaws that bite, the claws that catch!
> Beware the Jubjub bird, and shun
> The frumious Bandersnatch!'
>
> He took his vorpal sword in hand:
> Long time the manxome foe he sought –
> So rested he by the Tumtum tree,
> And stood awhile in thought.
>
> And, as in uffish thought he stood,
> The Jabberwock, with eyes of flame,
> Came whiffling through the tulgey wood,
> And burbled as it came!

from *Jabberwocky*
in Lewis Carroll's *Through the Looking Glass*

(4) You will find that the membership of some classes is entirely English, while that of other classes is partly English and partly invented. Which classes are open to invented words and which are not? Why do you think some classes have no invented words?

Part three

Functional relations

17 Heads and modifiers: the encoding of dependency relations

Part One looked at the constituent structure of simple sentences. This part widens the discussion by looking at other aspects of the structure of sentences that have been traditionally the concern of grammarians. This chapter examines some of the different types of relationships that constituents bear to each other, and considers how these relations are marked in the grammars of different languages and whether all such relationships can be satisfactorily described in the type of constituent structure grammars we have been looking at. Chapter 18 examines notions like 'agent' and 'patient' as they might be applied to a sentence like *The policeman* (*'agent'*) *arrested the burglar* (*'patient'*) and sees how the relevant notions might be captured in a grammar. Chapter 19 examines the terms 'subject' and 'object'. Chapter 20 is concerned with some questions of word order as they apply to connected text.

17.1 Heads and modifiers

We have considered how constituents group together to form larger constituents; words combine to form phrases; phrases combine to form clauses or even larger phrases; and clauses combine to form sentences. Although the constituent structure diagrams used in earlier chapters show only the arrangements of constituents, the relationships among the latter are quite complex. Consider the phrase *very large dogs*. Applying the procedures discussed in the previous chapter, we see that *very* can be replaced by various words, such as *really, unbelievably* and *amazingly*; *large* can be replaced by words such as *fierce, tiny*, or *stupid*. These two sets of words make up two form classes, or paradigms, and the words are said to be paradigmatically related. Paradigmatic relations are not displayed in constituent structure diagrams but are captured in a far more indirect fashion in dictionaries, where the entry for each word specifies which paradigm or form class the word belongs to.

The other major relationship among constituents is called syntagmatic.[1] 'Syntagmatic' comes from a Greek word meaning 'placed together' – and indeed is related to 'syntax', which derives from the Greek noun meaning 'placing together'. We have already seen in the first chapters that constituents are not placed together or combined randomly but that there are constraints on what types of constituent can combine and in what order they occur. For example, in English, determiners combine with nouns and not with verbs, and they precede the noun. We are about to discover that syntagmatic relations are more complex, and that there is more to them than just linear order.

The central idea in the following paragraphs is that any phrase contains a special constituent called the head, which is the central, characteristic and obligatory constituent (see pages 70–3, 260). For example, a sequence of words qualifies as an adjective phrase only if it contains an adjective; *very* does not constitute an adjective phrase but *very stupid* does. The adjective is the characteristic constituent in an adjective phrase. It is also central, in that it controls whether an intensifier can occur; adjectives such as *wooden* and *stone* exclude intensifiers such as *very, amazingly* and *rather* – assuming that, for example, *wooden* is not understood metaphorically as describing someone's expression.

The verb is the head of the verb phrase. Without a verb, a sequence of words does not constitute a verb phrase, and evidence that the verb controls the occurrence of other constituents in the verb phrase was presented in Chapter 5. Some verbs require either a noun phrase or an adjective phrase – *She became rich*; *She became the convener of the committee* – while many verbs exclude adjective phrases – **She reads rich*. Some verbs require a noun phrase, while others exclude noun phrases: *The dog squashed the cat* vs **The dog squashed* and *The dog growled* vs **The dog growled the cat*. There are verbs that allow two noun phrases, as in *We showed Celia the new house*, and verbs that require a noun phrase and prepositional phrase, as in *She pinned the notice to the board*.

To these examples can be added more subtle instances of verbs controlling nouns. Transitive verbs such as SCATTER require that the noun in the verb phrase be either a mass noun – *The children scattered sand over the table* – or a plural noun – *The children scattered the toys over the floor*.

Verbs have been described as requiring certain constituents – that is, the constituents are obligatory – or as excluding certain constituents. A much weaker link can be recognized, whereby a given verb merely allows a certain constituent. For instance, most verbs allow adverbs of time, as in *Fiona posted the parcel on Monday*. The time adverb *on Monday* is optional, and because time adverbs are optional with so many verbs, they are generally thought to be a type of modifier that is not relevant to subcategorization. This is not correct; there are verbs, in particular the copula BE, which need to be complemented by some constituent, a noun phrase, an adjective phrase, or a prepositional phrase functioning as an adverb of time or place, as in *The concert was on Monday*. With the copula, adverbs of time are required – that is, are complements – whereas with other types of verbs they are optional and therefore adjuncts.

In languages with case, where nouns take different affixes, the verb determines or governs the affix assigned to the noun. For example, in Russian the verb *nenavidit* 'hates' requires the object noun to have the accusative case suffix, as in *Ivana* 'Ivan', but the verb *ljubuetsja* 'admires', requires the object noun to have the instrumental case suffix, as in *Ivanom*. Verbs can also govern which prepositions can occur; we send a letter *to* someone but not *from* someone, and we put the blame *on to* someone but not *near* them or *round* them or *on top of* them.

The head of a prepositional phrase is the preposition. Note first that certain prepositions allow other prepositions to follow them, as in *from behind the door* and *in under the cupboard*, but not *above behind the door* or *to behind the door*. Consider now phrases such as *was near* or *walked behind*. If we are prepared to analyse *near* and *behind* as prepositions, as opposed to the traditional analysis as adverbs or particles, we can treat them as special prepositions that do not require a noun phrase. (The full meaning will be clear from the context; thus, *She stood near* (*us, the band, the car*, and so on.))[2]

In languages with case, prepositions govern the inflectional affixes that occur on the noun; in Russian, *pod* 'under' requires the instrumental case, as in *shkafom* 'cupboard', while *v* 'in' requires the locative, as in *shkafu*. (As always, the situation is actually more complex, but the complexities are of no concern here.)

Languages such as English, with auxiliary and main verbs, pose serious problems for dependency analysis. Consider the sentence *The story was written up/is getting written up in the local paper. Was* and *is* are usually described as auxiliary verbs, chiefly because they are relatively devoid of content and are seen as merely helping out the main verb *written up*, which denotes the action central to the situation. From a syntactic point of view, however, we see that *was* and *is* agree in number with the subject noun. In addition, *was* and *is* can be seen as requiring specific types of constituent; they can be followed by a passive participle, such as *written up*, or by a present participle, such as *getting*. In turn, GET requires certain constituents: an NP or an AP or, as above, a passive participle such as *written up*. Modal auxiliary verbs such as CAN, WOULD and MIGHT can be seen as requiring a following constituent to be a verb stem, as in *might write*, whereas HAVE requires the following constituent to be a past participle, as in *has arrived*. Similarly, modal verbs exclude participles; HAVE excludes the verb stem, and so on. The evidence suggests that the auxiliary verbs, though minor in meaning, are in fact the syntactic heads.

It is usually assumed that the head of the noun phrase is the noun. This analysis turns out to be harder to establish than for the adjective, verb and preposition, but for present purposes we will assume that it is correct. The evidence supporting this view is of the same sort as above. A sequence of words typically does not qualify as a noun phrase unless it contains a noun, and the noun can be seen as controlling the other constituents in the noun phrase. Mass nouns neither require nor exclude determiners; cf. *Sand is heavy*; *That sand is very wet*. Proper nouns typically exclude the definite and indefinite articles: **The Jane loves cycling*. (Note that this restriction is stated with respect to English; in Italian, proper nouns are preceded by the definite article, while in French personal names do not take the definite article but names of countries do: *La France est belle*, literally 'The France is beautiful'. Mass nouns exclude the determiners *many* and *few*, and many abstract nouns exclude the definite and indefinite articles, as in *an electricity.

In languages with gender the noun in a given noun phrase controls the shape of adjectives and determiners. In French *plage* 'beach' is feminine, and requires the feminine form of the articles, *la* 'the' and *une* 'a'. In contrast, *mariage* 'marriage' is masculine and requires the forms *le* and *un*. Conversely, *mariage* excludes *la* and *une*, while *plage* excludes *le* and *un*. Note the forms of the adjective in *une belle plage* 'a beautiful beach' and *un beau mariage* 'a beautiful marriage'. German nouns are in three classes. *Hund* 'dog' is masculine and requires the masculine forms of the articles, such as *der* 'the'; *Frau* 'woman' is feminine and requires, for example, *die* 'the'; and *Kind* 'child' is neuter and requires, for example, *das* 'the'. Notice too the differing forms of the adjective in the following noun phrases with the indefinite article: *ein kleiner Hund* 'a small dog', *eine kleine Frau* 'a small woman' and *ein kleines Kind* 'a small child'.

The data above are all examples of unilateral dependency, where a head constituent combines with modifying constituents. We must recognize two fundamental things about such relationships: first, that they are abstract relationships between sentence constituents; and secondly, that they are functional relationships indicating the syntactic and semantic function of constituents in their relationships with other constituents. Obviously a language needs to find ways of marking a particular relationship, and different languages select different ways of marking; the relationships themselves, however, are in principle independent of any particular aspect of word or sentence form. Two examples illustrate the point. One example of head–modifier dependency is the attribute–entity relation expressed by adjectives and nouns. The relationship is typically realized in English in the order Adj + N (*the red book*) but in French in the reverse order, N + Adj (*le livre rouge*), without affecting the dependency. Another example of head–modifier dependency is the possessor–possessed relation, in which the head is the noun denoting the possessed item. This relation can be expressed in two ways in English, as in *the son of the king* and *the king's son*. The dependency relation is the same in both constructions, but the word order is different and each construction requires different 'markers' (*of* and -*s*) to show the relationship.

The fact that the relationships are functional means that we need more labels for the different types of relationship: head–modifier, attribute–entity, possessor–possessed, and so on. These relationships are independent of constituent structure. It is true that particular languages arrange heads and modifiers in specific orders, but different languages have different orders, and we have seen that one and the same relation may be expressed by two completely different structures, as shown by the English possessor–possessed constructions. To conclude this section of the discussion, we should note two important facts. Dependency relations are essentially independent of constituent structure. All languages have dependency relations, but some languages have much looser arrangements of constituents than we are accustomed to in English. Indeed, some Australian aboriginal languages appear to have no hard-and-fast ordering of constituents at all. Earlier in the book constituent structure diagrams were also used to display dependency relations, but the two facts just stated raise the large question of whether constituent structure diagrams can be satisfactorily adapted for dependencies, or whether dependencies should be displayed in a separate representation. This question goes far beyond the scope of this book, but it is worthwhile drawing attention to it.

Constructions of unilateral dependency contrast with constructions of co-ordinate dependency, in which neither constituent depends syntactically on the other; in distributional terms each constituent has the same distribution as the construction as a whole. Examples are *Jack and Jill went up the hill* (co-ordinated NPs), *The house has been repaired and redecorated* (co-ordinated passive participles) and *The tigers are large and hungry* (co-ordinated adjectives). With respect to distribution, *Jack went up the hill* and *Jill went up the hill* are equally good sentences of English, and similarly for the other examples. *Jack* and *Jill* enjoy equal status in the noun phrase; neither controls the other, hence the term co-ordinate. Typically, co-ordinate constructions include a marker of co-ordination like *and* or *or* (*My husband AND I; You OR your wife*). Not all co-ordinate constructions show such a marker, as in the example *the little red hen*, where the head noun *hen* is modified by two adjectives that are co-ordinate, *little red*. Another case of co-ordinate dependency with no marker is appositive structures: *President Kennedy; Professor Miller; Mr Bun, the baker; Our father, which art in Heaven.* These examples show that the distributional definition for co-ordinate constructions is less convincing than with the other types of construction we have mentioned.

Heads of constructions allow, require, or exclude types of constituent. Relations of exclusion are important in so far as they are useful in defining particular grammatical categories. Thus, for example, verbs of state in English do not in general occur with progressive auxiliary verbs, and this is one of their defining characteristics. We find no sentences like **I am knowing Chinese* or **Bill is seeming ill*. Proper nouns in English do not typically co-occur with the definite article (**the Susan*), except when they co-occur with a relative clause (*the Susan I used to go out with twenty years ago*). Mass nouns do not co-occur with plural expressions (**these butter, *Rice are grown in India*).

The discussion has made clear the importance of dependency relations. Such relations lay behind the classification of verbs in Chapter 5; the strict subcategorization frames we established were statements of dependency. Similarly, dependency relations lay behind our discussion of modifier head relations among NP constituents in Chapters 6 and 7, and of adverbs in Chapter 7. We commented above on the problem of whether dependency relations and constituent structure can be successfully handled together. We need not be surprised that dependency relations cannot always be captured in a straightforward fashion in constituent structure grammars; constituent structure grammars are constructed in terms of formally established categories and the constructions they form; whereas dependency relations are, as the name suggests, relations. Furthermore, even if we can adequately represent these relations in constituent structure terms, we need additional interpretive machinery to interpret the relations from constituent structure trees, or constituent structure rules, or both.

There are approaches to description in which dependency relations are more central, but to discuss them here would take us too far out of our way. The interested reader is referred to the brief discussion of 'categorial grammar' in Lyons (1968, pp. 227–31) and to Allerton (1981).

At the beginning of this section we noted that different languages employ different formal means of marking dependency relations – word order, the use of 'markers', case inflections, and so on. In the sections that follow we discuss some of these.

17.2 Encoding: word order and marking

All languages use word order to a greater or lesser extent as a marker of various functional relationships, but different languages impose different ordering restrictions and within any one language some ordering restrictions are strict and others admit of a greater or lesser degree of latitude. It is usually possible to determine, for some particular area of some language, that a particular order is the 'normal' or 'unmarked' order; deviations from this, where they are permitted, usually have some particular stylistic or communicative effect.

In addition, all languages use a number of forms, free or bound, as markers of particular relationships; these markers often have little or no lexical meaning – their function being entirely to mark relationships. This, in English, we find the *-s* used to mark the genitive relation (*John's book, the old man's dog*, and so on) and the *by* found in passive sentences to mark the agent (*The village was destroyed by an earthquake*).

We will consider word order and the use of markers in four constructions in English, and then look briefly at comparable constructions in three other languages: Akan, Scots Gaelic and Turkish.

17.2a   Noun phrases in English

The unmarked order for NP constituents in English is: Determiner, Numeral, Adjective, Noun. The noun is the head of the construction and the other constituents are unilaterally dependent on it. As far as determiners are concerned the ordering is strict; they can only occur initially in the NP, and no reordering is permitted at all. Numerals almost invariably precede adjectives and nouns. Old King Cole, it may be remembered, called for *his fiddlers three*, but this particular ordering seems dictated by the rhyme scheme and is not an option usually available in contemporary spoken English; I can hardly *feed my cats two*! Occasionally we find NPs like *the big four* or *the silent three of St Botolph's*, but the numeral here is perhaps best treated as a nominalization. *The big four* derives from *the four big powers*, where *powers* is elided and may be contextually recovered, just as in *your two will be quite grown up by now, I expect* the word *two* is held to refer to 'children', 'dogs', and so on, as the context dictates (see the discussion on pages 239–40).

In English the unmarked position for adjectives is preceding the noun. There are a few exceptions. When the head noun is an indefinite pronoun, ending in *-body*, *-one*, *-thing*, and so on, then adjectives follow the noun: *somebody clever*, rather than *clever somebody* (a typical 'goon show' usage!). A few adjectives characteristically follow rather than precede the head noun, or regularly have a slightly different meaning from 'the same' adjective when it precedes the head noun:

1   Any *proper* university these days will have a flourishing department of linguistics
2   The school of shorthand is not part of the university *proper* but is closely associated with it

More usually, reordering involves a particular stylistic effect.

Some postposed adjectives, especially those ending in *-able* or *-ible*, retain the basic meaning they have (when they precede the noun) but convey the implication that what they are denoting has only a temporary application. Thus, *the stars visible* refers to stars that are visible at a time specified or implied, while *the visible stars* refers to a category of stars that can (at appropriate times) be seen (Quirk *et al.*, 1985, p. 249).

In sentences like

3   He prefers his mistresses unmarried

his mistresses unmarried is not an NP containing a postposed adjective. *Unmarried* is, rather, a different constituent from the NP *his mistresses*; it may be called a complement. Note the different paraphrase relations between **3** and:

4   He prefers his unmarried mistresses

Paraphrases like:

5a   He prefers his mistresses to be unmarried
5b   He prefers that his mistresses should be unmarried

relate to **3**, and a paraphrase like:

6   He prefers those of his mistresses who are unmarried

relates to **4**.

In English, while adjectives precede the noun, there are also ordering restrictions on adjectives themselves. Thus, for example, we will find *a nippy little red sports car*, but hardly **a red little nippy sports car*. The restrictions in this case relate to subclasses of adjectives which can to some extent be defined semantically – see the exercise on page 87. Subclasses defined in terms of order are known as order classes. We noted in Chapter 7.3 that adverbs also fall into order classes, though restrictions there are less rigorous.

17.2b   *Prepositional phrases in English*

English prepositional phrases are bilaterally dependent constructions. The preposition must always precede the NP, sometimes referred to as the 'object' of the preposition. A preposition can sometimes be separated from its object, as in relative clauses like:

7   The knife which he cut the salami with

but the general pattern is for them to be closely connected and strictly ordered.

17.2c   *Genitive constructions in English*

English has two genitive constructions, both unilaterally dependent. Genitive constructions can be used for a variety of functional relationships in English and in other languages; consider the variety of meanings that can be attached to an expression like *Myron's statue*, which may be: 'possessive' (the statue which Myron owns); 'subjective' ('the statue made by Myron'); 'objective' ('the statue of Myron'); and so on. We shall consider only the 'possessive' sense, both for English and the other languages we look at. One genitive construction uses the marker -*s*, as in:

8   Charlie's book; Pharaoh's daughter

Here the NP marked by -*s* is distributionally equivalent to a possessive pronoun (*his, her, my*, and so on). This NP, which we call the 'possessor', is the modifier of the 'possessed' NP, which is, distributionally, the head of the construction, and must always follow the possessor. The other structure involves a prepositional phrase with *of*:

9   The daughter of Pharaoh; The roof of the car

This time the NP in the genitive construction is distributionally equivalent to a pronoun like *mine* or *hers*, and the possessed precedes the possessor. However, it is still the possessor that is marked, here by the use of *of*. In both cases the head of the construction is the possessed noun – the obligatory noun and the one which controls number concord when such phrases are used as subjects in a sentence. To a certain extent these structures are interchangeable, as an old riddle shows:

10   Is the daughter of Pharaoh's son the son of Pharaoh's daughter?

but this is not always the case. Whichever construction is chosen, there is a strict ordering restriction, though the direction of the ordering is different in each case.

17.2d Sentence constituents in English

In English the unmarked word order of sentence constituents is Subject – Verb – Object, which we abbreviate as SVO. Circumstances when this particular order can be changed are examined in Chapter 20.

The ordering relations found in English for these four constructions do not apply universally. We will examine such structures briefly in three other languages: Akan, Gaelic and Turkish.

17.2e Noun phrases in Akan

In Akan, as in English, NP constructions are unilaterally dependent with the noun as the head of the construction. The normal order of constituents is Noun, Adjective, Determiner (the reverse of the English construction):

11 Gyinamoa ketewa bi
    cat   small   a   *a small cat*
    Onipa   kɛseɛ no
    man   big   the   *the big man*

Even in NPs which contain a relative clause the Determiner is frequently the last NP constituent:

12 Onipa aa   te   ha   no (ye me nua no)
    man   relative he-lives here the (is my brother)
    the man who lives here is my brother

17.2f Prepositional phrases in Akan

Prepositional phrases are bilaterally dependent constructions. Akan has a distributional class of items similar in sense and function to English prepositions, but this class always follows rather than precedes the NP with which it is in construction; they are often called 'postpositions':

13a Ofie   no   ho
house   the   exterior   *outside the house*
13b Ahina no   mu
pot   the   inside   *in the pot*
13c pono no   so
table   the   top   *on the table*

17.2g   Genitive constructions in Akan

In genitive constructions, the possessor precedes the possessed. No separate morph shows this relationship, but, in most genitive constructions, the possessed undergoes a tonal modification:[3]

14 Kofí   *Kofi* (personal name) [_ ‾]   me   *my* [_]
ponkɛ́   *horse* [_ _ ‾]   nantwíé *cow* [_ _ ‾ ‾]
Kofí pónkɛ́   *Kofi's horse* [_ ‾ ‾ _ ‾]
Kofí nántwíé   *Kofi's cow* [_ ‾ ‾ _ ‾ ‾]
me pónkɛ́   *my horse* [_ ‾ _ ‾]

As will be seen, the possessed noun acquires a high tone on its first tone-bearing unit. The tonal modification is a necessary marker of the genitive construction, since order alone does not suffice; this can be seen by considering the following examples, which contrast a genitive construction and an adnominal construction:

15a nsá   *beer* [_ ‾]   tumpáń *bottle* [_ _ ‾ ‾]
ɛsiáḿ   *flour* [_ _ ‾ ‾]   kotokuó *bag* [_ _ ‾ ‾]
15b *genitive*
Nsá túmpáń *beer bottle* [_ ‾ ‾ _ ‾ ‾]
ɛsiáḿ kótokúó *bag of flour* [_ _ ‾ ‾ ‾ _ ‾ ‾]
15c *adnominal*
Nsá tumpáń *bottle of beer* [_ ‾ _ _ ‾ ‾]
ɛsiáḿ kotokuó *bag of flour* [_ _ ‾ ‾ _ _ ‾ ‾]

17.2h   Sentence constituents in Akan

The unmarked order for sentence constituents is, as in English, SVO:

16a Kofi resua   Twii
Kofi is-learning Twii   *Kofi is learning Twii*
16b Kofi kumm gyata no
Kofi killed lion   the   *Kofi killed the lion*

Constituent order in Gaelic is different from both English and Akan.

17.2i Noun phrases in Gaelic

The normal order for NP constituents is Determiner, Noun, Adjective, as we noted in Part One; the noun is the head of the construction:[4]

17a	An iolair	mhór	
	the eagle	big	*the big eagle*
17b	An coi-neanach	beag	
	the rabbit	little	*the little rabbit*
17c	Am fear	beag	
	the man	little	*the small man*
17d	A' chaileag	mhór	
	the woman	big	*the big woman*

17.2j Prepositional phrases in Gaelic

Within the prepositional phrase the preposition precedes its NP object:

18a	anns	an sporran	
	in	the purse	*in the purse*
18b	aig	a' chladach	
	at	the shore	*at the shore*
18c	air	a' chreig	
	on	the rock	*on the rock*

17.2k Genitive constructions in Gaelic

In genitive constructions, the possessed precedes the possessor. The possessor is marked by appearing in the genitive case. Rules for the formation of cases in Gaelic are extremely complicated (the reader is referred to a Gaelic grammar, for example, Mackinnon, 1971) but the principle is clear from the examples; note that in Gaelic the article, as well as, or instead of, the noun may inflect for case:

19	an cat	*the cat*	(nominative, singular)
	a' chait	*of the cat*	(genitive, singular)

nan cat   *of the cats*   (genitive, plural)
an ceann *the head*   (nominative singular)
na cinn   *the heads*   (nominative plural)
Ceann a'chait (head of the cat) *the cat's head*
Cinn nan cat (heads of the cats) *the cats' heads*

(The article is not used with the possessed noun.) Possession is often expressed not with a construction of the sort illustrated above, but in constructions of the following sort:

20a Bha peann aig Màiri
         Was a pen at Mary   *Mary had a pen*
20b Tha cù dubh aig Calum, ach tha cat bàn   aig Màiri
         Is dog black at Calum but is cat white at Mary
         Calum has a black dog, but Mary has a white cat

These may be analysed as V + NP + PP, where the PP is expanded as Prep + NP. Structures of this sort may equally be used to express location:

21 Tha Calum aig a'   chladach
        Is   Calum at the shore   *Calum is at the shore*

(Many languages, including English, show relations between 'locative' and 'possessive' constructions; see the discussion in Chapter 18.4.

17.21   Sentence constituents in Gaelic

The unmarked word order for sentence constituents is VSO:

22a Reic Seumas an car
         Sold James   the car   *James sold the car*
22b Ghlas Màiri an dorus
         Locked Mary the door   *Mary locked the door*

and we have already seen that in structures like **20** the subject immediately follows the verb.

Typical word order patterns in Turkish differ from those we have already examined.

17.2m   *Noun phrases in Turkish*

The typical order of constituents in an NP in Turkish is Adjective, Determiner, Noun:

23   Adj   Art N
     Büyük   bir ev
     big   a   house   *a big house*
     Zeki   bir kız
     intelligent a   girl   *an intelligent girl*

17.2n   *Prepositional phrases in Turkish*

Turkish, like Akan, has postpositions, rather than prepositions – these, obviously, follow the NP:

24a   Karakola   yakin
      police station   near   *near the police station*
24b   sizler   için
      you (pl) for   *for you*

Many expressions that in English translate into prepositional phrases are represented in Turkish by case suffixes, as in Latin. Prepositions in Turkish govern particular case forms; in the examples *yakin* governs the dative, and *için* the absolute, case.

17.2o   *Genitive constructions in Turkish*

There are a variety of genitive constructions, depending on such features as whether the possessor is definite or indefinite, whether it is a 'full NP' or pronominal, and so on. (The interested reader is referred to a Turkish grammar, such as Lewis, 1967.) In all cases the possessor precedes the possessed. If the possessor is definite, both nouns are marked for the relationship; the possessor is in the genitive case and the possessed is marked with a possessive suffix:

25a   Müdürün odası
      director   his-room   *the director's room*
      (*genitive*)

25b   Kızların odaları
girls   their-rooms   *the girls' rooms*
(*gen pl*)

17.2p   *Sentence constituents in Turkish*

Word order in a Turkish sentence is usually SOV. If the subject is a personal pronoun it is usually omitted since the verb is marked for person. Thus:

26a   Ahmet otomobili aldı
Ahmet the car   took   *Ahmet took the car*
26b   Mehmet biraz para   istedi
Mehmet some money wanted
Mehmet wanted some money

The preceding discussion has exemplified four dependency relations in four different languages. The relations remain the same from language to language, but different languages mark the dependencies in different ways. In all of them word order is an important marker of the relation, but word order alone is not always sufficient. In most cases a formal marker of some kind is necessary in addition to word order; sometimes an additional word (like *of* in the English genitive construction); sometimes a morph (like *-s* in the other English genitive construction); sometimes case marking (as in Turkish and Gaelic genitive constructions); sometimes a tonal modification (as in the Akan genitive construction). Sometimes the marker is the only feature differentiating between constructions – as with the genitive and adnominal constructions in Akan.

In many of the constructions exemplified, the dependency relations can be captured in constituent structure terms. For example, prepositional phrases are formed by rules like:

27a   PP → Prep + NP (for English and Gaelic)
27b   PP → NP + Prep (for Akan and Turkish)

When the preposition governs the noun in a certain case, then this too can be captured by an interpretation of these rules.

In other examples the dependency relations are not so easily captured in constituent structure terms. We have already seen that rules like:

28a S → NP + VP
28b VP → V + NP

can account for the constituent structure of English sentences, and through such rules we can reasonably, though not entirely, successfully capture the relevant dependency relations: subject and predicate (**28a**); transitive verb and object (**28b**); and so on. Indeed, we carried out the strict subcategorization of verbs by appealing to different predicate types – different expansions of VP. Such rules seem reasonably adequate for a SVO language like English. Similarly rules like:

29a S → NP + VP
29b VP → NP + V

seem satisfactory for SOV languages like Turkish. In these terms, Gaelic is more difficult, as it has VSO word order; the copula and its complement and the transitive verb and its object are discontinuous around the subject.

In Gaelic, just as in English, verbs can be classified in terms of their predicate type. Thus we find copula + complement:

30 Bha – an cù – dubh
    V   NP   Adj
    (Was – the dog – black) *The dog was black*

(the sentences are analysed into their constituents); copula + locative complement:

31 Bha –Tearlach –anns an Fhraing
    V   NP   PP
    (Was – Charlie – in the France) *Charlie was in France*

intransitive verb:

32 Bhàsaich –Tearlach (Died – Charlie)
    V   NP   *Charlie died*

transitive verb + object:

33   Ghlac –Calum –breac (Caught – Calum – a trout)
    V   NP   NP   *Calum caught a trout*

The above characterizations, like those established previously for English, rely on 'predicate' types – reflected in co-occurrence relations between a verb and some other constituent in the sentence (an intransitive verb in Gaelic, as in English, occurs with one NP, the subject; a transitive verb occurs with two NPs, subject and object; and so on). However, do we want in Gaelic to establish a constituent VP? If we do, then we need a reordering rule to take the verb and place it at the beginning of the sentence in front of the subject NP; do we really want such a drastic structure-changing rule to be involved in the generation of simple sentences? It seems that in Gaelic dependency relations are not as readily interpretable from constituent structure configurations as they may be in English.

A similar problem arises in 'free word order' languages. Latin is often said to be such a language since the translation equivalents of a sentence like 'The boy loves the girl' include:

34a   Puer puellam amat (the boy – the girl – loves, SOV)
34b   Puer amat puellam (SVO)
34c   Amat puer puellam (VSO)

and any other permutation of the three constituents involved.[5] (Latin is not a language in which anything goes with respect to word order – prepositions and their objects are strictly ordered, for instance.) The grammatical relations of subject and object are marked in Latin by case (the subject takes the nominative case and the object, for most verbs, the accusative case, as in the example) rather than order, but the relations remain as relevant as they are in English! AMO is a transitive verb, and in a relation of bilateral dependency with its object NP. Clearly we can decide that one of these orders is basic, either a priori or on some other grounds, frequency of occurrence, for instance. So we might decide that the order shown in **34a** is 'basic' and postulate rules like:

35   S → NP + VP
    VP → NP + V

This analysis enables us to identify in constituent structure terms which NP is the subject and which the object and makes the assignment of the appropriate case relatively straightforward, but involves postulating a transformation 'scrambling' the constituents into any of the permissible orders. But such a description may only be a convenience, and one which derives from an 'English' view of word order.

The point at issue is this. Since grammatical relations of dependency, and so on, are crucial in the description of a language, we need to know which constituents are dependent on which other constituents, and just what type of dependency relation is involved. On the one hand, such relations seem, to an extent which varies between different languages, independent of the facts of word order, and so on; on the other, constituent structure is also important. Both need to be accommodated in a linguistic description. It happens that in English many dependency relations can be described in terms of constituent structure relationships. In some other languages this does not seem the case. Clearly it is possible to force a description of dependency in constituent structure terms on any language (as by the use of rules for Gaelic and Latin like those suggested above), but is this legitimate or appropriate?

A final comment on word order is required. There appears to be a tendency in languages for certain types of ordering restrictions to occur together. In an influential article Greenberg (1966, pp. 73–113) writes:

Linguists are, in general, familiar with the notion that certain languages tend consistently to put modifying or limiting elements before those modified or limited, while others just as consistently do the opposite. Turkish, an example of the former type, puts adjectives before the nouns they modify, places the object of the verb before the verb, the dependent genitive before the governing noun, adverbs before adjectives which they modify, etc. Such languages, moreover, tend to have postpositions for concepts expressed by prepositions in English. A language of the opposite type is Thai [or, as we have seen in this section, Gaelic] in which adjectives follow the noun, the object follows the verb, the genitive follows the governing noun, and there are prepositions. The majority of languages, as for example English, are not well marked in this respect . . . More detailed consideration of these and other phenomena of order soon reveals that some factors are closely related to each other, while others are relatively independent.

These facts about order lead Greenberg to postulate a number of universal tendencies, some of which are:

Universal 1: In declarative sentences with nominal subject and object, the dominant order is almost always one in which the subject precedes the object. This means that although six orders are possible (SVO, SOV, VSO, VOS, OSV and OVS), only three orders occur frequently (SOV, VSO and SVO) and the other three are rare.

Universal 2: In languages with prepositions, the genitive almost always follows the governing noun, while in languages with postpositions it almost always precedes.

Universal 3: Languages with dominant VSO order are always prepositional.

Universal 4: If a language has dominant SOV order and the genitive follows the governing noun, then the adjective likewise follows the noun.

The interested reader is referred to Greenberg's book (1963) for further discussion and exemplification of these universals.

17.3   Linkage: agreement and government

Under the general heading of linkage (a term deriving from Hockett, 1958) we may group together a number of grammatical constructions whose function is to show that two constituents are grammatically or referentially related. We will briefly exemplify two types of linkage, 'pronominal cross-referencing' and 'concord' or 'agreement'.

Pronominal cross-referencing can be illustrated in English with the sentence:

36 John thinks that he is intelligent

The sentence has two possible readings: 'John thinks that he (John) is intelligent' and 'John thinks that he (someone else) is intelligent', depending on whether *John* and *he* are used to refer to the same individual, or co-refer, or refer to different individuals.

We indicate reference by subscripts; if two items co-refer, then they will have the same subscript; if they do not, they will have different subscripts. Thus the two readings of our sentences are:

37 $John_1$ thinks that he_1 is intelligent (he = John)
38 $John_1$ thinks that he_2 is intelligent (he ≠ John)

We suppose that a sentence like **36** is produced by the grammar and that later rules are able to identify co-referentiality. Exactly how these rules operate is complex and not yet fully understood, but the following two informal generalizations account for many, though by no means all, of the curious features of English cross-reference:

(1) If a 'full' NP *precedes* a pronoun, then they may be co-referential.
(2) If a 'full' NP *commands* a pronoun, then they may be co-referential.

The relation of 'command' can be most straightforwardly illustrated with respect to 'main' and 'subordinate' or embedded sentences. An NP in the main sentence commands an NP in a subordinate sentence if the S that immediately dominates the main sentence also dominates the subordinate sentence.[6]

The first generalization is met in **36**: *John* precedes *he*, so they may be co-referential, as is marked in **37**. The qualification 'may' is introduced since the two do not have to be co-referential, as is shown by **38**. The second generalization is illustrated in Figures 17.1 and 17.2. In Figure 17.1 the NP in the subordinate sentence, S2, precedes but does not command the NP in the superordinate sentence, S1, so by generalization (1):

39 After $John_1$ came into the room, he_1 took off his_1 hat

is well formed. In the same figure the NP in S1 commands, though it does not precede, the NP in S2, so by generalization (1):

40 After he_1 came into the room $John_1$ took off his_1 hat is also well formed. In Figure 17.2 the NP in S1 both precedes and commands the NP in S2, so:

    41   John₁ took off his₁ hat after he₁ came into the room

is well formed. But the fourth possibility:

    42   *He₁ took off his₁ hat after John₁ came into the room

is not well formed, since the NP in S2 neither precedes nor commands the NP in S1. In general 'forwards' cross-referencing, as in **39** and **41**, is well formed, since the full NP precedes, and may or may not command, the pronoun, but 'backwards' cross-referencing is only possible when the pronoun is commanded by a full NP; thus

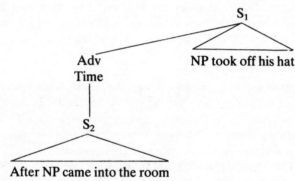

Figure 17.1

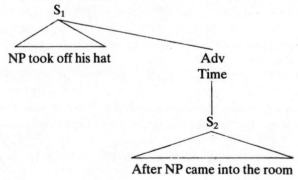

Figure 17.2

40 is well formed, but **42** is not. So, to return to our original example, **36** is well formed since *John* precedes and commands *he*; but

43   *He_1 thinks $John_1$ is intelligent

is ill formed since *John* does not command *he*. (Both **42** and **43** are, of course, well formed if *he* and *John* are not understood to be co-referential.) Note that in co-ordinate structures like that illustrated in Figure 17.3 forward cross-referencing is possible, by generalization (1); but since neither NP commands the other, backwards cross-referencing is not:

44a $John_1$ came into the room and he_1 took off his hat
44b   *He_1 came into the room and $John_1$ took off his hat

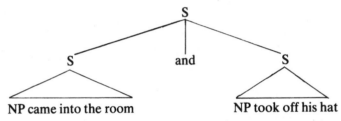

Figure 17.3

Our two generalizations will account for the well-formedness or otherwise of the following:

45a $Mary_1$ married someone she_1 met at college
45b   *She_1 married someone $Mary_1$ met at college

46a $John_1$ said that he_1 wanted to go
46b   *He_1 said that $John_1$ wanted to go

47a   The insinuation that $John_1$ was stupid angered him_1
47b   The insinuation that he_1 was stupid angered $John_1$
47c $John_1$ was angered by the insinuation that he_1 was stupid
47d   *He_1 was angered by the insinuation that $John_1$ was stupid

We will not pursue the mysteries of English forward and backward pronominalization further. We must, however, make one further observation about generalization (1), since it needs a modification to cover instances like:

48 $John_1$ injured $himself_1$
49   *$John_1$ injured him_1

In a simple sentence, when all the constituents are dominated by the same S, as in **48** and **49**, a full NP and a following non-reflexive pronoun cannot be co-referential (there are a few exceptions to this generalization in sentences like *John kept the book near him (self)*). In such circumstances co-referentiality depends on the presence of a reflexive pronoun, as in **48**.

The types of cross-referencing shown for English seem also to occur in many other languages. Some languages, however, can draw distinctions that English does not. Thus, several of the Kwa languages, spoken in West Africa, employ morphologically distinct pronominal forms in some constructions involving 'verbs of reported speech' to distinguish between reference to the speaker and reference to other parties. Thus in Efik, a Nigerian language, the two senses of the sentence:

50a $Okon_1$ agreed that he_1 would pay the debt
(Okon = he)
50b $Okon_1$ agreed that he_2 would pay the debt
(Okon ≠ he)

are differentiated by the use of two different pronouns:

51a   Okon enyime ete $imɔ_1$ eyekpe   isɔn oro
Okon agreed that he   would pay debt the (= **50a**)
52b $Okon_1$ enyime ete $enye_2$ eyekpe   isɔn oro
Okon agreed that he   would pay debt the (= **50b**)

The 'obviative' pronoun *imɔ* is only found in embedded sentences like **51a** where it cross-refers to the subject of a verb of reported speech.

In many languages the main verb may be marked for cross-reference to the subject. Thus in the Latin sentence:

52   Puer puellam amat
boy girl   he loves   *the boy loves the girl*

the form of the verb indicates cross-reference to the subject *puer*.

In such languages, a sentence need not contain an NP subject expression. Thus:

53 puellam amat
      girl   he loves   *he loves the girl*

is well formed. In such a case we say that the verb has 'deictic reference'. This may be to an NP elsewhere in the linguistic context – in a preceding sentence perhaps – or to an individual in the non-linguistic context. In those languages in which verbs are marked in this way, intransitive verbs may, of course, form a complete single-word sentence – this is the case with many modern European languages, like Italian. (This causes problems for a constituent structure grammar of the sort we examined in Part One.)

We now turn our attention to 'concord' or 'agreement'. Two, or more, constituents are said to be 'in concord' when they are both, or all, marked for the same grammatical category. Thus in English demonstratives and the head noun are said to be in concord within the NP: *this book: these books; that book: those books*. The singular form of the demonstrative can only co-occur with the singular form of the noun, and the plural form of the demonstrative with the plural form of the noun – there are no NPs like **these book*. In such constructions one constituent is the 'controller' of the concord (in the case illustrated above it is the head noun), and the other constituents are 'in concord' with the controller; so we say that demonstratives in English concord in number with the head noun within an NP. The reasons why the head noun in English is held to be the controller were explored in Chapter 14.2.[7]

In cases like *these books* the concord category is overtly marked on the controller (*books* has a plural marker). This is not always the case; sometimes the controller is not overtly marked for the category which controls the concord. Thus in French GARÇON is not overtly marked for gender, but it is 'inherently' masculine. This covert category controls concord on other NP constituents, like the article – *le garçon*, not **la garçon*. Similarly in German MANN and FRAU are not overtly marked as masculine and feminine respectively, yet this covert categorization controls concord on articles, adjectives, and so on, within the NP – *ein junger Mann, eine junge Frau*.[8]

In many languages concord is particularly to be noticed in the following constructions:

(1) NP constructions: articles, adjectives and other noun modifiers often concord with the head noun; concord may be for number and/or gender and/or case, and possibly other categories as well.

(2) Subject + main verb constructions: the main verb is often in concord for number with the subject; often other categories, like gender in Arabic and Hebrew, can also concord.

(3) Copulative constructions: the complement is often in concord with the subject, often in number and gender.

English has a limited degree of concord. Some, but not all, NP constituents show concord, as we have seen. Subject–main verb concord does operate:

54a My father (sing) lives (sing) in Somerset
54b My parents (pl) live (pl) in Somerset

but only in a patchy way. There is number concord in copulative constructions with NP complement:

55a This man (sing) is a fool (sing)
55b These men (pl) are fools (pl)

Many languages show no concord at all, or very little. Thus in Akan we find:

56a Onipa kɛseɛno (man big the)   *the big man*
         Nnipa kɛseɛ no (men big the)   *the big men*
56b Onipa no rekasa (man the is-speaking)
         the man is speaking
         Nnipa no rekasa (men the are-speaking)
         the men are speaking
56c Onipa noyɛ kɛseɛ (man the is big)   *the man is big*
         Nnipa noyɛ kɛseɛ (men the are big)   *the men are big*

(Number is shown on the noun by the alternation in the form of the prefix – *o-nipa* 'man', *n-nipa* 'men'.) These examples show no concord at all.

By contrast, some languages show very extensive systems of concord. An example is Luganda (cf. Chapter 14, exercise 2). All nouns in this language have a structure prefix + stem. The prefix shows two things: the gender class to which the noun belongs, and the number of the noun, singular or plural. Luganda, like other Bantu languages, divides nouns into a large number of gender classes; we note only three and refer to them as the *omu-aba, en-en* and *omu-emi* classes, since these are the forms of the singular and plural prefixes taken by the classes in question. First we illustrate concord within NP, which has the constituent order N + Adj + Demonstrative + Numeral. As you will see, Adjectives, Demonstratives and Numerals concord for number and gender class with the head noun:

57a Omu-kazi omu-lungi o-no
     woman   pretty   this   *this pretty woman*
57b Aba-kazi aba-lungi ba-no aba-satu
     woman   pretty   this   three
                                     these three pretty women

58a En-jovu en-kadde ey-o
     elephant old   that   *that old elephant*
58b En-jovu en-kadde ez-o es-satu
     elephant old   that three
                                     those three old elephants

59a Omu-ti omu-tono gu-no
     tree   small   this   *this small tree*
59b Emi-ti emi-tono gi-no e-satu
     tree   small   this   three   *these three small trees*

Two observations are in order. First, while the concord prefixes for the noun head and the adjective modifier are the 'same', different forms of concord prefix may be found on the demonstrative and numeral modifiers. Secondly, while the singular noun and adjective concord prefix is the same for the *omu-aba* and the *omu-emi* classes, the demonstrative and numeral concord prefixes are differentiated for each class. Similarly, the singular and plural noun and adjective prefixes are the same for the *en-en* class, but the demonstrative and numeral prefixes differ. This sort of pattern is very common in Bantu languages.

In sentence constructions there is cross-reference between the subject NP and the main verb. The verb word always carries a subject prefix, which is always the initial morph. This subject prefix not only cross-refers to the subject of the sentence, but it must also be in number and gender concord with the subject NP. In the following examples the verb has the structure subject prefix + tense marker + verb stem:

60a	Omukazi o-no a-li-fa		
	woman this she-future-die	*this woman will die*	
60b	Aba-kazi ba-no ba-li-fa	*these women will die*	

61a	En-jovu ey-o e-ri-fa		
	elephant that it-will-die	*that elephant will die*	
61b	En-jovu ez-o zi-ri-fa	*those elephants will die*	

62a	Omu-ti gu-no gu-li-fa		
	tree this it-will-die	*this tree will die*	
62b	Emi-ti gi-no gi-li-fa	*these trees will die*	

As in Latin (see the discussion of examples **52** and **53**, pages 280–1), and for the same reasons, the verb word in Luganda can form a one-word sentence. In this case we say that the pronoun prefix has deictic reference. So *erifa* (see **61a**) is appropriate if the speaker refers to a single elephant, cow, or other object which nouns of the *en-en* class are used to refer to. Similarly, *gulifa* (see **62a**) is appropriate if the speaker refers to a single tree or some other item which *omu-emi* class nouns are used to refer to.

We now turn to consider patterns of concord and cross-reference in transitive sentences. Basic constituent order is Subject–Verb–Object (SVO). In SVO sentences the verb carries a pronoun prefix which cross-refers to the subject and is in concord with it for number and gender class. There is no cross-reference shown in the verb to the object:

63a	Omu-kazi a-li-goba	en-koko	
	woman she-will-chase	chicken	
		the woman will chase the chicken	
63b	Aba-kazi ba-li-goba	omu-sota	
	women they-will-chase	snake	
		the women will chase the snake	

(-koko 'chicken': class *en-en*; *-sota* 'snake': class *omu-emi*).
Now consider sentences like:

64a Omu-kazi a-li-gi-goba
woman   she-will-it-chase
the woman will chase it (sc. chicken)
64b Aba-kazi ba-li-gu-goba
woman   they-will-it-chase
the women will chase it (sc. snake)

Comparing the sentences in **63** and **64**, we see that when a transitive verb has no object NP expression, the verb carries an object pronoun between the tense marker and the verb stem. This has deictic reference to some appropriate object in the context, and must be in the appropriate form for the gender class and number of the noun which is used to refer to such an object. Object pronouns do not occur within the verb word in sentences of basic SVO constituent order. Let us give some more examples:

65a Omu-sota gu-li-goba   omu-kazi
snake   it-will-chase woman
the snake will chase the woman
65b Omu-sota gu-li-mu-goba
snake   it-will-her-chase
the snake will chase her (sc. woman)

66a En-koko e-li-goba   omu-sota
chicken it-will-chase snake
the chicken will chase the snake
66b En-koko e-li-gu-goba
chicken it-will-it-chase
the chicken will chase it (sc. snake)

In Luganda, unlike English, object pronouns in such sentences are not found as separate constituents, but are rather infixed into the verb word.

Both subject and object may be represented by pronouns within the verb word; then we get one-word sentences like:

67a A-li-gi-goba   *she (sc. woman) will chase it (sc. chicken)*
67b A-li-gu-goba   *she (sc. woman) will chase it (sc. snake)*
67c Gu-li-mu-goba   *it (sc. snake) will chase her (sc. woman)*

67d   Gu-li-gi-goba   *it (sc. snake) will chase it (sc. chicken)*
67e   E-li-gu-goba   *it (sc. chicken) will chase it (sc. snake)*

and so on.

Finally, we discuss a case where the system of concord and cross-referencing can be used for a particular communicative effect. When the order of sentence constituents is SVO we have seen there is no object pronoun within the verb word. Now note these sentences, where this basic word order is disturbed; pronoun referencing within the verb allows the speaker and his or her hearer to keep track, as it were, of 'who is doing what to whom'. The English translations are an attempt to indicate the emphasis, and so on, that these sentences carry (small capitals indicate stress in English):

68a   Omu-kazi a-li-goba en-koko (SVO)
         the woman will chase the chicken
68b   Omu-kazi a-li-gi-goba (SV(O))
         the woman will chase it
68c   Omu-kazi en-koko a-li-gi-goba (SOV)
         the woman will chase the CHICKEN
68d   En-koko omu-kazi a-li-gi-goba (OSV)
         it's the CHICKEN *the woman will chase*
68e   En-koko a-li-gi-goba omu-kazi (OVS)
         it's the CHICKEN *that will be chased by the woman*

Technical terms

agreement	endocentric
command	exclusion
concord	government
controller (of concord)	linkage
co-ordinate dependency	marker
co-reference	paradigmatic
cross-reference	pronominal cross-reference
deictic reference	reflexive
dependency	syntagmatic

Notes

1   Other terms that relate to the same area are stucture and system and chain and choice. These relationships are very general and can be applied to all levels of linguistic description; they apply equally to phonological and semantic descriptions as they do to syntactic ones. We shall, however, only concern ourselves with such relationships in the grammar.

2   Prepositions must be distinguished from homophonous items that are verbal particles:

He added up the bill *but*	He ran up the hill
He added the bill up	*He ran the hill up
He added it up	*He ran it up
*He added up it	He ran up it

3   High tones are marked with an acute accent; low tones are unmarked. Tone-bearing units are: every consonant vowel sequence, and every consonant and vowel left over (*tw* is, phonologically, a single consonant; compare *sh* in English)'. Thus *Kofí* has two tone-bearing units, and *ponké* has three (*po-n-ké*) and so on. High tones are realized at a higher pitch than low tones but in a sequence HLH the second high tone is usually at a slightly lower pitch than the first. The pitch pattern for the examples is as shown after each example, except that this 'lowering' effect is not represented. In the examples that follow, the pattern of tones is represented by dashes enclosed in square brackets, one dash for each syllable. The height of the tones is represented by the height of the dashes inside the square brackets. Nasals – *m* and *n* – may carry a tone.

4   The variant forms of the article depend on the initial consonant or vowel of the noun stem they precede.

5   There is also the problem that we can find sentences like *puellam amat* 'he loves the girl', where no separate word is identifiable as the subject. Since the Latin verb is marked for 'person' (*amo* 'I love', *amas* 'you love', *amat* 'he loves', and so on) the subject is not usually realized as a separate constituent when it is 'pronominal'. We do not consider this complication further.

6   The notion derives from Langacker (1969), who formulates the relation more precisely. The interested reader is referred to this article for further discussion of this interesting area of English grammar.

7   It is possible to take a different view. We have taken the view that number is a category of the noun in English, and that other constituents are in concord with the head noun for number. We might instead assert that number is a category of the NP as a whole, and that all relevant constituents within the NP must be marked for this category. To some extent these different views can be accommodated in different rules. Thus a rule like:

NP → Art + Noun
Noun → N + Number

shows number unambiguously as a category of the Noun. But a rule like:

NP → Art + N + Number

can imply that Number is a category of the NP as a whole.

8 Some writers distinguish between 'concord' and 'governmental concord' depending on whether the concord category is overt (concord) or covert (governmental concord) on the controller. Thus in French, gender is an instance of governmental concord, since gender is covert – there is nothing in the shape of, for example, *plage, maison,* or *ville* to signal that they are feminine. (There are some patterns – for instance, most nouns ending in *-age* are masculine, with a handful of exceptions – but it is none the less true that there is no specific morph signalling the gender of a given noun.) In contrast, number is a matter of simple concord, since number is overt: *le garçon* 'the boy': *les garçons* 'the boys'.

Exercises

These two exercises illustrate concord systems in two languages, Russian and Gaelic. The Gaelic builds on the previous exercises on pages 53–55.

(1) *Russian*

The following examples illustrate concord between nouns and verbs. Assume that any other combinations of nouns and verbs are incorrect. Analyse the examples and answer the questions set out at the end. The following abbreviations are used: sg: singular, pl: plural, 3: 3rd person, 2: second person, 1: first person, nom: nominative case, acc: accustative case, dat: dative case.

1 Tanja znaet Mašu
   Tanja know-3-sg Mašu-acc   Tanja knows Masha
2 Maša vidit Tanju
   Maša see-3-sg Tanja-acc   Masha sees Tanja
3 Devuški znajut Petra
   Girl-nom-pl know-3-pl Peter-acc   The girls know Peter
4 (My) vidim Tanju
   We see-1-pl Tanja-acc   We see Tanja
5 (Ty) znaeš' Masu
   you-sg know-2-sg Masa-acc   You (sg) know Masha
6 (Ja) vižu Tanju
   I see-1-sg Tanja-acc   (I) see Tanja
7 Devuški vidjat Petra
   girl-nom-pl see-3-pl Peter-acc   The girls see Peter

8 (vy) znaete Tanju
    you-pl know-2-pl Tanja-acc   You (pl) know Tanja

9 (my) znaem Mašu
    we know-1-pl Maša-acc   We know Masha

10 (ja) znaju Tanju
    I know-1-sg Tanja-acc   I know Tanja

11 (ty) vidiš' Masu
    you-sg see-2-sg Maša-acc   You see Masha

12 Tanja i Maša vidjat Petra
    Tanja-nom and Maša-nom see-3-pl Peter-acc

13 Tanja pomagaet Maše
    Tanja-nom help-3-sg Maša-dat   Tanja is helping Masha

14 Tanja boitsja Mašy
    Tanja-nom fear-3-sg Masa-gen   Tanja fears Masha

15 Tanja vidit devušku
    Tanja-nom see-3-sg girl-acc   Tanja see a/the girl

16 Tanja vidit krasivuju devušku
    Tanja-nom see-3-sg pretty-acc   Tanja sees the pretty
    girl-acc   girl

17 Tanja pomogaet krasivoj devuške
    Tanja-nom help-3-sg pretty-dat   Tanja helps the pretty
    girl-dat   girl

18 Krasivaja devuška pomogaet Tanje
    Pretty-nom girl-nom help-3-sg   The pretty girl helps
    Tanja-dat   Tanja

19 Tanja pomogaet krasivym devuškam
    Tanja-nom help-3-sig   Tanja helps the pretty
    pretty-dat-girl-dat   girls

20 Tanja vidit krasivyx devušek
    Tanja-nom see-3-sg pretty-acc   Tanja sees the pretty
    girl-acc   girls

Questions:

(a) List the different verb forms.
     State a general rule controlling the occurrence of the verb forms.
(b) List any instances of grammatical conditioning
(c) List the noun forms.
(d) What controls the affixes added to the noun?
(e) List the combinations of noun and adjective.
(f) What controls the affixes added to the adjective? (NB. Some
     information is missing from the glosses of (19) and (20).)

(2)   *Gaelic*

Previous exercises examined NPs of the structure NP →
Art + N; the following NPs contain adjectives as well:

an taigh bàn	the white house
an ràmh gearr	the short oar
an tunnag bhàn	the white duck
an nàbaidh math	the good neighbour
an duilleag mhór	the big page
an sgadan beag	the little hern-rig
an ramh geàrr dubh	the short black oar
an sgoil bheag dhona	the small bad school
an tunnag bheag bhàn	the little white duck
an sgadan beag math	the good little herring
an luinneag mhath	the good song
an là fada	the long day
an sgoil bheag	'the little school'
an nighean gheàrr	'the short girl'
an duine mór	'the big man'
an oidhche fhada	'the long night'

(a)   Write a constituent structure rule that generates the NPs
in these data.

(b)   How many gender classes are there in Gaelic? Assign the
Nouns to your gender classes.

(c)   In the data given, which word class inflects for gender?

(d)   You will discover that inflection for gender (as illustrated
in the data) involves changing the initial consonant of
some words. This process is generally known as *lenition*.
Orthographically lenition is often marked by 'adding an
h' (for example, *bàn*: *bhàn*). Phonologically lenition is
manifested in various ways. In the data the correspond-
ences are as follows – the orthographic forms are shown
first (and in italics); the phonological realizations are
shown in phonemic brackets:

b: /b/ *bh*: /v/ *m*: /m/ *mh*: /v/ *f*: /f/
g: /g/ *gh*: /ʋ/ *d*: /d/ *dh*: /ʋ/ *fh*: 0

(e)   Describe the rule for gender concord within the NP.

(f)   Previous Gaelic exercises examined some sentences
using the 'attributive copula' verb form *bha*. Refer to

those data and your analysis. Here are four more similar sentences:

bha an taigh beag	the house was little
bha an duine math	the man was good
bha an oidhche fada	the night was long
bha an nighean dona	the girl was bad

What is the rule for concord in these sentences between the subject noun and the adjective?

(g) On the basis of your analysis of earlier questions, analyse the following sentences:

bha an tunnag bheag ban	the little duck was white
bha an tunnag beag ban	the duck was little and white
bha an sgoil mhór dona	the big school was bad
bha an sgoil mór dona	the school was big and bad
bha an duine mór dubh	the big man was black/
	the man was big and black
bha an taigh beag bàn	the little house was white/
	the house was little and white

(h) Notice that no ambiguity arises in the first two pairs of sentences, but that the last two sentences are ambiguous. How do you account for this?

(i) Draw two tree diagrams for the final sentence which will show how the ambiguity arises.

18 Processes and participants

18.1 Introduction

This chapter is concerned with the 'propositional structure' of the sentence. This term relates to:

(1) the type of 'state' or 'action' described by the sentence – this we call the 'process' of the sentence, and it is largely associated with the verb;
(2) the 'participant roles' involved in the state or action – these are typically associated with NPs in construction with the verb.

Chapter 7 introduced nuclear and non-nuclear constituents in a sentence. Nuclear constituents are typically obligatory; non-nuclear constituents are typically optional. Corresponding to the nucleus of a sentence are the notion of process and the participants in it; together they form the 'propositional nucleus'. Depending on the number of participants that can be identified, the propositional nucleus can be described as 'one-place' (for example, *John ran*), 'two-place' (*John sharpened the knife*), or 'three-place' (*John gave a book to Mary*).

In the syntactic structure of the sentence, non-nuclear constituents may accompany the nucleus. It is useful to recognize 'circumstantial' roles which correspond to the non-nuclear constituents and which are associated with the propositional nucleus. These are typically adverbs of time, place, manner, and so on, and are optional in the propositional structure. *John sharpened the knife in the woodshed last night* involves a two-place propositional nucleus with circumstantial constituents of place and time.

From now on we will use the term 'participants' even when referring to constituents of place and time, and so on, but our major concern is the propositional nucleus. The sorts of processes and participants we identify are probably common to all languages, though their syntactic realization differs from language to language. Our discussion focuses on English.

18.2 Actions and states

Let us begin with the sentences:

1 John sharpened the knife
2 The knife was sharp

In simple constituent structure terms these sentences are dissimilar; **1** is a transitive and **2** a copular sentence. In propositional terms they are more closely related; **1** describes an action ('sharpening the knife') that brings about the state of affairs described in **2** ('the knife being sharp'). The link is reflected in the lexical relations between the sentences. The NP *the knife* is the object in the [action] sentence but the subject in the [state] sentence, and the verb SHARPEN is morphologically related to the adjective SHARP.

The distinction between sentences describing actions and those describing states is fundamental. It is relevant to other pairs of sentences that we will examine and is reflected in various syntactic phenomena. The progressive is typically excluded from [state] sentences:[1]

3a John is sharpening the knife
3b *The knife is being sharp

Only [action] propositions containing an [agent] can be realized as imperative sentences:

4a Sharpen the knife
4b *Be sharp!

4b is possible if *sharp* has the figurative meaning of 'mentally alert', but note the peculiarity of *Be tall!* or *Be beautiful!*.

Only [action] propositions are typically associated with [instrument] (**5**) and [benefactive] (**6**) roles:

5a John is sharpening the knife with a whetstone
5b *The knife is sharp with a whetstone

(The [instrument] role is realized by *with a whetstone*; note that [instrument] roles are frequently identifiable by the use of the preposition *with* – we note the frequent association of roles with particular prepositions.)

6a   John is sharpening the knife for his mother
6b   *The knife is sharp for his mother

(The [benefactive] role is realized by *for his mother* – she is the participant who 'benefits' from the action; it can frequently be identified by the preposition *for*.) [State] propositions cannot usually be associated with circumstantial roles of manner, place and intention:

7a   John is sharpening the knife carefully
7a^1   *The knife is sharp carefully   (manner)
7b   John is sharpening the knife in the woodshed
7b^1   *The knife is sharp in the woodshed   (place)
7c   John is sharpening the knife intentionally
7c^1   *The knife is sharp intentionally   (intention)

Circumstantial roles of manner and intention seem characteristically tied to the occurrence of [agent], as *John was careful in sharpening the knife*; *John acted intentionally in sharpening the knife*. One might attest **7c^1**, but only if it has the sense 'it was someone's intention (agentive) that the knife should be sharp'; this sentence can hardly be construed with the sense 'the knife had the intention of being sharp'. Place participants, on the other hand, appear tied to the proposition as a whole: *Where John sharpened the knife was in the woodshed*. *Where the knife was sharp was in the woodshed* is nonsense – it implies that it wasn't sharp elsewhere!

18.3   Agent and patient: range, result and neutral

Let us now turn to some distinctions that can be drawn between the various types of [action] proposition. They can typically be questioned by:

8   What happened?

Thus:

9a What happened?
9b John sharpened the knife
9c John ran a race

and so on.

This is not possible for [state] propositions. *What happened?* does not allow the answer *The knife was sharp*, though the latter sentence can be the answer to questions such as *What was the knife like?* or *Can you describe the knife?*. [Action] propositions with [agent] can typically be questioned by:

10 What did [agent] do?

Thus:

11a What did John do?
11b He sharpened the knife
11c He built a house

and so on.

We have not yet encountered [action] sentences without [agent], but this generalization can be tested when we do. [Action] propositions with [agent] and [patient] can typically be questioned with:

12 What did [agent] do to [patient]?

Thus:

13a What did John do to the knife?
13b He sharpened it

14a What did John do to the dog?
14b He beat it

but hardly:

15a ?What did John do to the house?
15b ?He built it

and so on. Similarly, we find the question

16   What happened to [patient]?

as in:

17a   What happened to the dog?
17b   John beat it

but not:

18a   *What happened to the race?
18b   *John ran it

15 and **18** are peculiar because the propositions they express do not involve an agent acting on a patient. The house in **15** results from the building process, whereas the dog in **17** can hardly be described as the result of the beating. The object of BUILD, and also verbs such as DIG, BURN, PAINT, is [result], as in **19**:

19a   The dog is digging a hole
19b   The cigar burnt a hole (in the carpet)
19c   Velasquez painted the Rokeby Venus

The process of running has a [range]. In **18** the range is a race (distance not mentioned), but in **20** the distance is specified:

20   Harold ran a mile

Other processes, such as playing and singing, are also appropriately described as having a [range]. In **21** the playing ranges over a game, and the singing ranges over a song. Note that the agent is not doing anything to either the game or the song; they are not affected by the action:

21a   Peter is playing tiddlywinks
21b   Mary sang a song

[Range] participants occur with [state] processes too, as in **22**:

22a   The painting cost £5,000
22b   The statue weighs 20 tons
22c   His jump measured 29 feet

Some verbs can take either a [result] or a [patient] participant:

23a I painted a picture [result]
23b I painted the sitting room [patient]

24a Celia burned a hole in the carpet [result]
24b Celia burned the garden rubbish [patient]

The difference between [patient], [result] and [range] participants is reflected in syntax. As shown above, only a sentence with a [patient] participant can be an appropriate answer to *What did agent do to X?*. Only [patient] and [result] participants can occur freely as the subject of passive sentences.

25a The dog was beaten by its master
25b The picture was painted by Velasquez
25c Tiddlywinks was played by John

25c is acceptable only if it describes a habitual state of affairs but it is decidedly odd as a description of a single occasion.

22 contains a [range] participant and a [state] verb. The first NP is a [neutral] participant, [neutral] indicating that it is difficult to label the first NP either [agent] or [patient]. Other sentences relating to [state] processes require yet other participants:

26a Monica had the house in the South of France
26b Miranda knew all the answers
26c Gill believed the salesman

These examples do not describe actions, but they do not describe straightforward [state] processes either. The equivalents of 26 in other languages often involve special case affixes and prepositions, different from the case affixes that attach to agent nouns. Note that 26a and 26b have unusual paraphrases, in which the subject NP becomes the object of a preposition:

27a The house in the South of France belonged to Monica
27b All the answers were known to Miranda

We will say that in 26 *Monica* and *Miranda* are [dative] participants, the label reflecting the fact that in a number of languages the nouns would be in the dative case. Similarly, *Gill* in **26c** is [dative]. The second participant in each of the examples in **26** is [neutral] – clearly not [agent] but not obviously [patient] either. Other verbs that take [dative] and [neutral] participants are UNDERSTAND, OWN, SEE and HEAR.

Just as verbs describe [action] or [state] processes, so adjectives fall into two classes. Typically, adjectives describe states and only states: for example, TALL, UGLY, SLEEPY and WOODEN. A small number of adjectives can describe states or actions. Interestingly, whereas some verbs describe actions and others describe states, there are no adjectives that describe only actions. They either describe states only, or have a dual use, as in **28** and **29**:

> **28a** The children are being polite (= are behaving politely)
> **28b** The children are polite
>
> **29a** Billy is being silly (= is behaving in a silly fashion)
> **29b** Billy is silly

In the **a** examples the subject noun is [agent], but in the **b** examples it is [neutral].

Some [state] adjectives take a [dative] participant; they describe psychological states, as in **30**, or some physical states involving bodily sensation, such as COLD, HOT, HUNGRY, or THIRSTY. The participant is called [dative] because in a number of languages the noun is in the dative case:

> **30a** Celia is cold
> **30b** Frank is ashamed
> **30c** Alfred is sad

[Agent], [patient], [result], [range], [dative] and [neutral] participants are central to processes. Other types of participants can be recognized which are not so central and can be omitted, but which are clearly marked by prepositions:

> **31a** Alan burned a pattern in the wood with a hot poker
> **31b** John bought some books for Michael
> **31c** The vase was knocked over by Harry

With marks the [instrument] participant, and *for* marks the benefactive participant; that is, the participant who benefits from an action; *by* marks the [agent].

18.4 Location and motion: locative place, goal, source and path

[Action] and [state] verbs fall into a number of different subclasses. Here we can mention only one or two more important classes, beginning with verbs which are [state] + [location] and verbs which are [action] + [motion]. [Location] verbs take [locative place] participants:

32a   The casserole is in the oven
32b   The dog is under the table
32c   There is a wall round the garden

In, under and *round*, along with many other prepositions, signal [locative place]. A detailed account of [locative place] prepositions in English, and other languages, would have to describe the meaning and use of the different prepositions, but there is no space here for such an account.

[Motion] verbs allow [locative goal], [locative source] and [locative path] participants:

33a   They are going to Denmark
33b   A visitor has come from Xanadu
33c   We flew via Islamabad

To signals [locative goal], *from* signals [locative source], and *via* signals [locative path].

Other participant roles are clearly analogous to the locative ones but are not identical with them. They are signalled by the same prepositions but are not given exactly the same interpretation:

34a   This book gave the idea to John
34b   I learned this from her letter
34c   I received the news via Susan's mother

34a describes a situation in which an idea is conceived of as moving a book to a person. The movement cannot be observed but 34a is analogous to 33a. Similarly, 34b is analogous to 33b, and 34c to 33c.

To capture the analogy, *John* is labelled [goal], *letter* is labelled [source] and *Susan's mother* is labelled [path]. The absence of 'locative' indicates that 'abstract' rather than 'concrete' movement is involved.

[Motion] verbs can be accompanied by all three participants exemplified in **33**:

> **35**   We flew from London to Peking via Islamabad

18.5   Inchoative and causative-inchoative verbs

18.5a   (Causative-) inchoative verbs and participants

Two other subclasses of [action] verbs must be discussed: [inchoative] and [causative-inchoative]. Propositions with [inchoative] verbs describe an entity changing from one state to another; propositions with [causative-inchoative] verbs describe one entity acting on another so as to make it change state. The different classes of verbs take different types and numbers of participants.

The sentence:

> **36**   The shirt is torn

contains a [state] verb – or verb plus passive participle – *is torn* and describes the state of the shirt. In contrast, the sentence:

> **37**   John is tearing the shirt

contains the [causative-inchoative] verb *is tearing* and describes John acting on the shirt so as to make it torn. The verb in **36** is one-place, and takes a [neutral] participant, the shirt being neither [agent] nor [patient]. The verb in **37** is two-place, and takes an [agent] participant, *John*, and a [patient] participant, *the shirt*.

A propositional structure that seems to be intermediate between **36** and **37** is:

> **38**   The shirt is tearing

The verb is one-place. It is [action], since **38** is an appropriate answer to the question *What is happening?* and even to *What is* *happening to the shirt?* The latter question indicates that *the shirt* is [patient]. That is, **38** has a propositional structure with a one-place verb, like [state] propositions, but with a [patient], like [action] propositions.

18.5b   States and (causative-) inchoative verbs in English

A very large number of sentences in English can be related to each other in the manner shown in **36–8**. Some lexical items that are related in this way are shown in Figure 18.1; readers are invited to check this by constructing appropriate sentences. In Figure 18.1 the three columns are to be understood as relating, from left to right, to the propositional structure of **36, 38** and **37**.

	state (= 36)	*action* *inchoative* (= 38)	*action directed* *causative-inchoative* (= 37)
(a)	RIPE	RIPEN	RIPEN
	WIDE	WIDEN	WIDEN
(b)	YELLOW	YELLOW	YELLOW
	COOL	COOL	COOL
(c)	TORN	TEAR	TEAR
	CLOSED	CLOSE	CLOSE
(d)	MOLTEN	MELT	MELT
	ROTTEN	ROT	ROT
(e)	SHARP	—	SHARPEN
	MOIST	—	MOISTEN
(f)	LARGE	—	ENLARGE
	BOLD	—	EMBOLDEN
(g)	PASSIVE	—	PASSIVIZE
	BEAUTIFUL	—	BEAUTIFY
(h)	DEAD	DIE	KILL
	HIGH	RISE	RAISE
(i)	—	VANISH	—

Figure 18.1

A number of observations can be made about the sets of items in Figure 18.1. The relationship typically involves an adjective (left-hand column), an intransitive verb (central column) and a transitive verb (right-hand column). Sometimes (a, e, f, g) there is a morphological relationship of derivation (RIPE: RIPEN, and so on);

sometimes (b) the 'same' form is used in all three columns (YELLOW); sometimes (c) the 'adjectival' form is the same as the passive participle of the corresponding verb (TORN: TEAR); sometimes (d) the adjectival form is a former passive participle (MOLTEN: MELT); sometimes (h) there is a suppletive relationship between the adjective, and one or more of the verb forms (DEAD: DIE: KILL). There are also cases where there is a causative form, but no corresponding inchoative (SHARP: SHARPEN).

In some of the cases involving asymmetries an alternative expression, as it were, 'fills the gap'. Thus, for example, corresponding to:

> **39a** The gap is narrow
> **39b** The gap is narrowing
> **39c** John is narrowing the gap

we find:

> **40a** The gap is large
> **40b** The gap is getting larger/the gap is becoming larger
> **40c** John is enlarging the gap

but there is no sentence:

> **41** *The gap is enlarging

Corresponding to sentences like **39b** we can have:

> **42a** The gap is getting narrow
> **42b** The gap is becoming narrow

The different types of proposition are related in interesting ways. [State] propositions are realized by the copula BE, though other copulas, such as SEEM, are equally appropriate. The [inchoative] proposition can be realized in two ways; either the [inchoative] component is incorporated in the adjective, which becomes a verb, as in **39b**, or it is realized as a separate verb, GET or BECOME, as in **42a** and **42b**. Similarly, the [causative] component can be incorporated into the inchoative verb as in **39c** or realized as a separate verb, such as MAKE: *John is making the gap larger/large.*

Note that the [inchoative] and [causative-inchoative] forms are not available to every lexical item. There are no such forms for LARGE, though INCREASE has them:

43a The gap is increasing
43b John is increasing the gap

On the other hand, there is no adjective corresponding to INCREASE.

18.5c (Causative-) inchoative motion verbs

The relationship between [state], [inchoative] and [causative-inchoative] propositions is to be observed in [motion] verbs too:

44a Bill is in Glasgow [state]
44b Bill went to Glasgow [inchoative]
44c Celia sent Bill to Glasgow [causative-inchoative]

Strictly speaking, **44a** describes Bill's location rather than Bill's state, but there are parallels; just as *Bill became ill* implies *Bill was ill*, so *Bill went to Glasgow* implies *Bill was in Glasgow*. Just as *John narrowed the gap* can be paraphrased as *John made the gap (become) narrow*, so *Celia sent Bill to Glasgow* can be paraphrased as *Celia made Bill go to Glasgow*.

A word of caution is called for; *caused X to go* and *sent X* are not identical in meaning. *Caused Bill to go* has a wider range of application than *sent Bill*, since it can be used in circumstances where Celia organizes the event indirectly and even at long range, say by writing to Bill's parents or Bill's boss. In contrast, *sent Bill* is appropriate only where Celia directly orders Bill to go to Glasgow.

A number of [motion] verbs occur in both [inchoative] and [causative-inchoative] propositions:

45a The ball rolled into the corner
45b Jane rolled the ball into the corner

46a The boat floated on to the beach
46b We floated the boat on to the beach

Like GO and SEND are FALL/FELL; like ROLL and FLOAT are SLIDE and DROP. PUSH, DRAG and SHOVE are only [causative-inchoative], while DESCEND, DISAPPEAR and VANISH are [inchoative] only.

18.5d   Knowing and possessing

To round off the discussion of [inchoative] and [causative-inchoative] propositions, we can usefully note that the distinctions are relevant to [state] verbs that take [dative] participants:

> **47a**   Mary knows German [state]
> **47b**   Mary is learning German [inchoative]
> **47c**   Regina is teaching Mary German [causative-inchoative]

> **48a**   Alison has a car [state]
> **48b**   Alison is buying a car [inchoative]
> **48c**   The salesman sold Alison the car [causative-inchoative]

48c is interpretable as [causative-inchoative] only with respect to a particular sense of SELL; the salesman persuades Alison to buy the car. Normally, the [causative] component has to be realized as the separate verb MAKE:

> **49**   Jane made Alison buy the car

18.6   [State] propositions: description and identification; neutral and attribute

At the beginning of the chapter [state] propositions were mentioned and [state] sentences with [neutral] participants, the copula BE and adjectives were introduced. It is time to return to these examples, beginning with the observation that such propositions can be labelled [descriptive]. The noun is [neutral], neither [agent] nor [patient] and not obviously anything more positive. The adjective too has a role to play in the proposition and the sentence; that role we will call [attribute]. We have seen above that such [state], [descriptive] propositions have [inchoative] and [causative-inchoative] counterparts.

The examples of [state] propositions have all been realized as [state] sentences containing BE + Adjective. Another realization of [state] propositions is as sentences with BE and an indefinite NP.

These propositions/sentences too can be [state], [inchoative] and [causative-inchoative]:

50a Findlay is a real busybody [state]
50b Findlay has become a real busybody [inchoative]
50c These experiences turned Findlay into a real busybody
[causative-inchoative]

The final set of sentences to be examined are also [state], but not descriptive:

51a Fiona is the convener
51b The convener is Fiona

52a The committee elected Fiona convener
52b The committee elected Fiona as the convener
52c The committee elected Fiona to be the convener

Our sentences are once more related as [state] to [action]. The first two sentences we may describe as involving [identification]; Fiona is identified as the person who occupies a certain position, or plays a certain role, that of convener. The second set of sentences all describe an action that can cause such a state.

Let us look first at the sentences **51**; it is suggested that these are [identification] sentences. In order to discuss some of the peculiar characteristics of such sentences we can best compare them with sentences like **2** (*The knife was sharp*) where we were dealing with the attribution of a quality to an object; in the particular case of **2** we were concerned with the attribution of 'sharpness' to 'the knife'. Here we are concerned with the identification of 'Fiona' as filling the particular role of 'convener'. The distinction between [attribute] and [identification] can be seen more clearly in a slightly different example:

53 My wife is tall and beautiful
54 My wife is that tall and beautiful woman over there

53 describes my wife; **54** identifies her. Note that **54**, but not **53**, reasonably answers the questions:

55 Who is your wife?
Which one is your wife?

Questions like **55** are asking for an identification, not a description.

[Identification] sentences have certain syntactic peculiarities. We concern ourselves with two of them. First, both NPs are characteristically definite; they are usually either proper names, like *Fiona*, or NPs with the definite article, like *the convener*. Definite NPs usually refer uniquely to some individual in the context of utterance. With descriptive sentences, the subject NP is often definite, but the other constituent usually either is an adjective or, if it is an NP, does not contain the definite article:

> **56** My wife is a good cook, teacher, etc.
> My wife is tall and beautiful, etc.

In these examples, the adjectives and non-definite NPs do not refer; they rather describe. Thus, for example, in **51** both *Fiona* and *the convener* are NPs that could be used to refer; whereas in **56** the NP *my wife* can be used to refer to a unique individual, but *a good cook* cannot.

The second characteristic is that the NPs in identification sentences are reversible round the verb. Thus, for example, in answer to the question:

> **57** Which one is Fiona?

we might find:

> **58** Fiona is the conVENer
> The conVENer is Fiona

The capitals indicate that *con*VEN*er* is the word that appropriately in this context receives the sentence stress – it is the centre of the intonation contour. Note that whichever word order is used, the stress centres on conVENer – the NP that answers the identifying question. This particular characteristic of such sentences complicates our description, since the question can be phrased the other way:

> **59** Which one is the convener?
> **60** FIONA is the convener
> The convener is FIONA

where the intonation placement is exactly reversed. We clearly need to know what is intended by a particular sentence before we can properly assign a propositional structure to it: thus we say that with respect to the sequence **57** and **58** *convener* is the NP that is identified with the function we describe as [role]; whereas in **58** and **59**, it is clearly *Fiona* that has this function. The other NP we describe as realizing a [neutral] function.

What now of the sentences in **52**? Here *the committee* can be assigned the role [agent] and Fiona the role [neutral, patient]. *Convener* we describe as [role] as before.

18.7 Conclusion

We have obviously described only a part of the propositional structure of English – some exercises at the end of the chapter invite the reader to explore some of the many other areas that lend themselves to a description of this sort – but the part we have described includes some of the most important and fundamental relationships among propositions that are to be found in English. Although we have concentrated on English, remember that relationships of this sort are found in many languages – indeed, possibly in all languages.

To close, we briefly consider two questions. How redundant are the specifications? How many propositional roles, and so on, are we to recognize? As to the first question, it is clear that there is a certain amount of redundancy; for example, all [causative] structures involve an [agent]. The redundancy can be removed, but we prefer to keep it, partly for the sake of clarity, and partly because role features cannot always be predicted on the basis of process types, or vice versa; and until a full classification is developed in these terms it is unclear exactly what redundancy can be removed.

The second question is more difficult. We can choose either to reduce the number of roles, thus achieving an apparently 'simpler' system, or to multiply the number of roles, thus achieving a descriptively more accurate system. For example, we can collapse together the 'locative' roles ([Lplace], [Lgoal] and [Lsource]) and the 'dative' roles ([dative], [goal] and [source]). A justification for this is their very close relation, both semantically and grammatically. Typically we choose a 'dative' characterization for an animate noun, otherwise a 'locative' characterization. Furthermore, it seems that nuclear propositions cannot contain both a [dative] and a 'locative' participant (a dative proposition may, of course, be associated with a locative circumstantial role – *John gave Mary the money in the park* – but that is a different matter). On the other hand, there are grammatical differences between the two types of proposition, and they define different classes of verb (for example, 'locative' and 'verbs of motion', and 'dative' and 'verbs of giving and receiving'). A case where we might choose to multiply roles is [agent], which involves a number of notions that might be stranded out – 'initiator', 'actor', and so on:

> **61a**   Harry chopped the logs [actor]
> **61b**   Harry jumped the horses over the fence [initiator]

As so often in linguistic descriptions, a balance must be sought between maximum generality (the 'reductionist' approach, which leads to numerous instances requiring some special treatment – as with our [agent] role) and maximum explicitness (which leads to a proliferation of roles and might eventually lead to identifying a unique structure for every use of every verb, since presumably all verbs differ, however slightly, in their grammatical and semantic behaviour). We justify our description by its offering a degree of both generality and particularity. This conclusion is uncomfortable, since it has no easily defended validity, but there seems to be no alternative in the current state of knowledge. We can only take refuge in the fact that it is a position shared by anyone who attempts a description along these lines, and it seems to reflect the somewhat indeterminate nature of this aspect of language.

Technical terms

analytic;   circumstantial   roles;   incorporation;   proposition; propositional nucleus; propositional structure.

Process terms

action; causative; descriptive; directed; identification; inchoative; locative; possessive; state.

Participation role terms

agent
attribute, neutral, patient, result, role
dative goal, path, source
locative goal, path, place, source
benefactive, instrument, range

Examples of processes and participants

[action]	Agent		She was singing
	Patient		The string broke
	Agent	Patient	John sharpened the knife
	Agent	Result	The dog is digging a hole
	Agent	Range	Harold ran a mile
	Agent	Locative Goal	Susan went to Denmark
	Agent	Locative Source	Yasuko is arriving from Kyoto
	Agent	Locative Path	Helen travelled via Samarkand
	Agent	Patient Goal	She gave the book to Bill
	Agent	Patient Source	I got the cassette from David
	Agent	Patient Path	I contacted Jane via her sister
[state]	Neutral	Range	The painting cost £5,000
	Dative	Neutral	Miranda knew all the answers
			Harriet owns a cat
	Dative		Celia is cold/sad
	Neutral		The child is sleeping
	Neutral	Attribute	The town is dirty
	Neutral	Role	Fiona is the convener

Note

1 For prominence, labels for type of process and type of participant will be put in square brackets in the text.

Exercises

(1)   On page 297 the sentence *Miranda knew all the answers* is analysed as describing a [state] process. The participant roles are [dative] for *Miranda* and [neutral] for *answers*.

    (a)   Consider the following English sentences and decide which are acceptable, which are unacceptable and which are merely peculiar.

         (i)   Miranda is knowing all the answers [progressive]
        (ii)   What Miranda did was know all the answers [pseudo-cleft]
       (iii) Know all the answers [imperative]
       (iv)   Miranda knew all the answers in order to pass the exam [purpose]
        (v)   Miranda not only knew the answers on Friday but was still at it on Saturday [BE AT IT]
       (vi)   Miranda enthusiastically knew all the answers [manner adverb]

    (b)   Consider now the following sentences. Which ones can be converted to the constructions exemplified above? You may find that some of the sentences cannot be converted to any, or can be converted only to some, of the constructions. The tests pick out verbs describing [state] processes – stative verbs – but we may have to recognize a scale of 'stativeness'. The more stative the verb, the greater its 'resistance' to the constructions.

         (i)   Jane wrote a letter
        (ii)   Kirsty owned a flat in Heriot Row
       (iii) Brian washed the dishes
       (iv)   Bill understood the problem
        (v)   Susan heard the noise outside
       (vi)   The judge heard the case yesterday
      (vii)   Isabella saw Long's Peak against the dawn sky
      (viii) Isabella saw her solicitor last week
       (ix)   The crowds believed the Party's message

(2)   Consider these Russian examples and answer the questions below.

   (i)   Boris tolknul Mikhaila   Boris pushed Mikhail

   (ii)   Mikhail tolknul Borisa   Mikhail pushed Boris

  (iii) Boris dal kljuch Mikhailu Boris gave the key to Mikhail

  (iv) Mikhail vernul kljuch Borisu Mikhail returned the key to Boris

   (v) Borisu izvestno, chto Mikhail brosil plan Boris knows that Mikhail abandoned the plan

  (vi) Mikhailu veritsja, chto perestroika nuzhna Mikhail believes that perestroika is necessary

 (vii) Borisu stydno, chto lgal Boris is ashamed that he lied

(viii) Mikhailu xolodno Mikhail is cold

  (ix) Mikhailu vypalos' vvodit' perestroiku It fell to Mikhail to introduce perestroika

Questions:

(a)   Assign roles to the nouns in sentences (i)–(iv).

(b)   Say how these roles are marked in the nouns.

(c)   On the basis of the translations, assign a role to the nouns (v)–(viii).

(d)   Say how this role is marked.

(e)   Comment on the marking of the role in (v) and (vi), the marking of the roles in (i)–(iv) and the roles in (ix).

(3)   We have examined sentences expressing [action] pro-positions: for example, *John is sharpening the knife*. The roles are [agent] for *John* and [patient] for *knife*. The sentence can be made passive: *The knife is being sharpened by John* – note also *The knife is being sharpened*.

Questions:

(a)   When the sentence is made passive, what is the effect on the [agent] noun?

(b)   What is the effect on the [patient] noun?

(c)   Consider the examples:

    (i)   The gardener planted the garden with roses

   (ii)   The gardener planted roses in the garden

Can both of the sentences be made passive?

(d)   Assign roles to the nouns in the two sentences in (c).

(e)   Would you use both or only one of the sentences in (c) to describe the following situations?

    (i)   The gardener planted roses over the entire garden.

    (ii) The gardener planted roses only in one part of the garden.

(f)   Which of the following verbs are like PLANT and occur in constructions similar to (i) and (ii) in question (c)? (Possibly with different prepositions.)

    SPRAY, SPREAD, ENGRAVE, FESTOON, LOAD

(g)   Which of the above verbs are like PLANT in allowing a change of meaning when there is a change of construction?

19   Grammatical functions

The traditional apparatus of grammatical description includes the set of terms: subject, object, oblique object, indirect object, complement and adjunct. Their definitions are typically an amalgam of features deriving from their grammatical characteristics, from syntactico-semantic characterizations as discussed in the preceding chapter and from characteristics of their behaviour in texts. Criteria of the first two sorts, grammatical and syntactico-semantic, are chiefly involved in this chapter. We cannot entirely avoid textual criteria, but largely leave these until the next chapter. We shall be concerned to establish whether any or all of these notions has or have a special role in grammatical description. The discussion concerns itself with English, since the grammatical characteristics of these notions vary from language to language; the general principles involved, however, do seem to be widely applicable.

19.1   Subject

A distinction is frequently drawn between the 'grammatical' subject (characterized by grammatical considerations, such as being the controller of number agreement), the 'logical' subject (characterized by syntactico-semantic considerations – in sentences with an [agent] NP this is usually held to be the logical subject) and the 'thematic' or 'psychological' subject (characterized by textual considerations – 'this is what the sentence is about'). These can be illustrated in the sentences **1a–c** where G, L and T indicate respectively the grammatical, logical and thematic subjects:

1a   John (G, L, T) took the largest kitten
1b   The largest kitten (G, T) was taken by John (L)
1c   The largest kitten (T), we (G, L) gave away

As can be seen, the three characterizations do not necessarily coincide. We defer consideration of the thematic subject until the next chapter, and concentrate here on the notions of grammatical and logical subject.

We first consider the grammatical subject. All full declarative sentences must have a subject. This is an NP. With few exceptions the grammatical subject immediately precedes the main verb and is in number concord with it. Grammatical subjects are never marked with a preposition. NPs that fulfil these characteristics we call grammatical subjects. As we have seen before, for some actual sentence the structural configuration 'NP that is immediately dominated by S' typically identifies the grammatical subject.

The subject is frequently a 'full' lexical NP, like *John* or *the largest kitten* in **1a** and **1b**, or a pronoun, like *we* in **1c**, but it may also be a nominalized sentence or sentence-like constituent, as in:

2a   *That Edinburgh's New Town is magnificent* is undeniable
2b   *For you to run off with Mary* would be madness

Sometimes when no such constituent is available to act as subject a 'dummy' subject is supplied; this is the case with 'weather' expressions:[1]

3   *It* is raining

and in cases like **4b** where a nominalized sentence is 'extraposed' (see pages 358–60):

4a   *That Edinburgh's New Town is magnificent* is undeniable
4b   *It* is undeniable that Edinburgh's New Town is magnificent

The main verb concords in the singular with the dummy subject *it*. *It* does not, however, have the full range of syntactic possibilities of a full subject – questioning is impossible; no sense is made by asking:

5a   What is raining?
5b   What is undeniable that Edinburgh's New Town is magnificent?

Another item that operates like a dummy subject is *there* in sentences like:

6a There is a glass on the mantelpiece
6b There are glasses in the drinks cupboard

Sentences like these are called 'existential' because they are typically used to assert the existence of something. We call this use of *there* the 'existential' *there*, distinct from another use of *there* in sentences like:

7 There is the glass

which we call the 'deictic' *there* because sentences like **7** can be used to point to something.

Existential *there* has several curious features. It does not control number agreement on the verb, as can be seen in **6a** and **6b**. Unlike the deictic *there*, it cannot be stressed:

8a *There* is the glass (deictic)
8b **There* are glasses in the drinks cupboard (existential)

Connected with this is the fact that it is almost invariably pronounced in a 'reduced' form: / ðəz / 'there is', / ðərə / 'there are': the deictic *there* is usually non-reduced: / ðɛərɪz / 'there is' / ðɛərə / 'there are'. Thus / ðəz ə glas / 'There is a glass', with the reduced form, is understood as existential and not deictic. Finally we note that existential *there* is always in subject position:

9a There are glasses in the drinks cupboard
9b **Glasses in the drinks cupboard are there

(*It* may, of course, occur as subject of an embedded sentence: *It appears that there are a number of problems.*) By contrast, deictic *there* need not necessarily be subject:

10a *There* is the glass
10b The glass is *there*

Existential *there*, unlike deictic *there*, cannot be questioned:

11a Where is the glass? (deictic)
11b *Where are the glasses in the drinks cupboard? (existential)

Finally, existential *there* is typically restricted to sentences with an indefinite NP:

12a The glass is on the table
12b ?A glass is on the table
12c ?There's the glass on the table
12d There is a glass on the table

(**12c** is to be understood as the reduced, existential *there*; it is acceptable as the stressed deictic *there*.)

Some arguments that tend to the view that subject has a special status in the grammar of English can be derived from a transformational approach to description. In this approach we distinguish an underlying from a surface level of description. Suppose that the sentence:

13 Everyone believes that Charlie is handsome

is derived from an underlying structure which we represent as:

14 Everyone believes (Charlie is handsome)

Suppose too that the sentence:

15 Everyone believes Charlie to be handsome

is an alternative realization of this underlying structure. We now observe that whereas in **13** *Charlie* is clearly the subject of the verb *is* in the embedded sentence, in **15** *Charlie* appears to operate syntactically like the object of the verb *believe* in the matrix sentence.

Three pieces of evidence seem to support this observation. First, if we replace *Charlie* by a pronoun, then we must have *he*, the subject form, in **13**, but must have *him*, the object form, in **15**:

16a Everyone believes that he (*him) is handsome
16b Everyone believes him (*he) to be handsome

Secondly, consider the following sentences with reflexive pronouns:

17a Charlie$_1$ believes that he$_1$ (*himself) is handsome
17b Charlie$_1$ believes himself$_1$ to be handsome
17c Charlie$_1$ believes him$_2$ to be handsome

We have followed here the convention of marking subscripts on co-referential items. The distribution of the reflexive and non-reflexive pronouns here strongly suggests that *himself* is the object of *believe*. Thirdly, we note that the passive sentence:

18 Charlie is believed by everyone to be handsome

is well formed. The passive is largely restricted to objects – and this suggests that *Charlie* can be considered to have been at some stage the object of *believe*. There is, of course, no passive corresponding to **13**:

19 *Charlie is believed by everyone that is handsome

If we accept that such sentences are related to the structure shown in **14**, then it seems that this structure has been 're-analysed' along the lines shown in **20**:

20a Everyone believes (Charlie is handsome)
20b Everyone believes Charlie (to be handsome)

Transformational grammarians postulate a rule of 'subject raising' to account for this.[2] The rule only applies to subjects, as its name implies. Consider the following sentences:

21a Everyone believes (Charlie has killed Mary)
21b Everyone believes Charlie (to have killed Mary)
21c Charlie is believed by everyone (to have killed Mary)

22a Everyone believes (Charlie has killed Mary)
22b Everyone believes (Mary has been killed by Charlie) (Passive in embedded S)
22c Everyone believes Mary (to have been killed by Charlie)
22d Mary is believed by everyone (to have been killed by Charlie)

Note that *Mary*, the object of KILL in **22a**, cannot be raised:

23   Everyone believes Mary (Charlie to have killed)

but once it has become the subject of the embedded sentence by passivization, then it can be raised – yielding **22c**, and subsequently **22d**.

Returning briefly to *there*, we note that this item also operates like a subject for these purposes:

24a   Everyone believes (there is a solution to this problem)
24b   Everyone believes there (to be a solution to this problem)
24c   There is believed (to be a solution to this problem)

The argument suggests that the grammatical subject has an important role. Another argument offered by a transformational approach can be illustrated by the following sentence:

25   John$_1$ expected that the committee would choose him$_1$/him$_2$

The subscripts indicate two possible readings, one in which *him* cross-refers to *John*, and another where *him* refers deictically to some other individual in the context (see pages 379–80). Let us suppose that **25** is related to the underlying structure:

26   John expected (the committee would choose him)

after the fashion already established in discussing **13–15**. In the same spirit as before we consider the sentence:

27   John$_1$ expected the committee to choose him$_1$/him$_2$

is another way of describing the same situation. As before, *him* can have two interpretations. Let us now passivize the embedded sentence:

28   John expected (he would be chosen by the committee)

which is realized as:

29   John$_1$ expected that he$_1$/he$_2$ would be chosen by the committee

Then *he* has two readings, as in **25**. However, if we passivize the embedded sentence in the structure corresponding to **27** we get:

30 John$_1$ expected him$_2$ (*him$_1$) to be chosen by the committee

Him can only have one reading, with deictic reference. It cannot cross-refer to the subject of *expected*. But the sentence:

31 John expected to be chosen by the committee

has the other reading; that is, *John* is understood not only as the subject of *expected* but also as the subject of *be chosen*. There is, however, no overt subject present.

For the purposes of discussion we represent this situation like this:

32 John$_1$ expected θ_1 to be chosen by the committee

Once again we see that the subject, in this case an 'understood' subject, has a special role.[3] This relationship is quite general:

33a I$_1$ expect θ_1 to go to America this summer
33b Gill$_1$ wants θ_1 to come with me
33c Gill$_1$ expects her$_2$ (*her$_1$) to go with me

Our concern is not with the machinery of the putative transformational rules involved, but with the observation that the grammatical subject seems from the discussion to have a special status in English grammar.

So far all our discussion has involved declarative affirmative sentences. Let us briefly consider interrogative sentences. These can be illustrated by the **b** sentences here:

34a Katie is writing a French essay
34b Is Katie writing a French essay?

35a Sarah plays the trombone
35b Does Sarah play the trombone?

We have discussed the formation rules for interrogative sentences on pages 129–32. In outline, the rule is: invert the first auxiliary verb (*is* in **34**) and the grammatical subject; if there is no auxiliary supply an appropriate form of DO, as in **35**. Note that after the operation of this rule, the subject NP still precedes the main verb, and it still controls number agreement on the auxiliary, or DO. Subject–auxiliary inversion is also typical of certain sentences involving certain 'negative adverbs':

> **36a**   Never have I heard such nonsense
> **36b**   Seldom have I tasted a more magnificent claret

Our final observation on the grammatical subject is that there are a few constructions in which it follows rather than precedes the main verb. Thus we find:

> **37**   Down comes the flag, off goes the gun and away go the boats

Such sentences have a distinctly literary flavour, and we consider them to be a stylistic device, discussed further in the next chapter. Note that number concord between subject and verb is preserved even though the subject follows rather than precedes the verb.

The arguments strongly suggest that, for English at least, the grammatical relation of subject has a special role in grammatical description.

We now turn to the notion of logical subject. This, as we observed on page 313, usually relates to the question of the participant role a subject realizes. As the preceding chapter made clear, the grammatical subject can realize any of a number of such roles. Perhaps the most typical role for the subject is agentive:

> **38a**   John beat the dog
> **38b**   William invaded England in 1066

Instrumental subjects can be seen in:

> **39a**   The axe smashed the door
> **39b**   A brush could clear those drains

The fact that such subjects are instrumental is established by the passive forms of the sentences, where the instrumental preposition *with* occurs:

40a The door was smashed with an axe
40b Those drains could be cleared with a brush

Dative subjects are shown in:

41a Harry knows that his wife is unfaithful
41b I am interested in linguistics

and this description is supported by paraphrases with *to*:

42a That his wife is unfaithful is known to Harry
42b Linguistics is interesting to me

where the dative preposition *to* occurs.
Goal subjects are to be observed in:

43a Harry received a gold medallion from the Royal
Society
43b Charlie obtained a licence from the local authority

and this analysis is supported by the fact that the preposition *to* occurs in sentences like:

44a The Royal Society presented a gold medallion to
Harry
44b The local authority issued a licence to Charlie

Source subjects are to be seen in **44**; and note the paraphrase with the preposition *from* in **43**.
Locative place subjects occur in sentences like:

45a Edinburgh is cold, wet and windy
45b This box contains fifty-two matches

where alternative formulations of the proposition contain a locative proposition:

46a It is cold, wet and windy in Edinburgh
46b Fifty-two matches are contained in this box

Patient subjects are found in the sentences:

47a   The butter is melting
47b   The ice is cooling

Finally, we note neutral subjects in:

48a   Mary is very tired
48b   Harry is the Professor of Linguistics

All the participant roles identified in Chapter 18 may occur in some sentence as the grammatical subject. The traditional notion of logical subject is usually related to sentences involving an [agent] participant. Thus in:

49   William invaded England in 1066

William, the [agent] participant, is referred to as both the logical and the grammatical subject. In the corresponding passive sentence:

50   England was invaded by William in 1066

William remains the logical subject, but *England* is now the grammatical subject. The notion of logical subject appears to relate to the unmarked subject choice in some particular propositional structure. By analogy *the axe* and *a brush* are the logical subjects in **39**, *Harry* and *I* in **41**, and so on. We should note here that, given the participant roles [agent], [instrument] and [neutral], the active declarative sentence chooses the [agent] participant as subject over the [instrument] and the [neutral], and the [instrument] over the [neutral]; these choices are reflected in **38** and **39**. Similarly, given [dative] and [neutral], the most unmarked order, all other things being equal, chooses [dative] as subject, and this is reflected in **41**. These facts suggest that if we introduce the notion of participant roles together with appropriate statements about unmarked subject choice we can dispense with the notion of logical subject, since this new machinery gives a more precise characterization of the notions involved.

19.2   Object

The grammatical object, like the subject, is realized by an NP. In active declarative sentences with unmarked word order four grammatical features characterize the object: (1) it directly follows the verb; (2) it is not in construction with a preposition; (3) it can become the subject of the corresponding passive sentence; and (4) it is an obligatory constituent with transitive verbs.

The most clear-cut cases of objects are those constituents traditionally referred to as the direct or affected object. These are NPs that realize what we called (page 295) [neutral, patient] participant roles in two-place propositions where the verb is a verb or directed action, causative or non-causative, and the other participant, which must become subject in active sentences, is described as [agent]:

51a *Samson smote
51b *The forester split

In such constructions no possible paraphrases involve prepositions; the relevant NPs can become the subject of the corresponding passive sentences; and the direct object is an obligatory constituent. We do not find:

52a Samson smote
52b The forester split

where only an [agent] participant is realized.

Traditional grammars also recognize other types of object in two-place sentences. The names usually given to them reflect the type of propositional role that the object realizes. All of them are, to a greater or lesser extent, unable to meet the four criteria outlined above. Thus, the following sentences involve an 'object of result' (also called an 'effected' or 'factitive' object):

53a Mary wove that blanket
53b The workmen are digging a hole

Objects of result can typically become the subject of a passive sentence, and there are no paraphrases involving prepositions. Many verbs that occur in such sentences can also appear in one-place sentences with an agent subject but no object:

54a Mary is weaving
54b The workmen are digging

Sentences like:

55a   Mary sang a song
55b   I dreamed a strange dream (last night)

are sometimes described as involving 'cognate objects', since the relevant NP usually contains a noun morphologically derived from (and hence cognate with) the verb stem. We identified such participants as [range] participants but noted that, while there are no paraphrases involving prepositions, they do not always felicitously become the subjects of passive sentences.

Some grammarians have identified the object in sentences like:

56a   Harold is eating his lunch
56b   Patricia is reading *War and Peace*

as an 'object of concern'; they are clearly neither affected (direct) nor effected (resultant) objects. Such objects do not always appear as subjects of passive sentences with the same degree of acceptability as the other objects we have looked at and, like objects of result, are often omissible.

The cases examined so far suggest that there is a hierarchy of 'objecthood'. The prime exemplar is the direct object. This has a particularly close tie to the main verb; it is an obligatory sentence constituent; it immediately follows the main verb; it will not occur in a paraphrase involving a preposition; and it can be the subject of the corresponding passive sentence. Other objects (of result, concern, and so on) do not meet one or more of these criteria.

We now consider sentences like:

57a   The Russians supplied arms to the Vietnamese
57b   The Russians supplied the Vietnamese with arms

These sentences contain the same nouns and verbs: RUSSIAN, VIETNAMESE, ARM, SUPPLY. They differ with respect to their function; in **57a** ARM is a direct object, whereas in **57b** it is an oblique object. In **57b** VIETNAMESE is a direct object, whereas in **57a** it is an oblique object. Because the two sentences are close in meaning – they both describe events of supplying arms – many analyses see them as containing the same roles (agent, patient, neutral) and differing only with respect to which role is chosen as direct object and thereby presented as more central, because more closely related to the verb.

The [agent] becomes subject of the active sentence. There is, however, a choice as to whether the [goal] or the [patient] participant immediately follows the verb. Whichever is chosen, that participant is realized as an NP without a preposition, and the other participant is realized as a prepositional phrase. We refer to the NP that immediately follows the verb as the object. Note that it operates syntactically like an object. It cannot occur with a preposition in this position:

58a   *The Russians supplied with arms to the Vietnamese
58b   *The Russians supplied to the Vietnamese with arms

It may become the subject of the corresponding passive:

59a   Arms were supplied to the Vietnamese by the Russians
59b   The Vietnamese were supplied with arms by the Russians

Furthermore, it is no longer omissible:

60   *The Russians supplied with arms

whereas the PP is omissible:

61   The Russians supplied arms
62   The Russians supplied the Vietnamese

We call the NP in the prepositional phrase an 'oblique object', recognizing that the NP in the prepositional phrase might, as it were, have become the object, had the other NP not done so. The oblique object is omissible, as we have observed, and cannot generally become the subject of a passive sentence:

63   *The Vietnamese were supplied arms to by the Russians

In the case of verbs like SUPPLY neither of the non-agent participants is, as it were, the 'designated' object; one of the participants may become an object, but it may be either. The effect of becoming an object is important. The syntactic effect we have already discussed; but there is also a semantic effect, which varies from cases like **57** where there seems to be little semantic effect to cases with considerable semantic implications:

64a   An archer shot at William with an arrow
64b   An archer shot William with an arrow
64c   An archer shot an arrow at William

SHOOT may occur with two oblique objects, or with a direct and an oblique object. The semantic effect may be so great here that the reader may be disinclined to treat all three sentences as deriving from the same propositional structure.

19.3   Indirect object

We now turn to 'indirect objects'; their status is very ambivalent. The term is used when a verb is followed by two NPs, neither of which is associated with a preposition. In these structures the first NP is the indirect object, and the second the direct object:

65   John gave Mary (IO) a book (DO)

A sentence like **65** can be paraphrased as:

66   John gave a book to Mary

Here the direct object directly follows the verb; what was the indirect object is now introduced in a prepositional phrase. If the direct object immediately follows the verb, then the other NP must be introduced by a prepositional phrase[4] – there is no sentence:

67   *John gave a book (DO) Mary (IO)

Frequently the prepositional phrase in a sentence like **66** is also referred to as an indirect object. We shall not, however, do this, reserving the term indirect object for the first of two NPs in sentences like **65**. Instead we call it, as before, an oblique object.

From a semantic point of view, the indirect object frequently realizes a [goal] participant, as in **65**. But not always. We find a [benefactive] in:

68a Mary baked me a cake
68b Mary baked a cake for (to) me

a [comitative] in:

69a Mary played John tiddlywinks
69b Mary played tiddlywinks with (*for, *to) John

and perhaps a [source] in:

70a John asked Mary a favour
70b John asked a favour from (*to, *for) Mary

Sometimes the [goal] : [benefactive] distinction is unclear:

71a Mary sang me a song
71b Mary sang a song to/for me

We call all the participants realized in prepositional phrases oblique objects and, if necessary, distinguish between a 'benefactive oblique object', a 'comitative oblique object', and so on.

The peculiarity about structures of this sort seems to be that one participant is, as it were, the 'designated' direct object. It retains this function even when the NP in the oblique object 'becomes' an object too – thus giving rise to a V + NP + NP structure. Before demonstrating this, let us inquire how widely the process of what we may call 'indirect object formation' applies. We illustrate with 'benefactive oblique objects', and invite the reader to determine which of the following are possible:

72a Cash me a cheque (a cheque for me)
72b Buy me a beer (a beer for me)
72c Catch me a butterfly (a butterfly for me)
72d Do me a favour (a favour for me)
72e Change me a fiver (a fiver for me)
72f ?Run me an errand (an errand for me)
72g ?Purchase me a beer (a beer for me)
72h *Feed me the cat (the cat for me)
72i *Beat me the carpet (the carpet for me)
72j *Pursue me the postman (the postman for me)

328 Part three: Functional relations

(We indicate our judgements, as before, with ? for questionable, and * for impossible.) Some of these structures were acceptable in earlier states of English, and some, for some speakers, still are acceptable. This variability seems to occur with other indirect object constructions.

We now apply our criteria for objecthood to the direct and indirect objects in these sentences. We have already seen that the indirect object may occur as an oblique object, and that this is not possible for the direct object. We now observe that the indirect object, or its corresponding oblique object, can usually be omitted without affecting the grammaticality of the sentence, but the direct object cannot be omitted:

73a   John gave Mary a book
73b   John gave a book
73c   *John gave Mary (except in another sense)

74a   John bought me a beer
74b   John bought a beer
74c   *John bought me (except in another sense)

Consider now the problems of passive formation in these sentences. When the direct object immediately follows the verb, it can become the subject of the corresponding passive:[5]

75a   John gave that book to Mary
75b   That book was given to Mary by John

Similarly, the indirect object, the NP immediately following the verb, can usually become the subject of the corresponding passive:

76a   John bought Mary a new car
76b   Mary was bought a new car by John

77a   Mary baked me a cake
77b   I was baked a cake by Mary

78a   John bought me a beer
78b   I was bought a beer by John

but not always:

79a John asked Mary a favour
79b ?Mary was asked a favour by John

80a John caught me a butterfly
80b *I was caught a butterfly by John

81a Mary played John tiddlywinks
81b *John was played tiddlywinks by Mary

Once again the bounds of acceptability are not entirely clear.

A further difficulty is that in indirect object constructions (V + NP + NP) the direct object can still sometimes become the subject of the passive sentence:

82a My grandfather gave me this watch
82b This watch was given me by my grandfather

83a John bought me that bottle of Glen Grant
83b That bottle of Glen Grant was bought me by John

The NP in the oblique object cannot, however, become subject of the passive sentence (unless, of course, it has first 'become' indirect object):

84a My grandfather gave this watch to me
84b *I was given this watch to by my grandfather

The NP that immediately follows the verb has a privileged status, both syntactically and semantically. When only one NP is available for this role (that is, in two-place propositions) there would seem to be a hierarchy of 'objecthood'. When two NPs are available for this role (that is, in three-place propositions), the situation is more complex. Sometimes one NP seems to have what we have called a 'designated' object role, and retains many of its object-like features even when displaced from the position immediately following the verb (that is, in indirect object + direct object constructions). In other circumstances neither of the NPs is a designated object, and then either one of them must become an object (for example, with SUPPLY– pages 324–5) or neither of them need become an object (for example, with SHOOT – page 326). The hierarchy of objecthood can be extended to accommodate this. Direct objects are most 'object-like', in terms of the criteria established at the beginning of this section, followed by objects of result, indirect objects, objects of concern, and so on, eventually arriving at oblique objects.

We should not leave this discussion of objects without mentioning briefly 'phrasal' verbs, since their syntax clearly intersects with our observation on oblique objects. Phrasal verbs are items like BLOW UP in:

85   The commandos blew up the bridge

In such cases UP seems to be related to BLOW rather than to be a constituent with *the bridge* and the syntax of these constructions supports such an analysis. Furthermore, the constituent *the bridge* operates syntactically like the direct object in such constructions. It is an obligatory constituent; it can occur immediately following the verb; and it can be the subject of the corresponding passive:

86a   *The commandos blew up
86b   The commandos blew the bridge up
86c   The bridge was blown up by the commandos

The interested reader is referred to Quirk *et al.* (1985) for general discussion; to Bolinger (1971) for a perceptive analysis of many different constructions of this type; and to Jespersen (1929) for his many examples.

19.4   Complement

Traditional grammars distinguish between a number of different complement types.[6] The names given to them, like the names given to different types of object, relate to the propositional roles that they realize. In two-place sentences, the primary distinction is between 'attributive', 'identity' and 'locative' complements; we discuss each in turn.

The italicized constituents in **87** are attributive complements, so called because they describe the class membership of the subject noun, or ascribe an attribute to it:

87a   Roses are *red*
87b   Roses are *flowers*

Because such complements relate back to the subject noun, they are called 'subject complements', a relationship sometimes described as 'intensive' to the subject. Further distinctions can be profitably drawn. In **87b** the noun *flowers* is a 'nominal complement'. The complements in **87** are 'state complements' since they are found in stative sentences and describe states, in contrast to the complements in inchoative sentences like:

88a The leaves are turning brown
88b Sir Charles became a soldier

which are known as 'result complements'. The variety of terminology in this area relates to the complex propositional status of such constituents, discussed in the last chapter. It also reflects syntactic differences between the various types of complements, and between the complements and the direct object. The complement is an obligatory constituent and always follows the verb. The nominal complement is almost always an indefinite NP, and concords in number with the noun to which it is intensive (*He became a soldier*; *They became soldiers*). The complement cannot become the subject of a passive sentence. Some copular verbs (BE, SEEM) are restricted to stative sentences, others (BECOME, TURN) to non-stative sentences.

The identity complement can be illustrated in:

89 Harold is the man with the arrow in his eye

and is always a definite NP. The two constituents in such a sentence can be reversed round the copular verb:

90 The man with an arrow in his eye is Harold

In these circumstances, which constituent is to be identified as the complement depends on textual considerations (pages 305–7). In sentences in isolation the NP following the verb is most usually identified as the identity complement:

91 Harold is (to be identified as) the man with the arrow in his eye

The prepositional phrase in a sentence like:

92   Mary is *in bed*

is called the locative complement. The locative complement is usually a prepositional phrase, as in **92**, or a place adverb like *upstairs* or *over there*. The locative complement is typically, but not invariably, an obligatory constituent, and can be found with a variety of verbs in state sentences:

93a   The newspaper is lying on the floor
93b   Your coat is hanging in the cupboard
93c   The Scott Monument stands on Princes Street

Corresponding to the locative complements in **92** and **93**, we can also recognize a 'directional complement' in sentences like:

94a   The ball rolled under the bed
94b   The car skidded across the road

If we distinguish between locative and directional complements, then we may also note that the latter typically occur only in non-state sentences.

These three complement types correspond to three of the basic types of propositional structure identified in Chapter 18:

95a	attributive	John is a fool (state)
		John is clever
		The litmus paper is turning red (result)
95b	identity	John is chairman
95c	locative	Mary is in London (place)
		The ball rolled under the bed (direction)

It is interesting, and somewhat curious, that another basic type:

96	possessive	Mary has a little lamb
		Mary has red hair

is not also described as involving a complement – but it isn't. (It may be observed that *Mary is a redhead* does involve a complement!) We return briefly to this point below.[7]

We now turn to sentences like:

97a I consider John *a fool*
97b I consider John *clever*
97c Acid will turn litmus paper *red*
97d The committee elected John *chairman*

The italicized constituents are 'object complements' – so called because they are intensive to the object. The distinctions 'state', 'result', 'nominal', and so on, that we drew for the subject complements in **87** and **88** can also be drawn here. In the sentences illustrated the complement is usually obligatory; constituent order is usually as shown; the nominal complement agrees in number with the NP to which it is intensive; and so on.

Many of the sentences in **97** correspond to paraphrases like:

98 I consider John to be a fool

This suggests that such sentences might be seen as derived from an embedded predication. We can illustrate this by the following sequence:

99 I consider (John is a fool)
I consider that John is a fool
I consider John to be a fool
I consider John a fool

100 They elected John (John is chairman)
They elected John to be chairman
They elected John chairman

In the case of a sentence like **97c** a more abstract representation might be more suitable:

101 Acid CAUSE (litmus paper turn red)

where CAUSE is a representation of the causative status of TURN. Such representations remind us of a similar analysis discussed in Chapter 18.5b. They also make very obvious the parallel between the two-place constructions set out in **95**, and the corresponding three-place sentences in **97**.

Before turning to three-place sentences with locative complements, we should note that the italicized constituents in the sentences in **102** are also often called complements:

102a	Jane returned home *safe*
102b	Harriet danced the tango *naked*
102c	I always drink my coffee *cold*
102d	I always buy my meat *fresh*
102e	They painted the fence *yellow*

Some of these items are intensive to the subject, **102a** and **102b**, and others to the object, **102c** and **102d**; the state : result distinction can be drawn. In these sentences the complements seem to have a looser syntagmatic tie to the verb than do the complements previously discussed. They are, to begin with, both omissible and not relevant for strict subcategorization. Furthermore, their status seems to be more 'adverbial' than that of the object complements of **97**; in some cases they can be substituted by adverbs (*safely* instead of *safe* in **102a**). Other cases relate to a variety of different paraphrase constructions – I *always drink my coffee after it has become cold*; *Harriet was naked when she danced the tango*; and so on.

Consider now the following three-place locative sentences:

103a	John put the book on the table
103b	John rolled the ball under the bed

The prepositional phrase constituent is still described as a locative complement, and the place : direction distinction observed in **95c** still applies. As before, the relationship between the two- and three-place sentences is a causative one. We can represent this with the abstract formulation:

104a	John CAUSE (PUT) the book (the book BE on the table)
104b	John CAUSE (ROLL) the ball (the ball GO under the bed)

BE and GO represent, respectively, the place and directional nature of the embedded predications concerned. These abstract representations are rather distant from the actual surface form of the sentence; it is not suggested that the representations might be underlying structures, in the sense that we used this term in Chapter 10.

We now close this section by returning to the possessive construction mentioned earlier:

105 Mary had a little lamb

106a The shepherd gave Mary a little lamb
106b The shepherd gave a little lamb to Mary

The constituent *a little lamb* is not usually described as a 'possessive complement' or the like, either in **105** or in **106**. Indeed, in **106** this constituent is called the direct object, and in **106a** *Mary* is the indirect object, as we have seen (pages 326–9). We also saw that the status of the indirect object is less clear than that of the direct object. It is now clear that the relationship between the sentence in **105** and that in **106** is not very dissimilar from the relationship between the two-place locative sentences in **95c** and their three-place counterparts in **103**. We might represent this with abstract representations like:

107 Mary HAVE a little lamb

108a The shepherd CAUSE (GIVE) Mary (Mary HAVE a little lamb)
108b The shepherd CAUSE (GIVE) a little lamb (a little lamb GO to Mary)

The different orderings in the embedded sentence correspond to the two different surface orderings in **106**, and perhaps correspond to a different nuance of meaning. An analysis of this sort may also go some way towards explaining the apparent difference in meaning surrounding the choice of object with verbs like SUPPLY and SHOOT discussed on pages 325–6, but to pursue this matter further would take us too far out of our way.

19.5 Adjuncts

Subjects, objects and complements form the nucleus of a sentence. They are nuclear in at least two senses, both of which are complementary. They are the constituents which, in constituent structure terms, are either obligatory or are introduced by an expansion of the VP, and hence relevant to strict subcategorization. They are also to be identified with nuclear participants in the sense discussed in the preceding chapter; many of the names given to different types of subject and object reflect this.

All other sentence constituents we call adjuncts. Adjuncts are usually adverbials, whether they are adverb phrases, prepositional phrases, adverbs, or subordinate clauses of time, place, manner, and so on, that distributionally function like adverbials. They are typically optional sentence constituents, and have a degree of mobility within the sentence denied to the nuclear constituents. Adjuncts are clearly a rather 'mixed bag', in that syntactically there are numerous subclasses which have different and overlapping distribution, and they fill a variety of semantic roles, as can be seen by consulting the discussion of adverbs in any standard grammar of English – for example, Quirk *et al.* (1985).

19.6   Conclusion

In the preceding chapter we characterized sentence constituents in terms of their syntactico-semantic function within a sentence as [agent], [patient], and so on. We suggested that a propositional structure characterized in these terms is an abstract structure which could be realized by any one of a number of actually occurring sentences. A given propositional role may occur in a number of syntactic positions within the sentence without affecting the way in which the role is characterized, though there will be other syntactic phenomena that reflect the different sentence positions the role occupies. We also noted that the syntactico-semantic characterization can be used to control various grammatical features, like the ability of some roles to occur with the progressive auxiliary, its ability to occur in imperative sentences, and so on.

In this chapter we have looked at the functional roles of subject, object and complement, and at the various syntactic and semantic properties that can be associated with these functions. Of particular interest have been the various circumstances that permit an NP to take on the function of subject, object, and so on. From a transformational point of view, deriving the various different sentence orders from a single basic structure, the discussion may be seen to consider the ways in which sentences can be provided with subjects and objects.[8]

Suppose, for example, we establish a hierarchy of functional roles in outline like this:

109 subject – object – indirect object – oblique object

and suppose the underlying order of constituents in the sets of sentences in **110** and **111** is as shown in the first of each set of sentences, then the italicized constituent as it were 'climbs up' the hierarchy:

110 John gave the book to *Mary* (oblique object)
John gave *Mary* the book (indirect object)
Mary was given the book by John (subject)

111 The Russians supplied arms to *the Vietnamese* (oblique object)
The Russians supplied *the Vietnamese* with arms (object)
The Vietnamese were supplied with arms by the Russians (subject)

If we also consider subject raising to be within the grammar (cf. page 317), then a constituent can, as it were, climb to the front of its own sentence, hop up into a superordinate sentence and then climb up that:

112 S^1 ('People' allege S^2 (John gave the book to *Mary*))

By the process illustrated in **110** we get:

113 S^1 ('People' allege S^2 (*Mary* was given the book by John))

Raising produces:

114 S^1 ('People' allege *Mary* S^2 (to have been given the book by John))

Passivization of S^1, and the deletion of the indefinite 'people', then yields:

115 *Mary* is alleged to have been given the book by John

In this account, while the functional relation of the NP *Mary* changes from derivation to derivation, its propositional role does not – it is still understood as having a [goal] relation to GIVE. The conditions under which *Mary* climbed up its own sentence, hopped into the superordinate sentence and then climbed up that have little to do with its propositional role, but are instead related to its functional role as successively oblique object, indirect object, subject, and so on.[9]

There is very obviously a large degree of overlap between the two types of characterization – of propositional and of functional role. Are both types of characterizations necessary? Or could one type or the other not be 'enriched' so as to accommodate both sorts of description? The latter course is appealing, and indeed in the preceding chapter we remarked that the different names given to different types of object and complement reflect their propositional status. On the other hand, the two different characterizations do seem to control rather different sorts of syntactic phenomena, and in our present state of knowledge it seems best to retain both.

Technical terms

adjunct
complement – attributive, identity, locative, nominal
existential sentence
object – affected, cognate, of concern, direct, effected, factitive,
        indirect, oblique, of result
raising
subject – grammatical, logical, thematic

Notes

1   In terms of the terminology introduced in the preceding chapter, we might refer to the proposition which **3** realizes as a 'no place' proposition. In traditional grammars they are often realized by what are referred to as 'impersonal verbs'; cf. the single Latin verb *pluit* 'it is raining'. Not all languages permit 'no place' propositions; in Akan the sense of **3** would be realized as *nsuo tɔ* 'water falls', 'it is raining'.

2   As already remarked, this volume does not describe the formal machinery involved in a transformational grammar. For a discussion, see one of the books listed in the section 'Further reading' on page 372.

3   In early transformational grammar the phenomena briefly outlined here were treated by postulating a structure with two sentences: *John expect* and *John be chosen by the committee*. The two subject NPs being equal, a rule called Equi-NP Deletion deleted the second occurrence of *John* and the second sentence was realized as an infinitive. Nowadays a structure is postulated with two sentences, but with an empty subject NP in the second one: *John expect*: NP [Ø] *be chosen by the committee*. In spite of the change in treatment, this type of structure is still generally known as an 'Equi' construction. For present purposes what is important is that the phenomenon lends further support to the status of 'subject'.

4   There are some exceptions to this generalization. Normally the IO object is animate and the DO inanimate (reflecting that normally one gives 'things' to 'people'). This need not necessarily be the case: *John gave the school a library (a library to the school)*; *Etheldreda gave the nunnery her daughter (her daughter to the nunnery)*; *Fiona gave the nurse the child (the child to the nurse)*. In such cases the paraphrase with *to* seems preferred to the structure involving IO and DO; doubtless in order that the semantic relations should be clearly marked.

   Further observe that if we pronominalize the DO, then only the first of the following sentences is grammatical: *John gave it to the school*; **John gave the school it*. If, however, we pronominalize the IO, then both *John gave it a library* and *John gave the library to it* are possible. If we pronominalize both NPs, and both are animate or inanimate, sentences like *John gave it it* and *John gave her him* do not seem acceptable. If, however, one NP is animate and the other inanimate, then we can have *John gave it her* and *John gave her it* and whichever order is used, the animate is understood as the IO and the inanimate as the DO!

5   All sorts of problems arise in this area if we try to passivize indefinite NPs. Thus, *A book was given to Mary by John* seems less acceptable than *That book was given to Mary by John*. Here we deal only with definite NPs.

6   Sometimes all NPs that follow the verb are known as complements. In this usage, what we have called the 'direct object' is called an 'extensive complement', to distinguish it from the 'intensive complement', which relates back to the subject. We do not follow this usage.

   The term complement is also applied to the sentential objects that are associated with particular verbs. Thus, in the sentence *John believed that he was clever* the constituent *that he was clever* is a sentence complement. *That* is called a 'complementizer'.

7   In English the copula verb BE is used in all three types of complement construction. This is not the case in all languages. In Akan, for instance, we find:

attributive (Yɛ)   Kofi yɛ ɔhene bi (Kofi is chief a) *Kofi is a chief*
                    Kofi yɛ kɛseɛ (Kofi is big) *Kofi is big*

identity (Ne)   Kofi ne ɔhene no (Kofi is chief the) *Kofi is the chief*
                    ɔhene no ne Kofi   *The chief is Kofi*

locative (Wɔ)   Kofi wɔ ofie no mu (Kofi is house the in) *Kofi is at home*
This can cause, and has caused, translation problems; in a Bible translation, is the copula in *God is love* to be translated with *yɛ* (has the attribute) or *ne* (is to be identified as)?

   We should also observe that in this language we find:

possessive (Wɔ)   Kofi wɔ ofie yi *Kofi owns this house*
                    ofie yi wɔ Kofi *This house belongs to Kofi*

8 The transformational account can of itself only deal satisfactorily with the actual formal operations of providing subjects and objects, etc. It does not handle the semantic consequences of these operations very satisfactorily, unless additional interpretive machinery is provided somewhere in the total description to take account of the semantic consequences of the operations. As we have seen, these vary from verb to verb and may sometimes be considerable.

9 Participant roles (also called thematic roles) play a part in most formal models. One formal model takes grammatical functions such as subject, etc., as the basic items in the analysis, while one recent model (Lexical-Functional Grammar) assigns important parts to both roles and functions.

Exercises

(1) This chapter has shown that subject and object are important positions, in that the constituents occupying them are central to the clause and are prominent relative to the other constituents. The following two exercises illustrate two phenomena of English syntax relating to subject and object position and the constructions that allow particular constituents to appear in these central positions as opposed to some peripheral position.

(a) Rephrase each of the sentences below with the constituent in bold as the grammatical subject. Make whatever grammatical changes are necessary: introduction or deletion of prepositions, change of voice from active to passive, introduction of HAVE or BE. Do not change any major lexical items. List the various devices and find other verbs and adjectives that follow the same patterns.

   (i)   It is cold in **Edinburgh** in May
   (ii) It happened that **Shona** and I arrived at the same time
   (iii) It is foolish of **Judith** to smoke so much
   (iv) It is difficult to write **good rules**
   (v)   The new taxation system will benefit the **higher paid workers**
   (vi) They thought Susan had passed **the exam**
   (vii) Lunch-time shoppers thronged **the streets**
   (viii) The police know **the criminals**
   (ix) One piece of **the chess-set** is missing
   (x)   Someone sprayed paint on **the demonstrators'** faces
   (xi) Many of the group shook **the speaker's** hand

(xii)   There is no chair for **Kate** to sit on
(xiii) There are even more rhododendrons in **the Botanic Gardens**
(xiv)   It is unlikely that **Celia** will agree
(xv)   The freezer will keep **the coffee beans** fresh longer

(b) As pointed out on page 327, English has pairs of sentences such as *Susan bought the present for Dorothy* and *Susan bought Dorothy the present*. The difference is that in the first sentence *Dorothy* is in a peripheral position, as an oblique object, whereas in the second sentence *Dorothy* is in object position (albeit indirect object position). Consider the pairs of sentences below and decide in which pairs the second sentence is acceptable. Is there a scale of acceptability, with some examples being neither fully acceptable nor fully unacceptable? Do the examples point to a property that controls (or helps to control) the acceptability?

   (i)   Florence cooked a meal for her friends/Florence cooked her friends a meal
   (ii)   Reach down that book for me/Reach me down that book
   (iii) Bill mended some appliances for Fred/Bill mended Fred some appliances
   (iv)   Jane washed some glasses for Michelle/Jane washed Michelle some glasses
   (v)   Rita fed the cats for me/Rita fed me the cats
   (vi)   Marie watched the programme for Neil/Marie watched Neil the programme
   (vii) Louise opened the door for Sandra/Louise opened Sandra the door

See the other examples on pages 326–30.

(2) Subjects and objects can be recognized in languages other than English. Consider the following data and answer the questions. (Ronnie Cann very kindly allowed us to use the data.)

Sanskrit:
   (i)   *Ràkṣasaḥ gacchati*
          Rakshasa is going

(ii) *Canàkyaḥ gacchati*
      Canakya is going
(iii) *Ràkṣasaḥ vanaṃ prati Canàkyena gacchati*
      Rakshasa is going to the forest with Canakya
(iv) *Canàkyaḥ vanaṃ prati Ràksaṣena gacchati*
      Canakya is going to the forest with Rakshasa
(v)   *Ràkṣasaḥ Canàkyam tudyati*
      Rakshasa is hitting Canakya
(vi) *Canàkyaḥ Ràkṣasam tudyati pustakena*
      Canakya is hitting Rakshasa with a book
(vii) *Ràkṣasaḥ tudyate Canàkyena*
      Rakshasa is being hit by Canakya
(viii) *Ràkṣasaḥ tudyate pustakena*
      Rakshasa is being hit with/by a book
(ix) *Canàkyaḥ tudyate Ràkṣasena*
      Canakya is being hit by Rakshasa

Questions:
(a) Provide translations for all the words in the above sentences, apart from *vanaṃ prati*.
(b) Identify the grammatical subjects and say how these are marked.
(c) Identify the direct objects and say how these are marked.
(d) Identify the oblique objects and say how these are marked.
(e) Identify the [agent], [patient] and [instrument] nouns. Which grammatical functions are they associated with?
(f) Using the information you have collected, describe how the passive is formed in Sanskrit. (Note that word order is not syntactically significant.)

20   Sentences in texts

Notions like subject in the previous chapter were discussed by examining sentences in isolation. We now consider another use of the term subject: what can loosely be called the 'thematic subject', the 'psychological subject', or the 'subject of discourse'. To avoid confusion, we do not use the term subject in this connection (reserving it for the grammatical subject discussed in the preceding chapter), but instead introduce the terms theme, rheme and end focus, topic and comment, and given and new. We are concerned with those features of word order within sentences that are related to the communicative function of sentences within texts. The relevant notions clearly lead off into a study of the structure of text and it is not our intention to pursue this matter in detail.

'Theme', 'rheme' and 'end focus' refer to structural positions within the sentence. The two focal points in English sentences are the beginning and the end; the language has a number of processes that position a constituent either initially or finally. The constituent that occurs in initial position is the theme, and processes used to make some constituent initial are processes of thematization.

The theme is italicized in the following:

1 *Someone* parked a large furniture van right outside our front door last night
2 *A large furniture van* was parked right outside our front door last night
3 *Right outside our front door* someone parked a large furniture van last night
4 *Last night* someone parked a large furniture van right outside our front door

The propositional structure of each of these sentences is identical; they differ in terms of which constituent is thematized. Constituents other than the theme are the rheme. Obviously some constituent must be sentence initial, and the word order shown in 1 is usually thought of as being the 'most neutral' or 'unmarked' word order in a set of sentences like **1–4**; it is an active declarative sentence with place and time adverbs in end position. Such sentences we call thematically unmarked. The other sentences are thematically marked in one way or another, and some involve what one intuitively thinks of as a greater degree of markedness than others – **3**, for instance. We can also say that there is an unmarked order of constituents in the rheme. What the unmarked order is depends on which constituent is thematized; and we must use a somewhat intuitive notion of what we consider the unmarked or 'most neutral' order of rhematic constituents. It will probably be agreed that the rhemes in **1–4** show an unmarked constituent order, given that some constituent has been thematized.

Now, just as some constituent must be thematized, so some constituent must occur in final position. We call the final position the 'end focus'. If all the rhemes in **1–4** are in an unmarked word order, then all the end focuses are also unmarked. However, just as there are thematizing processes which produce marked themes, so too there are end-focusing processes that produce marked end focus. Consider:

5   Someone parked a large furniture van last night *right outside our front door*

6   It was parked right outside our front door last night, *a large furniture van*

7   Parked right outside our front door last night it was, *a large furniture van*

8   A large furniture van, right outside our front door last night, *parked!*

Some of these end focuses are clearly more marked than others, as the reader can confirm by reading them aloud – they involve a successively more indignant intonation pattern!

Considerations that govern which constituent is to be chosen as theme and which as end focus are related to communicative processes within text.

The terms 'given' and 'new' can only be understood in terms of text. In their most straightforward sense, these terms can be understood as information that has literally been 'given' in the preceding text and information that is 'new' to the sentence immediately under consideration. A number of linguistic features correlate with this. New information is characteristically spelled out in full – otherwise there is no way for the hearer or reader to get access to it. Given information is typically either assumed and not referred to at all, or referred to by the use of proforms or other cross-reference expressions.

For example, suppose you received a letter which contained:

9   I must tell you the news about John and Mary
10   They have just got married

9 introduces the new information that there is some 'news' about 'John and Mary'. When we come to 10 this can be treated as given; hence *they* cross-refers to *John and Mary*, and no mention is made of 'news', but a piece of new information is added – that the 'news' is that 'John and Mary have got married'. It would be unnatural if the letter read:

11   I must tell you the news about John and Mary
12   The news I have to tell you is that John and Mary have got married

where all the given information is spelled out in the second sentence. In a long text such a process eventually becomes impossible, since new information is constantly being added.

Given information need not always be overtly referred to in text. It may be information 'given' in the sense that both participants share it as speakers of the same language, it may be cultural information shared between members of a linguistic community, or it may even be information privately shared between two individuals. To illustrate this, suppose the 'letter' in 9 and 10 continued:

13   I must tell you the news about John and Mary
14   They have just got married
15   A very flashy reception with lots of extravagant presents on display
16   Dear old Charlie gave a toast-rack!
17   He does have a flair for the original!

The shared background of writer and reader includes the knowledge that marriages may involve receptions and the provision of presents. The way 'dear old Charlie' is introduced implies a certain type of relationship between the writer and 'Charlie', which is given to the reader. The last sentence can only be appreciated if one realizes that a 'toast-rack' is a totally conventional wedding present (not to say a literary convention). From a linguistic point of view, we note the pronominalization of 'given' information, and the elision of *They had* in **15** and of the goal participant in **16** . . . *gave (them) a toast-rack.*

The importance of the notions of given and new to a study of word order lies in the fact that what is given is very frequently the constituent that is thematized. The unmarked structure for text might be schematically represented as:

18   given new. given new. (given) new. etc.

where the given is pronominalized and thematized, and the new information occurs in the rheme. We see several examples of this in the letter: *they* in **14**, *he* in **17**. What is given may be elided; in **15** we find *(they had) a very flashy reception* . . . so that the resultant sentence is all new information. We might regard *a toast-rack* in **16** as an example of end focus (note the prominence given to this constituent by the exclamation mark). Another way of presenting the same information is: *A toast-rack from dear old Charlie*, where the 'given' (and understood) *They received*, or the like, is elided and *A toast-rack* is thematized.

The notions of topic and comment can be illustrated in the following way. By topic we mean the 'perspective' from which a sentence is viewed, what the sentence is 'about'. Topic seems to correspond to what people mean by 'psychological subject'. The comment then is something said about this topic. With sentences in isolation, we normally understand a sentence like:

19   John patted the dog on the head

as being a sentence which takes *John* as its topic and tells us something about what 'John' did. By contrast, the sentence:

20   The dog was patted on the head by John

seems to focus attention on 'the dog', and tells us something that happened to it. Frequently topic and theme coincide, as they do in **19** and **20**. Frequently, too, topic, theme and given coincide, as in **14** and **17**. So in **14**, for example, *they* is topic and theme and cross-refers to *John and Mary* in the previous sentence; the comment *have just got married* is then made on this topic.

Topic and theme need not, however, coincide. Consider:

21 There has been a lot of bullying in the school this term
22 The one who is always being picked on is Tom Brown

We might reasonably identify Tom Brown as the topic of **22**, yet here this constituent is in end focus. The effect of putting *Tom Brown* in end focus is precisely to delay identification of the topic, thus creating a particular communicative effect.

Before considering each of these three notions in more detail we should briefly mention the question of what 'meaning' attaches to them. At this point we enter a peculiarly difficult and shadowy area. Clearly sentences like **1–4** or **5–8** have an 'emphatic' or 'contrastive' effect, but it is difficult to characterize this with any precision. Similarly, the ability to recover 'given' information, as for example in the 'letter' in **13–17**, has communicative importance – but this again is difficult to characterize. Thematizing processes do not in general appear to affect what we may refer to as 'propositional meaning' – the underlying propositional roles of the various constituents – though even this statement needs some qualification, since, as we have seen, subject- and object-forming processes are often significant.

In one area thematization has a particular effect. This involves sentences where one or more of the NPs involved contains a quantifying expression (like *every, few, many*, or a numeral) or the sentence contains a negative element. So, for example, the sentence:

23 Everyone in this room speaks two languages

can be understood as asserting either that 'everyone' speaks the same two languages (say, French and German) or that everyone speaks two languages, but they may be different for each individual (say, French and German, Chinese and Hindi, and so on). The latter is the more usual interpretation; the sentence is understood as a comment on the linguistic ability of 'everyone in the room', which is the topic. By contrast, in the sentence:

24 Two languages are spoken by everyone in this room

the most usual interpretation is that just two languages, say French and German, are at issue and everybody speaks them.

Some support for this may be gathered by considering ways in which the sentences may be extended:

25   Two languages are spoken by everyone in this room and I understand neither of them

26   Everyone in this room speaks two languages and I understand neither of them

The first of these sentences seems immediately comprehensible. In the second the reader may be momentarily confused by the suspicion that 'everyone' comprises only two people (*neither of them*). In some cases this effect is so strong that pairs of sentences appear to differ in meaning; sometimes one sentence of a pair is almost incomprehensible:

27a   Many men love few girls
27b   Few girls are loved by many men

28a   Nobody speaks seventeen languages
28b   Seventeen languages are spoken by nobody

29a   A few men marry two women
29b   Two women are married by a few men

The 'focusing' effect of thematization is very noticeable in sentences like these, but it varies from case to case. 23 and 24 may fairly easily be understood in either sense, though one sense is probably preferred for each sentence. Each sentence in 28 appears to have a distinct interpretation, though with a little effort the reader can contextualize the other interpretation. In cases like 29, the b sentence is almost incomprehensible.

20.1   Theme, rheme and end focus

Of the notions just discussed, theme, rheme and end focus offer least descriptive and conceptual difficulty, because they are formal terms identifying structural positions within the sentence. The initial, thematic, constituent is where the sentence starts; and the final, end focus, constituent is the culmination of the sentence. In a sentence like:

30 Ice cream, that's the pudding I like best in the world

the speaker, as it were, announces what the topic of the sentence is and then goes on to make a comment on it. By contrast, in a sentence like:

31 The pudding that I like best in the world is ice cream

the speaker keeps the hearer in suspense as to what is liked until the very end. We can reasonably successfully specify the formal operations involved in forming sentences like **30** and **31**; it is much more difficult to say why a speaker might prefer **30** to **31**, or vice versa, since this involves the more difficult considerations of what sort of effect the speaker thinks will be achieved by using one or other sentence.

In this section we examine some of the formal machinery available in English to enable a speaker to thematize a constituent or bring it into end focus. We begin with declarative sentences; interrogative and imperative sentences function somewhat differently, so we defer consideration of these.

First we consider thematization processes. These fall into four very general types.

The first type we call 'subject selection rules'. These are cases where any one propositional role within a given propositional structure may be selected as grammatical subject, and the sentence remains an active declarative sentence:

32 Blood flowed in the gutters
33 The gutters flowed with blood

The second we call 'promotion to subject rules'. These are cases where a particular propositional role, which in an active declarative sentence would not be grammatical subject, is promoted to subject with some consequent alteration in the verb group (as is the case with the passive) or by the introduction of a pro-verb (like HAVE):

34a The managing director sacked the strikers
34b The strikers were dismissed by the managing director

35a   My auntie knitted a pair of gloves for me
35b   I had a pair of gloves knitted for me by my auntie

35b is to be understood as having the same general sense as **35a**, rather than in the causative sense 'I got my auntie to knit me a pair of gloves'.

The third general type is called 'left-movement rules'. These involve the thematization of a particular constituent without any consequent change of grammatical function; thus the subject function of *I* and the object function of *Christmas* do not alter in:

36a   I hate Christmas
36b   Christmas, I hate it

The fourth type we call 'clefting rules'. These involve the distribution of the constituents of some proposition into a copular sentence:

37a   I am very fond of marzipan
37b   It's marzipan that I'm very fond of
37c   Marzipan is what I'm very fond of

Before discussing these processes, some general comments can be made. We cannot possibly list all possible types and subtypes exhaustively in this chapter, nor are these four general types mutually exclusive – they are not and they interact in various ways. The characterization is merely a useful *ad hoc* typology. Nor do we claim a strict paraphrase relation between pairs of sentences examined, as for example any of the pairs of sentences noted above; it does seem, however, that the propositional relations involved remain the same. The thematization processes themselves may add emphases of meaning, or predispose the reader to a particular reading in preference to some other possible reading.

We can group a number of processes together under the general heading of 'subject selection rules'. The most obvious cases involve verbs like FLOW, illustrated in **32** and **33**, which are associated with two propositional roles, either of which may become subject. Another example is:

38a   His face streamed with blood
38b   Blood streamed down his face

and similar sentences can be constructed with verbs like CRAWL and BENEFIT.

A large class of verbs and related adjectives that refer to psychological states occur in structures like:

39a I am bored with writing
39b Writing is boring to me

40a I am excited at the prospect of Christmas
40b The prospect of Christmas is exciting to me

and similarly AMUSE, CONFUSE, DISGUST, EXCITE, FRIGHTEN, AMAZE, PUZZLE, WORRY, and so on. Under the general heading of subject selection we can also include cases of lexical suppletion, since these too permit one rather than another constituent to become grammatical subject, and the resulting sentences are, in general terms, paraphrases. Verbs such as LEND allow converse relations as in:

41a I lent my daughter five pounds
41b My daughter borrowed five pounds from me

and similarly with BUY : SELL, TEACH : LEARN, AMUSE : PLEASE, and so on. We may also, under this general heading, note a number of verbs where an 'indefinite and non-specific' agent role may not be realized at all, and some other constituent assumes the role of grammatical subject:

42a They produce a lot of whisky in Scotland
42b Scotland produces a lot of whisky

Similar verbs permitting this construction include GROW, MAKE and MANUFACTURE.

Perhaps the paradigm case of a 'promotion to subject' rule is the passive:

43a A bus knocked Mary down
43b Mary was knocked down by a bus

A very characteristic use of the passive is illustrated by:

44a Someone has eaten all the cheese
44b All the cheese has been eaten

where in the **b** sentence the indefinite and non-specific agent expression has been elided. Indeed, a sentence like:

45 All the cheese has been eaten by someone

is often held to be unacceptable, and is certainly stylistically marked. Such structures are also often used when the speaker is anxious not to mention a specific participant, or when it is contextually recoverable. Sentences involving modal verbs often lend themselves to loose paraphrases involving a promotion to subject:

46a You might buy a second-hand motor-bike for £200
46b £200 might buy you a second-hand motor-bike

The same sort of process is observable with many other verbs with a modal or aspectual meaning:

47a You need to have your car serviced
47b Your car needs to be serviced

48a This novel begins to interest me
48b I begin to be interested in this novel

'Raising' transformations (see the discussion on pages 317, 337) can also have the function of creating thematic constituents. Thus consider sentences like:

49a (John will go) is certain
49b That John will go is certain
49c John is certain to go

The subject of the constituent sentence is raised to become the subject of the matrix sentence; similar sentences can be formed with LIKELY, SEEM and HAPPEN. A similar operation can raise the object of a constituent sentence to become the subject of the matrix sentence:

50a (to please John) is difficult
50b John is difficult to please

and similar sentences can be formed with verbs and adjectives like
HARD, TOUGH, IMPOSSIBLE (but not POSSIBLE) and EASY.

Other promotion to subject rules involve the introduction of
proverbs like HAVE and GET. HAVE seems involved in a number
of constructions involving locative or benefactive roles, or participants that occur in genitive constructions:

51a There is a pond in my aunt's garden
51b My aunt's garden has a pond in it

52a There is an article by the Bishop of London in today's *Times*
52b Today's *Times* has an article by the Bishop of London
(in it)
52c The Bishop of London has an article in today's *Times*

53a The policeman twisted the criminal's arm
53b The criminal had his arm twisted (by the policeman)

54a Someone bought a gold watch for the dustman
54b The dustman had a gold watch bought for him

In **54b** we see once again the non-realization of an indefinite and
non-specific-agent participant. Paraphrases with TAKE and GET
often seem to involve goal roles:

55a The waves battered the ship
55b The ship took a battering from the waves

56a Parliament didn't approve the Sunday Opening Bill
56b The Sunday Opening Bill didn't get the approval of
Parliament last year

We turn now to our third set of rules – 'left-movement rules'.
Many constituents can be thematized by simply moving them to the
front of the sentence. We have already observed (**page 94**) that this
can be done with sentence adverbs:

57 Last night I proposed to Mary

58   On Hogmanay in Scotland few people go to bed before midnight

When constituents are thematized in this way it does not affect their status as grammatical subject, object, and so on:

59   Mary, I proposed to
60   That soup, I find totally disgusting
61   The kittens, we drowned

Sometimes a pronoun is 'left behind' in the slot from which a constituent is moved:

62   Jane, she'll be late home this evening
63   That soup, I find it totally disgusting

Rules of this sort often permit a constituent to be thematized from quite 'deep down' in an embedded sentence:

64   That man, I thought you told me you were never going to see him again

Our last general type of thematization operation is 'clefting'. Under this head we mention two types of operation. The first is called simply clefting:

65a   John gave the book to Mary
65b   It was John who gave the book to Mary
65c   It was the book John gave to Mary
65d   It was Mary John gave the book to

The syntax of cleft sentences is far from straightforward, and the reader is urged to do a little personal research into the extent to which the operation can be extended. It seems that almost any constituent can be clefted in English except the verb, and even this is possible in some dialects of English:

66a   ?It's singing John is
66b   ?It's delivering the mail the postman is

The distribution of tense, mood and aspect features in cleft sentences is also worth investigation:

67a John might have given the book to Mary
67b It might have been John who gave the book to Mary
67c It is John who might have given the book to Mary

Another structure of this general type is pseudo-clefting, illustrated by sentences like:

68a John loves Mary
68b The one who loves Mary is John
68c John is the one who loves Mary
68d The one who John loves is Mary
68e Mary is the one who John loves

69a John bought a screwdriver
69b What John bought was a screwdriver

In such sentences the participants from a simple proposition – for example, that relating to **68a** – are distributed into an equational sentence like **68b**. Equational sentences can be reversed round the copula (**68b** and **68c**), and some of the conditions for this reversal were discussed on pages 305–6. Simple cleft sentences, like **65**, cannot be reversed. Also note the forms *the one* and *what* in **68b** and **69b**; these form a particularly puzzling feature of pseudo-clefts, since we can also find sentences like:

70 The one/person/girl who John loves is Mary
71 What/the thing/the tool John bought is a screwdriver

We have discussed four types of operation that produce, or may produce, themes. The first two – subject selection and promotion to subject – have the consequence of making some constituent the grammatical subject. This frequently, but not inevitably, means that this constituent is also the theme. The third type – left-movement rules – necessarily produces themes, but has no effect on the functional relation (subject, object, and so on) of the thematized constituent. Clefting produces a theme which is the grammatical subject of the copular verb BE but does not affect the functional relations of the 'original' sentence, which now appears in a construction that resembles a relative clause.

Several syntactic consequences flow from these differences. Both subject-forming rules and left-movement rules can occur in the same sentence:

72a   Blood flowed in the gutters
72b   The gutters, blood flowed in them!

73a   I liked the novel, but I was disgusted with the musical
73b   The novel pleased me, but the musical disgusted me
73c   The novel I liked, but the musical I was disgusted with

Secondly, left-movement rules apply to a wider range of constituents than subject-forming processes. Many constituents cannot become grammatical subjects, but they can be thematized by left-movement rules. Thus adverbial expressions:

74a   Stealthily the cat stalked the mouse
74b   One dark and stormy night the robbers met

constituents like *up* in:

75   Up jumped John

or negative adverbs like *never* or *seldom*:

76a   Never have I heard such magnificent playing!
76b   Seldom have I tasted a more magnificent Stilton!

These particular constructions involve inversion as well as thematization. Perhaps most strikingly, however, note that subject-forming processes can only apply within the simple sentence (as, for example, the passive) or from a constituent sentence to the matrix sentence (in the case of raising rules).

Movement rules and clefting rules seem to be able to apply, within ill-defined limits, across sentence boundaries. Thus in:

77a   I am anxious that my dog will not keep on wanting to mate with *the mongrel next door*
77b   It's *the mongrel next door* that I am anxious that my dog will not keep on wanting to mate with

the clefted constituent comes from a deeply embedded sentence; no subject-forming rule could extract a subject for a higher verb from so deeply embedded a sentence.

A further difference between subject-forming and other

thematization rules concerns the category of definiteness in the NP. From a statistical point of view, subject expressions are more likely to be definite than indefinite, not surprising in view of our previous observations about the structure of given and new information; given information characteristically precedes new information. Given information, since it is given, characteristically involves a definite NP. This is not, of course, to say that subjects cannot be indefinite NPs, merely that they are more frequently definite. Themes created by left-movement rules, on the other hand, are characteristically definite – again not surprising, in view of the emphatic nature of many such sentences.

Consider subject NPs first. Both of the sentences:

78a My wife gave me that camera
78b That camera was given to me by my wife

seem perfectly acceptable; but of the sentences:

79a My wife gave me a camera
79b A camera was given to me by my wife

the latter seems much less acceptable, though it could be contextualized. If we now try thematizing the same constituents by a left-movement rule we find that:

80 That camera my wife gave me

is quite acceptable, but:

81 A camera my wife gave me

seems deviant. This is particularly true with indefinite expressions like *anybody* and *somebody*:

82a Somebody has stolen my socks
82b Somebody, he's stolen my socks
82c It's somebody who has stolen my socks

83a Anybody can ride a bicycle
83b Anybody, he can ride a bicycle

Just as a number of types of rules make some constituent thematic, so too there are rules which bring a particular constituent into end focus. It is not so easy to characterize these into general types, and many of them turn out to be, as it were, the obverse of theme-forming rules – clearly, since if some constituent is chosen as theme, then some other constituent must be placed in end focus. As before, we suggest four general types.

First, 'end focus selection rules', the simple obverse of subject selection rules:

84a   The changes in the income tax laws will benefit the lower-paid worker
84b   The lower-paid worker will benefit from the changes in the income tax laws

We do not discuss these further.

Secondly, what we may call 'postponement rules':

85a   Getting hold of a plumber these days is difficult
85b   It's difficult to get hold of a plumber these days

Many of these rules, like that illustrated, involve changing the grammatical function of a constituent; thus *Getting hold of a plumber these days* is the subject of **85a**, but not of **85b**.

Our third class of rules we call 'right-movement rules':

86a   Your mother has gone out shopping
86b   She's gone out shopping, your mother

These rules involve moving a particular constituent to the end of a sentence, but do not change its grammatical function. Finally, pseudo-cleft sentences, discussed on page 355, can be as easily considered rules producing an end focus, as they can be considered rules producing a theme (see examples **68** onwards on page 355). We do not discuss these again here.

Postponement rules transport a constituent to the right of the sentence. The most widespread such rule is 'extraposition', which takes a constituent, typically from subject position, and moves it to a position after the verb, leaving a dummy *it* subject behind:

87a That you enjoy reading linguistics books is amazing
87b It is amazing that you enjoy reading linguistics books

This operation is obligatory for a number of verbs – thus:

88a It happens that I am related to the Russian royal family
88b *That I am related to the Russian royal family happens

Even when it is not obligatory, it is particularly frequent when the NP involved is a 'heavy' NP: that is, when it is, in a literal sense, long – often the case when the constituent in question is an embedded sentence. Thus, while both **87a** and **87b** are acceptable, **87b** seems stylistically more acceptable. Why this should be is unclear, but it may have to do with 'processing' difficulties in understanding sentences. The point can be appreciated better if we make the subject constituent of *is amazing* even heavier:

89a That you can read a linguistics book when the rest of the family is watching the World Cup on television is amazing
89b It is amazing that you can read . . .

The **b** sentence is undeniably less difficult! The shifting of heavy constituents can also be seen in sentences like the following:

90a They presented a copy of the works of Bloomfield which was hand-printed on parchment and bound in red morocco to the retiring professor
90b They presented to the retiring professor a copy of the works of Bloomfield which was hand-printed on parchment and bound in red morocco

where the heavy direct object moves to the end of the sentence. Or again:

91 They presented a copy of the works of Bloomfield to the retiring professor which was hand-printed on parchment and bound in red morocco

where a heavy relative clause has been extraposed to the end of the sentence. (The reader is invited to consider the extent to which relative clauses can be extraposed, and what conditions permit or inhibit this.) In all cases the movement seems the consequence of a heavy constituent.

Right-movement rules typically operate on the subject constituent, and typically a pronoun copy is left behind:

92   It's disgusting, soup

Sometimes in addition to the constituent which is dislocated, a proverb copy of the verb is introduced:

93   He jilted her, John did

and frequently constituent and pro-verb are inverted:

94   He jilted her, did John

These processes are available in independent declarative sentences. We should briefly comment on thematization processes in non-declarative sentences and in dependent sentences. It can hardly have failed to strike the reader that one effect of thematizing operations is to bring some particular constituent into prominence – this usually involves making it appear as the topic of the sentence. So it is not surprising that the most usual thematic element in imperative and interrogative sentences is not the grammatical subject. Interrogative sentences are very frequently used to ask questions and in '*wh* questions' it is the *wh* word that is thematic:

95a   Who did I see you with last night?
95b   Where have you put my slippers?
95c   How are you?

The main thrust of a question is to discover the identity of the participant signalled by the *wh* word. With *wh* questions, if the *wh* word is not thematic, then, in speech, it usually bears heavy stress:

96   You put my slippers WHERE?

and is typically no longer a straightforward request for information, but rather a request for confirmation, an expression of surprise or the like:

97a   A: Where are my slippers?
97b   B: I put them in the dustbin
97c   A: You put them WHERE?

Note in passing that in terms of the four-way distinction drawn earlier, the formation of *wh* questions involves a left-movement rule; and the *wh* element can be thematized from a deeply embedded sentence:

98   Who do you suppose Mary told me she met yesterday?

Yes–no interrogatives are marked by the thematization of an auxiliary verb:

99a   Didn't we meet in Marakesh?
99b   Have you got a match?

In imperative sentences the thematic element is normally the main verb, perhaps not surprising if we think that imperative sentences are characteristically used as commands, and commands are typically requests for action:

100a   Go away!
100b   Shut up!

Sometimes a 'vocative' element is thematized:

101   Roger, give me a cigarette, will you?

presumably to attract the attention of the person being addressed, or to single him or her out from among a number of possible addressees.

Finally we mention thematic processes in subordinate clauses. Almost invariably subordinating conjunctions are thematized within their sentence; from a functional point of view, this marks both the fact and the type of subordination. Thus:

102a   *If* you don't stop, I'll scream
102b   *When* Charlie comes home, we'll have a party
102c   John gagged her, *so* she wouldn't scream
102d   I won't stop *until* you ask me nicely

Complementizers occur initially in their complement sentence, and relative pronouns and other relative markers are initial in their sentences:

>   **103a**   I know *that* my redeemer lives
>   **103b**   The man *who* believes that will believe anything

In the same connection, though not with respect to subordinate sentences, binding elements in general (*thus, for example, in conclusion*, and so on, see page 143) are usually thematic – again to mark the nature of the relation between sentences.

This section has looked at a number of syntactic processes available in the language that secure initial or final sentence position for some particular constituent. The function of such operations appears to be tied up with communicative processes of various kinds. It is not always easy in well-formed text to identify precisely what effect a given thematization has; it is, paradoxically, much easier in an ill-formed text to appreciate that the clumsiness springs, or can spring, from a failure to make an appropriate thematization. At the end of the chapter is an exercise based on this premise – to which the reader is invited to devote his or her ingenuity after reading the other sections.

20.2   Given and new

As was suggested in the introductory section to this chapter, a principal syntactic consequence of the distribution of information into that which can be held to be given for some sentences and that which is new to the sentence, lies in the fact that given information is 'reduced' in some way or not mentioned at all. Reduction processes that can be observed in written text include most obviously the use of proforms of various kinds – not only pronouns, but also such proforms as the various forms of DO. The auxiliary verbs, including the modals, can be used with a proform type of effect in sequences like:

>   **104a**   A: Are you going to Alan's party tonight?
>   **104b**   B: Must I?
>   **104c**   A: I think you should

a usage referred to by Palmer, following Firth, as 'code' (Palmer, 1974). In spoken discourse reduction is even more evident – given information is typically unstressed, and may be phonologically reduced in various ways, many of which are discussed in Brown (1990).

A lot of given information is not mentioned at all. This is illustrated in the example above, where the complements of the modal verbs in **104b** and **104c** have been elided, and can be recovered contextually. Elision results in sentence fragments, which, as we noted (pages 144–5), can only be understood by reference to 'fuller' forms, which can be recovered contextually.

When given information is mentioned, the effect is frequently contrast of some sort, or emphasis. Thus, for example:

105a A: I'm going to play squash this afternoon
105b B: Squash! I didn't know you played

106a A: Would you like a drink? There's whisky or gin
106b B: I think I'd like a whisky

20.3 Topics

It is appropriate to complete this chapter by returning briefly to the notion of topic. The discussion must be brief since a full examination of the issues involved leads to a consideration of the structure of text as a whole, and this is not the place for such a discussion.

Of all the notions discussed topic is the most difficult to come to grips with. We have suggested that we can view the topic as being 'what the sentence is about', the 'perspective from which the sentence is viewed', and so on. In many simple sentences we can identify the topic by asking what is the implicit request or question which the sentence would be an appropriate answer to. Thus, for example we might identify 'Edinburgh' as the topic in a sentence like:

107 Edinburgh is the most beautiful city in Scotland

if we assume it answers the implicit request:

108 Tell me something about Edinburgh

On the other hand, if **107** were to answer the implicit question:

    109   Which is the most beautiful city in Scotland?

then the topic would be 'the most beautiful city in Scotland'. We have used the phraseology 'implicit request or question' since **107** would not be a normal answer to either **108** or **109** if it were an actual question. In such circumstances we would rather find:

    110   It's the most beautiful city in Scotland

as the answer to **108**, and:

    111   Edinburgh is

or:

    112   It's Edinburgh

as the answer to **109** – illustrating the process of reduction consequent on the given – new distinction mentioned earlier.

This approach to the identification of topic is all right so far as it goes. Our observations suggest, correctly, that the notion of topic cannot be divorced from considerations of given–new (with the associated grammatical consequences of pronominalization, elision and so on) and from processes of thematization. It also suggests, correctly too, that there is no simple one-to-one correspondence between topic and theme (*Edinburgh* in **111** is theme, but not topic, if **111** is the answer to the implicit question **109**). Nor is there any necessary connection between topic and given, since **107** might be the initial contribution to a conversation, itself introducing a topic.

The approach seems reasonably satisfactory for simple exchanges but it meets with some difficulties when applied to longer passages in text; some of them relate to the difficulties experienced in trying to identify a sentence unit (pages 143 ff.). In the first place, a complex sentence can often be analysed as having either a complex topic, or several topics. Related to this is the problem of the units within which we wish to identify topics; for example, one might wish to say of this book that as a whole it has a topic, defined in general terms, that each part has a topic, down through chapters, sections, paragraphs, and so on. To regard topic as a notion restricted in its application to a single sentence is unrealistic, and the technique of asking 'implicit questions' can be applied as well to groups of sentences, paragraphs, and so on, as to single sentences. Let us briefly examine each of these two problems.

Consider first the problem of the identification of a topic in a complex sentence:

> **113** In everyday speech 'fitness' means suitability or adaptedness or being in good condition; 'evolution' means gradual change, with the connotation of unfolding; and as for 'inheritance', we may hope to inherit money, rights or property; we might inherit too a mother's eyes or a grandfather's gift for fiddling.
>
> **114** These are the meanings . . . of fitness, evolution and inheritance – the meanings for which scientists chose them when they were struggling to put their conceptions into words.[1]

The first orthographic sentence **113** might answer the implicit question:

> **115** What do scientists mean by 'fitness', 'evolution' and 'inheritance'?

But this seems to introduce three topics, each in turn topic for one of the succeeding clauses separated by semicolons. We can resolve this difficulty by supposing that the sentence could be dissolved into independent simple sentences (which would involve some amendment to the text and would destroy its stylistic characteristics!) each answering one implicit question (What do scientists mean by fitness? What do scientists mean by evolution? and so on). We then have the difficulty of identifying an appropriate topic for the final clause in **113**; perhaps it answers the implicit question, 'What else can you inherit?' But this does not seem helpful, since the function of this sentence is further to exemplify what is meant by 'inherit'. The second sentence, **114**, also presents a problem. It seems better to regard both of these sentences as relating to a single, complex topic: an elementary initial definition of what is meant by 'fitness', 'evolution' and 'inheritance'. The same sort of difficulty arises if we try to continue this method with the rest of the paragraph:

116   In the course of time those conceptions have become clearer . . . but the words which embody them have remained the same.

117   The change that has gone on is sometimes described by saying that scientists give the words a new precision and refinement . . .

118   The idea scientists now have in mind when they speak of 'fitness' can be explained like this . . .

It is perhaps appropriate to say that the topic of the two sentences 116 and 117 together answered the implicit question, 'How have scientists refined the definition of these terms?' The next paragraph, the beginning of which is shown in 118, goes on to offer a contemporary definition of 'fitness' that itself extends over a number of sentences.

Even with declarative sentences in text, then, there are problems in identifying topics in any straightforward way. Further difficulties arise if we try to identify the topic of interrogative sentences. Take the case of 109, for example. It seems hardly appropriate to ask what question this answers since it is itself a question. We might say it answers some implicit question like:

119   What question would you like answered?

but this is tautologous. A more appropriate approach is to suggest that instead of 'having a topic', overt interrogative sentences like 109 'introduce a topic'. This certainly seems the function of the 'rhetorical question' often found in expository texts:

120   'Inheritance' was the second of the three words of which I said that biologists use in special or unfamiliar ways.

121   Just what is inherited when geneticists speak of inheritance?

120, a declarative sentence, reintroduces as a topic something previously mentioned, and 121 establishes that the author is about to define what he means by this topic. The author is using the 'implicit question' technique we started this section with as an explicit technique for defining a topic – it then hardly seems sensible to inquire what the topic of this topic-introducing question is!

This approach to the identification of topics leads to the question of what unit it is within which we wish to identify topics; it is suggested above that it is appropriate to consider there to be a hierarchy of such units. The hierarchy starts, if this is appropriate, with the clauses of which a complex sentence consists (see the discussion of sentence **113**), goes through the orthographic sentence if this is relevant, and it may not always be so (see the discussion of sentence **114**), to groups of sentences, then to the paragraph, and so on. If this approach is appropriate it will be noted that the orthographic sentence may not necessarily be a unit that needs to be attended to, though it generally will be.

To illustrate what is meant by groups of sentences serving as a unit for the identification of topics, consider for instance the structure of the second paragraph in this section. The first sentence is introductory, the second offers an elementary definition, the third suggests a technique of identification, the fourth and fifth exemplify this technique, and so on. The implicit question technique works well on this paragraph, providing it is not applied to each individual sentence, but rather to groups of sentences as appropriate:

What is this section about?   (S1)
What do you mean by 'topic'? (S2)
How would I identify one?   (S3)
Can you give me an example? (S4, 5)

and so on. Note that this set of questions refers as much to what we might call the rhetorical structure of the paragraph as to the structure of individual sentences. In so far as it relates to rhetorical structure, it helps account for a number of facets of sentence construction, notably the distribution of the binding expressions noted on pages 143–5.

This approach to the identification of topics may assist in untangling some of the mysteries of word order. We have already noted that what is topic is frequently also what is thematic, but this statement needs to be qualified. The thematic element may relate to the topic of some unit larger than the sentence (as is perhaps the case when binding expressions are thematic – they often identify the function of the sentence: *for instance, thus, in conclusion,* and so on). Equally, the thematic element may have nothing to do with the topic, but be some other element of the message that the speaker wishes to foreground.

20.4   Conclusion

The phenomena considered in this chapter pose a peculiar difficulty for constituent structure grammars. Much of it, particularly the observations relating to theme and end focus, clearly has to do with constituent structure, but some of it, particularly that relating to topic, while it may have implications for constituent structure, cannot usefully be brought into a constituent structure grammar of any sort that we have discussed. Even the material clearly relevant to constituent structure is of a curious sort. Some of it, particularly the thematization operations that have to do with subject selection, seems relevant to what we may call centrally grammatical processes – processes like subject selection with verbs like RUN and STREAM (page 350). Other operations, particularly those like left-movement rules (pages 353–4 ff.), seem outside the centrally grammatical processes and have more to do with communicative effects in texts. Yet it is not as simple as that. Question formation resembles a left-movement rule (in that it can take a constituent embedded deeply in the sentence and thematize it), and we surely want to think of question formation as a centrally grammatical process. Conversely, the passive operation, often thought of as a central grammatical rule (transformational grammars often treat it as the first transformation to be taught), seems to have as much to do with communicative effects as anything else (see the very perceptive remarks on the functions of passivization in Jespersen, 1929).

One might think it convenient to be able to distinguish the centrally grammatical rules, whatever they may be defined to be, from those rules that are concerned with text-forming processes, but this is clearly impossible. Nor should this surprise us.

Technical terms

cleft sentence comment	left dislocation
given	left-movement rules
'heavy' NPs	new

Note

1   The quotations here and in examples **116–118**, **120** and **121** are from Medawar, 1960.

Exercises

(1)   Each of the following two texts contains much the same
      propositional matter; the propositions follow each other in the
      same order. Each text too exhibits thematization devices of
      various sorts. Identify the types of thematization operations
      involved. Account for the fact that while text (a) seems to
      be fairly coherently structured, text (b) is decidedly odd.

      (a)   (i) It was in 1960 that the cave was discovered. (ii) An old
            shepherd thought he heard 'water running underground'
            at the foot of a nearby mountain. (iii) He told a friend of
            his who lived in the nearby village of Petralona. (iv) The
            villager removed a few stones and literally fell into the
            cave. (v) A quick search showed that the floor was
            littered with animal bones. (vi) What he had found was a
            prehistoric habitation site. (vii) On a subsequent visit he
            found an entire human fossil, lying on its right side with
            its legs drawn up. (viii) He told other villagers that
            night that he had found the remains of a 'big monkey'
            in a cave.

      (b)   (i) What was discovered in 1960 was the cave. (ii) A
            shepherd who was old thought that 'water running
            underground' had been heard by him at a nearby
            mountain's foot. (iii) A friend of his who lived in the
            nearby village of Petralona was told by him. (iv) A few
            loose stones were removed by the villager and it was the
            cave he literally fell into. (v) That animal bones littered
            the floor was shown by a quick search. (vi) He had found
            a prehistoric habitation site. (vii) Lying on its right side
            with its legs drawn up, he found an entire human fossil on
            a subsequent visit. (viii) He told other villagers that night
            that the remains of a 'big monkey' had been found by him
            in a cave.

(2)   The dialogue below comes from genuine spontaneous
      conversation recorded on tape. Read through it and answer
      the questions. ('A69' and 'M59' mean the 69th contribution by
      A and the 59th contribution by M to this conversation. As
      these are transcriptions of tape-recordings, minimal
      punctuation has been inserted.)

A69:   we hear enough about golf in the common room with Richard

M59:   what's he going to do that boy anyway?

L59:   play golf

A70:   be a professional golfer

M69:   is he?

L60:   he would if he could . . . I think he's applied for a sports scholarship

M61:   in this country?

L61:   yeah

M62:   they're very few and far between aren't they? I mean there's millions of them in America, sports scholarships

L62:   that's what he's done . . . at the moment he's keeping his fingers crossed that he hears about it

M63:   what about the other ones? what are they doing?

Questions:

(a)   Discuss the treatment of given and new information with respect to the syntax.

(b)   Find examples of end focus.

(c)   List the themes in the passage. What types of constituent occur as theme?

Further reading

In this book we have provided an introduction to the basic concepts used in syntactic analysis. Since by its very nature our account can be neither exhaustive nor definitive, in this final part we indicate routes by which readers can explore particular topics in more detail, gaining new insights and new perspectives. Every area of syntax offers a sometimes confusing variety of analyses and models. There are different views on how many levels of constituent structure to recognize, on the relative importance of dependency relations and constituent structure, on the exact set of participant roles, on whether grammatical functions can be recognized in every language, on the exact nature of focus and given versus new, on the relationship between morphology and syntax, and on how the various concepts are to be applied to particular languages. The phrase-structure rules and the discussion of transformational relations are the gate to a huge area: the construction of rules for handling, not just individual constructions, but the relations among them, the interaction of morphology and syntax and the interaction of lexical items with syntactic structure.

This diversity of view is a cause for optimism. It is only through competing analyses that progress is made in any area of intellectual activity. And the diversity should not be allowed to obscure the large agreement among linguists about fundamental concepts. This book has introduced some of these concepts.

Introduction

We have not discussed many issues concerned with the nature of language in general; the reader is directed to Sapir (1921), Jespersen (1929), Bloomfield (1935) and the introductory chapters of Lyons (1968) and Hockett (1958). One excellent introductory textbook on linguistics in general is Yule (1985), while another useful overview is Fromkin and Rodman (1988). Interesting discussions of some of the problems of standard language mentioned in the Introduction are to be found in Milroy and Milroy (1985) and Devitt (1989).

Part one

One comprehensive discussion of syntax is in Radford (1988). It presents in some detail the X-bar treatment of constituent structure and dependency relations and also covers topics such as subcategorization, selectional restrictions and relations between constructions. The entire exposition relates to one recent formal grammar, but the first five chapters can be read with profit even by students with no interest in formal grammars.

Burton-Roberts (1986) gives a good, straightforward account of English syntax, covering constituent structure and dependency relations, phrases and clauses, and giving detailed illustrations from English.

Allerton (1981), Lyons (1968) and Matthews (1981) are for more advanced students. Allerton focuses on the problem of dependency relations and subcategorization, while Lyons (esp. ch. 6.1, ch. 4.2.1–4.2.8, ch. 6.2.1–6.2.2) and Matthews (chs 1, 4, 6, 7) offer more difficult accounts of the general issues connected with establishing constituent structure and dependency relations. Matthews, following good European (but not American) practice, argues the case for taking dependency relations as central in syntax. His book is excellent but requires great stamina.

Students who wish to see the theoretical concepts applied to English in detail should consult a reference grammar of English. The major work is Quirk *et al.* (1985), but Huddleston (1984) has wide coverage too. Remember that reference grammars such as that of Quirk and his colleagues are intended to be dipped into, not read from cover to cover, and do not present alternative analyses. Huddleston, however, does present and evaluate competing analyses.

Problems concerning the sentence (Chapter 11) are discussed in the introductory books mentioned above. The view presented here is much influenced by Lyons (1977a, pp. 29–31, 622–35), but see also Matthews (1981, ch. 2).

Students who wish to find out about generative grammar can read Radford (1988), who describes basic concepts of syntactic analysis and introduces Chomsky's Government and Binding model. The introduction is to be completed in a second volume which has not been published at the time of writing. General overviews of the major generative models are to be found in Horrocks (1987) and Sells (1985). The former is more suited to beginning students.

Part two

The study of morphology has undergone a renaissance since the first edition of this book, and various introductory textbooks have been written. Bauer (1988) is a good genuinely introductory text, while Matthews (1974) provides an excellent discussion of the basic theoretical issues for advanced students.

Parts of speech (form classes) and grammatical categories are also coming back into fashion, but there is no general introduction. The most comprehensive single account is still Lyons (1968, ch. 7.1–7.6). The best recent short discussions are in Shopen (1985a, b), in particular Schachter (1985) on parts of speech and Chung and Timberlake (1985) on tense, aspect and mood. These articles examine data from a wide range of languages. More particular and detailed studies of specific grammatical categories are Comrie (1976) on aspect, Comrie (1985) on tense and Palmer (1986) on mood and modality.

Part three

There are good discussions of heads and modifiers (in connection with dependency relations) in Burton-Roberts (1986, pp. 36–42) and Radford (1988, ch. 4.4–4.6, ch. 5.2–5.4).

Processes and participants, while part of traditional analyses of languages such as Latin and Greek, suffered loss of status in the 1960s and 1970s but are now again recognized as important. As with grammatical categories, a good introduction is lacking, but Lyons (1968, ch. 8.2) and Lyons (1977a, ch. 12.5–12.6) provide a short account. Somers (1987, chs 1, 7) deals with the handling of language by computer. Students with no interest in computing should not be put off; Somers' discussion is good (and might even kindle an interest in computing!). Our treatment in Chapter 18 omits certain interesting complexities which are dealt with by Schlesinger (1989) and Miller (1989).

Grammatical functions or relations have not only been the focus of much work in the last fifteen years but have been taken as central elements in two formal grammars. Good introductions are given by Lyons (1968, ch. 8.1) and Andrews (1985). Jespersen (1929) offers a general traditional account, and Matthews (1981, ch. 5) disposes of the idea that grammatical subject is applicable to all languages.

The structure of texts or discourse analysis is now a vast area roamed by linguists, psycholinguists and specialists in Artificial Intelligence. One very good introduction is Brown and Yule (1983), while an interesting and accessible study of how form and content are built up in texts is Halliday and Hasan (1989). Chafe (1976) is still the classic paper on focus and given versus new. Foley and van Valin (1985) survey the grammatical devices by which different languages encode focus, theme and given–new. An excellent synthesis of single-sentence syntax and discourse analysis is to be found in Halliday (1985).

Exercises

Gleason (1955), Nida (1949) and Langacker (1972) still provide the most useful collections of exercise materials.

References

Allerton, D. J. (1981), *Valency and the English Verb* (London: Academic Press).
Andrews, A. (1985), 'The major functions of the noun phrase'. In Shopen (1985a), *op. cit.*, pp. 62–154.
Bauer, L. (1983), *English Word-Formation* (Cambridge: Cambridge University Press).
Bauer, L. (1988), *Introducing Linguistic Morphology* (Edinburgh: Edinburgh University Press).
Bloomfield, L. (1935), *Language* (London: Allen & Unwin).
Bolinger, L. (1971), *The Phrasal Verb in English* (Cambridge, Mass.: Harvard University Press).
Brown, G. (1990), *Listening to Spoken English*, 2nd edn (London: Longman).
Brown, G., and Yule, G. (1983), *Discourse Analysis* (Cambridge: Cambridge University Press).
Burton-Roberts, N. (1986), *Analysing Sentences* (London: Longman).
Chafe, W. L. (1976), 'Givenness, contrastiveness, definiteness, subjects, topics and point of view'. In Li (1976), *op. cit.*, pp. 27–55.
Chung, S., and Timberlake, A. (1985), 'Tense, aspect, mood'. In Shopen (1985b), *op. cit.*, pp. 202–58.
Comrie, B. (1976), *Aspect* (Cambridge: Cambridge University Press).
Comrie, B. (1985), *Tense* (Cambridge: Cambridge University Press).
Devitt, A. J. (1989), *Standardizing Written English* (Cambridge: Cambridge University Press).
Foley, W. A., and van Valin, R. D. (1985), 'Information packaging in the clause'. In Shopen (1985a), *op. cit.*, pp. 282–364.
Fries, C. C. (1952), *The Structure of English* (New York: Harcourt Brace).
Fromkin, V., and Rodman, R. (1988), *An Introduction to Language*, 4th edn (New York: Holt, Rinehart & Winston).
Gleason, H. A. (1955), *Workbook in Descriptive Linguistics* (New York: Holt, Rinehart & Winston).
Greenberg, J. H. (1963), 'Some universals of grammar with particular reference to the order of meaningful elements'. In J. H. Greenberg (ed.), *Universals of Language* (Cambridge, Mass.: MIT Press), pp. 73–113.
Halliday, M. A. K. (1985), *An Introduction to Functional Grammar* (London: Edward Arnold).
Halliday, M. A. K., and Hasan, R. (1989), *Cohesion in English* (London: Longman).
Hockett, C. F. (1958), *A Course in Modern Linguistics* (New York: Macmillan).
Horrocks, G. (1987), *Generative Grammar* (London: Longman).
Huddleston, R. (1984), *Introduction to the Grammar of English* (Cambridge: Cambridge University Press).
Jespersen, O. (1929), *Philosophy of Grammar* (London: Allen & Unwin).
Langacker, R. (1969), 'On pronominalization and the chain of command'. In D. A. Reibel and S. Schane (eds), *Modern Studies in English* (Englewood Cliffs, NJ: Prentice Hall), pp. 160–186.

Langacker, R. W. (1972), *Fundamentals of Linguistic Analysis* (New York: Harcourt Brace).

Leech, G. (1971), *Meaning and the English Verb* (London: Longman).

Levinson, S. (1983), *Pragmatics* (Cambridge: Cambridge University Press).

Lewis, G. L. (1967), *Turkish Grammar* (Oxford: Oxford University Press).

Li, C. L. (1976), *Subject and Topic* (New York: Academic Press).

Lyons, J. (1968), *Introduction to Theoretical Linguistics* (Cambridge: Cambridge University Press).

Lyons, J. (1977a), *Semantics* (Cambridge: Cambridge University Press).

Lyons, J. (1977b), *Chomsky*, 2nd edn (London: Fontana).

Mackinnon, R. (1971), *Gaelic* (London: Teach Yourself Books).

Matthews, P. H. (1974), *Morphology* (Cambridge: Cambridge University Press).

Matthews, P. H. (1981), *Syntax* (Cambridge: Cambridge University Press).

Medawar, P. B. (1960), *The Future of Man* (London: Methuen).

Miller, J. (1989), 'Participant roles, synonymy and truth conditions'. In D. Arnold, M. Atkinson, J. Durand, C. Grover, and L. Sadler (eds), *Essays on Grammatical Theory and Universal Grammar* (Oxford: Oxford University Press), pp. 187–202.

Milroy, J., and Milroy, L. (1985), *Authority in Language* (London: Routledge & Kegan Paul).

Nida, E. (1949), *Morphology. The Descriptive Analysis of Words* (Ann Arbor: University of Michigan Press).

Palmer, F. (1974), *The English Verb* (London: Longman).

Palmer, F. (1986), *Mood and Modality* (Cambridge: Cambridge University Press).

Quirk, R., Greenbaum, S., Leech, G., and Svartvik, J. (1985), *A Comprehensive Grammar of the English Language* (London: Longman).

Radford, A. (1988), *Transformational Grammar. A First Course* (Cambridge: Cambridge University Press).

Robins, R. H. (1964), *General Linguistics, an Introductory Survey* (London: Longman).

Sapir, E. (1921), *Language, an Introduction to the Study of Speech* (New York: Harcourt Brace).

Schachter, P. (1985), 'Parts of speech'. In Shopen (1985a), *op. cit.*, pp. 3–61.

Schlesinger, I. M. (1989), 'Instruments as agents: on the nature of semantic relations'. *Journal of Linguistics*, vol. 25, pp. 189–210.

Sells, P. (1985), *Lectures on Contemporary Syntactic Theories* (Stanford, Calif.: Center for the Study of Language and Information).

Shopen, T. (1985a), *Language Typology and Syntactic Description*, vol. 1: *Clause Structure* (Cambridge: Cambridge University Press).

Shopen, T. (1985b), *Language Typology and Syntactic Description*, vol. 3: *Grammatical Categories and the Lexicon* (Cambridge: Cambridge University Press).

Somers, H. L. (1987), *Valency and Case in Computational Linguistics* (Edinburgh: Edinburgh University Press).

Yule, G. (1985), *The Study of Language* (Cambridge: Cambridge University Press).

Index